Chinese Occupational Welfare in Market Transition

Also by Ming-kwan Lee

CHANGING CHINESE SOCIETIES: Social Indicators Analysis (*co-editor*)

HONG KONG POLITICS AND SOCIETY IN TRANSITION

INDICATORS OF SOCIAL DEVELOPMENT: Hong Kong 1997 (*co-editor*)

INEQUALITIES AND DEVELOPMENT: Social Stratification in Chinese Societies (*co-editor*)

Chinese Occupational Welfare in Market Transition

Ming-kwan Lee

First published in Great Britain 2000 by
MACMILLAN PRESS LTD
Houndmills, Basingstoke, Hampshire RG21 6XS and London
Companies and representatives throughout the world

A catalogue record for this book is available from the British Library.

ISBN 0–333–77372–1

First published in the United States of America 2000 by
ST. MARTIN'S PRESS, LLC,
Scholarly and Reference Division,
175 Fifth Avenue, New York, N.Y. 10010

ISBN 0–312–23155–5

Library of Congress Cataloging-in-Publication Data
Lee, Ming-kwan, 1948–
Chinese occupational welfare in market transition / Ming-kwan Lee.
p.   cm.
Includes bibliographical references and index.
ISBN 0–312–23155–5 (cloth)
1. Industrial welfare—China—Guangzhou. 2. Working class—China–
–Guangzhou. 3. Labor—China—Guangzhou. 4. Employee fringe benefits–
–China—Guangzhou. I. Title.

HD7260.62.C6 L43   2000
331'.0951'275—dc21
                                                                                    99–088262

This book is printed on paper suitable for recycling and made from fully managed and sustained forest sources.

10   9   8   7   6   5   4   3   2   1
09   08   07   06   05   04   03   02   01   00

Printed and bound in Great Britain by
Antony Rowe Ltd, Chippenham, Wiltshire

In Memory of Dr Ng Mau-sang, 1948–94

Contents

List of Tables and Figures

Tables

Figures

A Note on the Romanization of Chinese

There are several systems for rendering Chinese words in the Roman alphabet. The most widely used today are the *pinyin* system, used in the People's Republic of China, and the older Wade-Giles system, which until recently was almost universally used in English-language publications. This thesis uses the official *pinyin* system. In a number of cases, renditions in Wade-Giles have also been given in parentheses.

Preface

Since 1978, reform in China has rapidly transformed this vast socialist country from a rigidly controlled and centrally planned economy into the vibrant and increasingly market-oriented economy that it is today. This reform process involves the dismantling of old institutions and the establishment in their place of institutions characteristic of a market economy. Emerging from these changes is increasingly a mixed economy with unique characteristics.

The 'iron rice bowl' – a unique package of near-permanent employment and occupational welfare for urban state-sector employees – is among the institutions that have been dismantled.

From the 1950s China had developed a system of occupational welfare which provided comprehensive 'cradle to grave' benefits and services to urban state-sector employees. Millions depended on their work-units, the *danwei*, for health insurance, retirement pensions, housing, various kinds of subsidies both in cash and in kind, various collective facilities and services such as nurseries, staff canteens, clinics, bathing facilities and, in large units, schools and hospitals. Chinese occupational welfare turned work-units into *gemeinschaftlich* communities, which provided for and controlled nearly every aspect of the life of their employees. It was a very rare and extreme situation of welfare dependence. Chinese occupational welfare provided an important means by which the communist regime gained consent for its rule from its urban citizenry. It underpinned and buttressed the state's dominance and control over society.

This study explains the origins and nature of this unique system of welfare, describes how it has undergone changes during market transition and discusses the socio-political implications of these changes in terms of citizenship rights, family solidarity and state–society relations.

Based on the case study of a large, state-owned enterprise, the study shows that in the course of market transition Chinese occupational welfare has undergone very radical changes. Empirical evidence and field data show that these changes have come about through three separate, yet interrelated processes at the individual, the work-unit and the state level: the process reshaping dependence, the process reshaping the *danwei* welfare economy and the process reforming Labour Insurance. The system emerging from these changes is no longer worked entirely through the *danwei* bureaucracy: it is no longer the exclusive privilege of a particular status group, the urban state employees. The new system has broken with the near-complete dependence of the past and it no longer exempts individual workers from their share of risks and responsibilities. Emerging from the change is a model of welfare pluralism with unique cultural and institutional characteristics.

The transformation of Chinese occupational welfare was at once symptomatic and constitutive of the transformation of contemporary China. It signified the end of the old and heralded the beginning of a new socio-economic and political order.

This book developed from my dissertation submitted to the London School of Economics in 1998. The research question I took with me to the LSE in January 1994 was on social stratification in China. I was eager to write a thesis on the *danwei*. The 'thesis' I had was that the *danwei* was the primary basis of urban stratification in pre-reform China. I argued that the 'bureaucracy situation' – the conceptual counterpart, in the redistributive economy, of the Weberian notion of 'market situation' – was the key concept for understanding and explaining social stratification and social class in China. The socialist work-unit was a *quasi-class,* a particular kind of 'redistributive grouping' (Giddens 1980), and 'class conflict' assumed the form of *politics of redistribution* in an officially classless society (Lee 1994).

Soon after I arrived at the Department of Social Policy and Administration at the LSE, I became fascinated with its policy concerns and its intellectual ethos, a tradition that went back to T. H. Marshall and R. M. Titmuss. Professor Robert Pinker, my supervisor, shared with me his many insights in and encouraged me to write about the *danwei* from the perspective of comparative social policy. I gladly altered my research plan and, with his guidance, set off for what promised to be a most rewarding intellectual journey. To Bob, teacher and friend, I owe my deepest gratitude.

I am also most grateful to Professor Howard Glennerster, who gave me perceptive and very useful comments on an early set of field notes and in important ways helped me develop the ideas for the thesis at the early stage of the study.

My thanks also go to friends and fellow researchers at the Guangzhou Academy of Social Science, who helped me gain entry into the field and were always there to keep me company and give me support throughout the field study.

I am also grateful to the 28 interviewees at the Dongfang Heavy Machinery Works who spared long hours talking to me about their *danwei*, their working lives, their families, their feelings, worries and aspirations. I must thank them for their trust, sincerity and openness without which the research process would not have been as smooth or as effective.

I must also take this opportunity to thank Professor Ian Gough, Professor of Social Policy and Director of European Research Institute at the University of Bath, for his insightful comments on the thesis and for encouraging me to get the thesis published.

Last but not the least, I am indebted to my wife, Clara, and my two children, Tania and Flora, for their love, support, patience and understanding, especially because I had to be away from home during three consecutive Chinese New Years.

M. K. Lee
The Hong Kong Polytechnic University

1
The Nature of Chinese Occupational Welfare

Introduction

This study is about 'occupational welfare' in the People's Republic of China: how it came about, how it works, its sociological, economic and welfare implications, and, in the latest phase of the country's economic reforms, how it responds to changes induced by market transition.

Since the 1950s, occupational welfare has been the predominant mode by which welfare benefits and services are distributed in China.[1] Work-units, or *danwei*,[2] provide their members with comprehensive welfare 'from the cradle to the grave'. Urban employees depend on their work-units for a wide range of benefits and services covering health insurance, retirement pensions, housing, nurseries, canteens, bathing facilities, various kinds of subsidies both in cash and in kind and, in large state organisations, hospitals and schools.[3] The work-unit is at once a workplace and an 'urban village' (Henderson and Cohen 1984: 5), a 'microcosm of an urban community and welfare organiza-tion' (Bian 1994: 177), a 'multi-functional' (Lu 1989; Li 1994) social structure and, in the view of some, a 'total community' (Shirk 1993: 31). Indeed, Chinese occupational welfare has turned work-units into 'mini-welfare states' (Leung 1992: 6), each assuming a wide range of welfare responsibilities.

Why was such a system of occupational welfare created in China? What are its economic implications for the work-units and sociological and welfare implications for their members? What in this system has changed since the introduction of economic reforms in 1978? In what ways have these changes altered workers' dependence on their units and affected their life-chances and ways of life? How are they reacting to these changes? These and related questions will engage and configure discussion in the chapters to follow.

The concept of occupational welfare

'Occupational welfare' includes 'those benefits that accrue to wage and salary earners over and above their pay, including those referred to as fringe benefits' (Bryson, 1992: 131) and covers, in Britain for example, such benefits as private pension schemes, paid holidays, sick pay, death benefits, subsidized meals, company cars and travel season tickets.[4] With few exceptions these are the 'prerogatives of the private sector' (Rein and Rainwater 1986: 7). Entitlement to occupational welfare is based not on citizenship, but on the job status which applies to selected groups of the working population according to merit, work performance and productivity (Abel-Smith and Titmuss 1974: 31; Taylor-Goodby and Dale 1981: 159–60).

Titmuss, as early as 1958, drew the field's attention to occupational welfare. He likened 'social welfare' to the visible tip of an iceberg with two other forms of welfare – 'fiscal' and 'occupational' – hidden from view, and made a strong case for considering all three of them. However, sticking to 'the principle of a unitary and institutionally dominant statutory welfare system' (Pinker 1992: 276), Titmuss has a very negative view of occupational welfare. In his opinion, occupational welfare raises 'questions of equity' and the 'whole tendency ... is to divide loyalties, to nourish privilege, and to narrow the social conscience' (1958: 52), 'simultaneously enlarging and consolidating the area of social inequality' (ibid: 55). He believed that only in the public sector could effective redistribution be achieved.[5]

This concern, that the private provision of welfare could produce inequitable outcomes, has been shared by Sinfield (1978), Field (1981), Hoven (1982), Reddin (1982), Walker (1984: 28), Green (1984) and many others, who point out that in addition to direct state welfare in cash and in kind there exist systems of private, occupational and charitable welfare within the general structure of state subsidy and regulation. The net effect of redistribution within these systems is regressive, towards the better-off and most powerful groups. Papadakis and Taylor-Goodby (1987) also draw attention to the social control implications of occupational welfare. Pension schemes, for example, 'might reinforce mechanisms of control which induce conformity by an employee to guidelines devised by the employer as a precondition for the realization of benefits' (Papadakis and Taylor-Goodby 1987: 176).

Yet 'most writers on the welfare state are silent on occupational welfare' (Bryson 1992: 132).[6] There are surprisingly few treatises on the subject and few attempts which study the 'ways in which the public and the private sector interact in the provision of social protection' (Rein 1982: 133). The preoccupation of welfare state writers with 'the idea of state responsibility for welfare' (Mishra 1984: 11) and their reluctance to recognize occupational welfare as an area for government intervention at all largely explains this phenomenon.

The origins of occupational welfare

Explanations of the origins of occupational welfare in Western capital-ist countries have mostly stressed either one or a combination of three factors: culture, internal labour market and worker power. Let me con-sider each in turn.

1. Culture

This view draws attention to the important part played by paternal-ism: 'a relationship between the agents in any economic organization in which the employer acts towards his employees in a manner some-what similar to that of a father toward his children' (Bennett and Iwaoshino 1963: 224). The relationship implies a pattern of mutual obligations which require the employer to be benevolent and employees obedient, loyal and subordinate. 'The *quid pro quo* ... is that the workers be loyal and committed to the company' (Doeringer 1984: 281). In Japan, where workers enjoy employment security and preferential welfare (Vogel 1979; Pinker 1986; but see also Sethi, Namiki and Swanson 1984; Kendall 1984; Oliver and Wilkinson 1988 for some more qualified positions), Dore (1973) notes that the ideo-logy of paternalism with its reciprocal responsibilities and duties had been refashioned into a conscious managerial strategy which attempted to resolve an acute shortage of skilled labour following the decision to industrialize in 1867. Paternalism is not, however, a Japanese trademark. In Britain, as Perkin (1969) has shown, paternal-ism was at the heart of the system of patronage and dependence which characterized pre-industrial society with its vertically struc-tured bonds of loyalty and allegiance. Russell's (1991) case study of occupational welfare in Britain similarly leads her to conclude that the 'paternalistic style of personnel management, with its emphasis on company-provided occupational welfare, has a long pre-history in Britain' (p. xi):

The paternalist's philosophy reflected a unitary concept of the occupational community where, ideally, harmony prevailed, each individual having his function, his symbolic duties, his reciprocal obligations, and his ties of dependency. Attention to the welfare … for deserving long-service employees was an expression of the paternalist's sense of responsibility and duty. From the viewpoint of labour management welfarism served as a means of encouraging reciprocal sentiments of gratitude, loyalty and co-operation on the part of the recipients. (Russell 1991: p. 271)

Welfarism was also popular in the United States in the mid-1920s. 'Welfare capitalism arose out of the corporations' concern for finding a way of creating in their workers a sense of loyalty', and welfare programmes became one specific part of a strategy that aimed at 'harmonizing' the interests of capital and labour (Edwards 1979: 91).

2. The Internal labour market

This view, expounded mainly by labour economists, explains fringe benefits by way of the concept of the 'internal labour market'. Traditional views on labour markets focus on external markets, seeing a market in which competing (potential) employers face competing (potential) employees. This implies a situation in which there are few attachments between workers and firms, and high labour turnover. As firms grow larger and more powerful, they try to bring more and more of their environments under control and 'internalize', so to speak, forces which can potentially upset their profits and existence. Hence the creation of 'internal labour markets' through which to arrange the purchase and sale of labour-power within the firms. Internal labour markets consist of such mechanisms and institutions as hierarchical job ladders, limited ports of entry, inducements to stay in the job, promotion ladders, and so on. Seen in this light, benefits and earnings are one part of the institutions and mechanisms which make up the internal labour market. But while non-Marxist economists regard earnings and benefits as a means for maintaining labour stability, which is seen to be essential to a firm's productivity (Doeringer and Piore 1971) and long-term profitability (Chandler 1977), neo-Marxists regard them as part of 'a system … contrived and consciously designed to perpetuate the capitalist's control over the firm's workforce' (Edwards, Reich and Gordon 1973: 5).

3.   Worker power

In this perspective, capitalists are not so much interested in as compelled by the organized power of occupational groups to provide more earnings and benefits to the employees (Kalleberg, Wallace and Althauser 1981). Elbaum's (1984) study of American iron and steel industry during World War I and the Great Depression, for example, concluded that 'the primary cause of internal labour market was pressure collectively exerted by workers for employment security and advancement with consequences that included rigid internal promotion rules and a wide range of freedom for competitive constraints and wage structure' (1984: 101). Benefits and welfare could also result indirectly from labour power. Jacoby's (1984) study of American manufacturing firms in the 1930s and 1940s noticed, for instance, that pecuniary welfare and fringe benefits had arisen out of competition with unions to secure employee loyalty. Firms which introduced such 'managerial innovations' 'refused to bargain over these benefits and stressed to employees that unions had not been responsible for them' (Jacoby 1984: 52).

Clearly not all of these perspectives are relevant for understanding the origins of occupational welfare in China. Internal labour markets, for instance, presuppose profit-seeking firms and external labour markets characterized by competition and mobility. Such capitalist institutions are largely non-existent in the planned economy. Indeed, before 1978, Chinese leaders ideologically rejected these institutions. They believed in the superiority of a planned socialist economy and were unwilling to grant ideological legitimacy to a labour market for state enterprises (Davis 1990: 88). Before 1978, there was strict administrative control over job assignment; wages and benefits were centrally regulated; salary increases were determined by state budgets; career promotions followed ranking systems imposed by central planners; employers were not allowed to lay off workers; and employment was virtually for life. There were neither external nor internal labour markets. It was only during the economic reforms of the 1980s that some limited labour markets began gradually to come into existence. Even then, in the urban state sector, there were 'extremely high levels of immobility' and 'state employees were "stuck"…, frustrated by their inability to take advantage of the reform leadership's stated goals of reducing bureaucratic controls over employment practices' (Davis 1990: 87). Chinese occupational welfare cannot be explained, therefore, in terms of the functions and logic of internal labour markets.

The worker power perspective is also largely irrelevant. There was no autonomous occupational power, and trade unions were under the leadership of the ruling Communist Party, co-operating with the government and workplace management to control rather than serve workers. Their jobs were to 'transmit the party line to workers, encourage production ..., engage in political education, and execute a range of welfare chores' (Hoffmann 1974: 134). Attempts by early leaders of All-China Federation of Trade Unions (ACFTU) to define for the trade union a more independent and pro-worker role were attacked, labelled as 'anti-Party' 'economism' and 'syndicalism', and politically stigmatized (Ouyang 1994). Trade unions were disbanded in 1967 and not formally reconstituted until 1974.

The culture perspective does appear to be relevant. Paternalism, as Walder (1986) points out, was inherent in the ideology and practice of the Chinese firms. Paternalism had also been found to be prevalent among former Soviet-type societies. It characterized the relationship between the state and state enterprises (Kornai 1986: 52–61) and had been the 'main mode of legitimation' (Fehér 1982: 69) for communism before its demise. In these societies, 'social benefits serve ... to inspire loyalty to the state' (Rimlinger 1971: 254) and, 'thanks to the social services, the state gains considerably in legitimacy and support' (Mishra 1977: 144).

In seeking to explain the origins of occupational welfare in China, this study has taken the position shared by such writers as Hall (1986), Skocpol (1985), Berger (1981) and Steinmo et al. (1992). This position, 'historical' or 'new institutionalism', maintains that one should bring the historical context of a national society in and examine a policy or an institution by situating it in both the context of political and societal institutions and a broader matrix of contesting interests and ideas.

Scholars (for example, Stark and Nee 1989) in the fields of China and East European studies insisting on this position are critical of approaches which regard these countries as either some variants of communist totalitarian states or as modernizing countries on an evolutionary course converging with modern industrialism. They question many of the fundamental assumptions underlying these approaches; for example, the image of an atomized citizenry in the totalitarian model and the idealized image of Western development in the theory of modernization. They criticize these overarching paradigms for their failure to attend to the complex realities and many diversities within these societies. Also, they were dissatisfied because, during the 1980s, 'the shift to attempted reforms dramatized the lack of fit between the analytical problems constructed by the competing theories and those faced in the societies themselves' (Stark and Nee 1989: 7). Turning away from these theories, the new institutionalists have instead subscribed to the view that state socialism represents a distinct social formation which has its own institutional logic and dynamics of development, and insisted that theories explaining processes and outcomes in state socialism must take into account the institutional arrangements specific to socialism.

This study of Chinese occupational welfare has been oriented by similar recognitions. In endorsing the new institutionalist position, it maintains that Chinese occupational welfare must be studied in its own national and historical contexts, and as part of an institutional configuration characteristic of state socialism. Great care has to be exercised, therefore, in applying and using concepts which derive meanings from very different societal, cultural and institutional contexts, concepts such as the internal labour market, occupational welfare and paternalism.

The nature of Chinese occupational welfare

Chinese occupational welfare follows from an employment relation distinctly different from that typical of a market economy. In the market economy, an employment relation is primarily a labour market relationship: 'a specific contractual exchange of efforts and skills for money and other compensation' (Walder 1986: 16). Occupational welfare is one component of an employer–employee exchange equation.

In China, employment in the state enterprise is not primarily a market relationship. It is, rather, 'a position that establishes the worker's social identity and rights to specific distributions and welfare entitlements provided by the state' (ibid.: 16). Occupational welfare follows from an employment relation which relates the individual to the state and which at the same time defines the former's rights and entitlements and the latter's obligations. Such rights and entitlements are not extended, however, to all citizens. They are limited to a selected sector of the citizenry – urban workers in employment in the state sector: in the early 1950s, around 80 per cent, in the late 1980s, around 70 per cent, and in 1996, 66.7 per cent of the urban labour force (State Statistical Bureau 1989: 101; Hu 1996: 126; see also Table 1.4).[7]

The *danwei* is therefore more than just a workplace. It brings the state and its state-sector urban citizens together and articulates a relationship of entitlements and obligations between them.

But the *danwei* is also more than just the meeting place between state and society. In a 'redistributive economy' (Polanyi 1977; Szelenyi 1983; Kornai 1984; Nee 1989, 1990; Walder 1992; Lee 1994), which collects and distributes goods through centralized decision-making and bureaucratic hierarchies, the *danwei* has become the principal organizational framework through which the socialist state allocates resources and redistributes income. *Danwei* membership is an important status because it entitles a worker to the goods and incomes 'redistributed' by the state to its urban population. In market economies, such goods and incomes are supplied basically through the market.

Occupational welfare is an integral part of such state-distributed goods and income.[8] It typically includes the following benefits and services (Leung 1992: 13–14; see also Chow 1988: 29–45; Guo et al. 1990: 3–4; Walder 1986: 59–67):

1. *Labour insurance*: This is a non-contributory scheme covering retirement, sickness, injury, medical care, invalidity and death, funeral expenses, survivorship, maternity and sick leave. The range of benefits under the scheme are 'mandated by the government and in principle meant to be fairly uniform across work-units' (Hussain 1993: 16). The provisions of main benefits covered by the scheme are as shown in Table 1.1.
2. *Allowances and subsidies*: These include allowances given out in cash, on a monthly basis, for example, for heating, travel expenses, food, single-child, as well as heavily subsidized benefits, such as for housing, electricity and water. Housing is easily the most important of these. State enterprises control about half of all the urban housing stock (Whyte and Parish 1984: 82) and state workers depend on their *danwei* for heavily subsidized living quarters, paying a monthly rent that 'rarely exceed the equivalent of one or two days' pay' (Walder 1986: 65). Employees who do not live in *danwei* housing but remain in private or municipally owned housing can receive cash grants from their enterprises to repair their quarters.
3. *Collective Welfare:* Most work-units provide free or almost free services in a number of the following: clinics, primary schools, bathing facilities, kindergartens, sports facilities, barber shops, canteens, club houses, recreational centres, old-age centres, reading rooms, child day-care and kindergarten, an important service for the typical family in which both spouses work. In general, the higher the level of government, the more resources there are, and the better the collective welfare programmes and facilities available to work-units

(Walder 1992; Bian 1994: 177–207). Schools and hospitals are common in large-scale units. In 1995, one-third of China's hospital beds were in work-unit hospitals and as many as 6.1 million pupils went to schools run by work-units (Ming Pao, 6 December 1995).

4. *Individual Welfare*: Provided mainly through union cadres at the cell-group level to workers who have personal or family problems, this includes job placement for the physically disabled, mediating family, interpersonal and industrial disputes, counselling delinquents, promoting family planning and family education, assisting impoverished households and caring for the retired elderly.

5. *In-kind distribution*: Workplaces are also points of distribution of ration coupons not only for highly sought-after industrial goods – sewing machines, bicycles, radios, watches and furniture – but also for additional coupons for grain and other foodstuffs above the rationed amounts. Before 1979 this was important simply to assure supplies. After 1979 it became important to obtain better brands and pay low state prices. Many enterprises also buy grain, fruits, meat, eggs, fish, clothes, furniture, and household goods and distribute them to their employees. One study has suggested that the distribution of consumer goods accounted for 10 per cent of the total personal income of employees in state enterprises (Guo et al. 1990: 5).

These benefits and services are generally non-contributory, non-fee-charging, and when fee-charging, on only a nominal basis. In general, these are distributed or made available to workers on an 'egalitarian' (Guo et al. 1990: 2) basis. Together they 'could add at least 50 per cent to money wages' (Hu and Li 1995: 168).

It is only too clear that, because of all these benefits and services, workers cannot but become highly dependent on their *danwei* to satisfy a broad range of their needs. Through the late 1970s, in China, such dependence was accentuated by the fact that there was also a scarcity of alternatives and no real 'exit' (Hirschman 1970) option: 'movement between enterprises was tightly restricted; residence controls were strictly enforced; housing and consumer goods were in extremely short supply; and common consumer items and even basic foodstuffs were rationed through the workplace' (Walder 1986: 17). Shortages were compounded by the fact that wages had been kept low and effectively frozen throughout the 1960s and 1970s (Parish 1981: 39). During these years, there were few commodities available in the market and little to buy with. Such shortages and controls eased in the 1980s. A major theme discussed in the chapters to follow is how the economic reforms

Table 1.1   Selected Labour Insurance Benefits Provided to Permanent Workers in State-owned Enterprises

Item	*Provisions*
Work-related injury or illness	100% cost of treatment, medicine, hospital, and travel.
	100% wage during treatment. Food two-thirds cost paid. Registration fee paid by patient.
Work-related disability	Pension 40–90% former wage until death or recovery. Partial disability resulting in change to lower-paying job: 10–30% of prior wage as supplement, up to level of former wage
Non-work-related injury or illness	Fees, costs, medicine paid. Employee pays for expensive medicine, travel and meals. 60–100% wage up to 6 months, 40–60% thereafter (amount depends on seniority).
Non-work-related disability	40–50% wage as a pension for permanent disability.
Injury or illness of dependants	Entitled to treatment at clinic or hospital attached to enterprise. 50% cost of treatment and medicine. Expensive medicine, travel, hospital room, meals, registration fee, examination fee and medical tests paid by family.
Death benefits	*Work-related*: Lump sum, 3 months' pay.
	25–50% pay to minor dependants until working age (16 years).
	Non-work-related: 2 months' pay as lump sum. 6–12 months pay, lump sum, to minor dependants.
Benefits for death of minor dependants	Lump sum half-month pay for child over 10 years; one-third pay month for child under 10; no benefit for child under 1 year.
Maternity benefits	90 days' leave at full pay (15–45 for miscarriage). Pre-natal care paid by enterprise, at factory clinic or hospital. 4 yuan supplement on birth of each child. 8 yuan for multiple births.
Old-age pensions	*Male*: At age 60, with 25 years' seniority, and 10 years with present enterprise, 60–90% pay, depending on seniority. If continues work after retirement age, 10–20% pay in addition to full pay.
	Female: Same, but retirement age is 50, with 20 years' seniority and 10 years in current job.

Table 1.1   Continued

Item	Provisions
Unemployment relief allowance	*Workers with five or more years of service*: up to 24 months' support; during the first 12 months, 60–75 per cent of standard wage; during the next 12 months, 50 per cent (the standard wage is calculated as the worker's average monthly wage over two years before leaving the enterprise); and for *workers with less than five years of service*: up to 12 months' support at 60–75 per cent of standard wage.

Source: Zhan (1993: 206–84); Walder (1986: 44).

begun in 1978 by the Chinese patriarch, Deng Xiao-ping, challenged and upset this pattern of dependence, creating new problems and possibilities for *danwei* workers.

The Chinese system of occupational welfare has resulted in a number of social and political consequences. One significant consequence is that it has provided an important source of regime legitimation in China. As Walder (1986: 249) points out: 'The extraordinary job security and benefits, the goods and services distributed by the state enterprise in a situation of scarcity that affects other sectors of the workforce more severely, is an important source of acceptance of the system.' Occupational welfare vindicates the 'superiority of socialism' and its care for the welfare of the working class (Saich 1984: 153). Indeed, the popular support that the Chinese Communist Party secured in urban areas in the early years of the Republic depended to no small extent on 'the ability of the new government to equitably and honestly distribute goods and services so that popular consumption needs would be met at low and stable prices' (Whyte and Parish 1984: 103).

A second consequence is that it has turned work-units into *gemein-schafts* – communities which encompass many aspects of the life of their members. As encapsulated in one popular expression, '*qiyie ban shehui*,' or in English, 'enterprises run the society' (Bian 1994: 177), each work-unit is in effect a 'small society' (*xiao she hui*), a microcosm of the urban community. It integrates in one structure such a wide range of functions and responsibilities, it no longer is just an economic organiza-tion. The Chinese saying, 'the mayor governs the factory managers, and the factory managers govern the society' (Leung 1992: 2), vividly high-lights this *gemeinschaftlich* character of the work-unit.

The *gemeinschaftlich* character of the work-unit is underpinned by two important conditions: it has 'a lifetime, relatively immobile mem-bership'[9] (Womack 1990: 324), and its tendency to reproduce member-ship by recruiting from among close kin and relatives (Leung 1992: 5; Davis 1988). There was preferential distribution of job opportunities to family members (Walder 1986: 66). Many spouses worked in the same unit (Henderson and Cohen 1984: 36) and, between 1978 and 1986, when *dingti* ('replacement') was allowed, many workers, on reaching retirement age simply passed on their jobs to their children. State-sector jobs became in effect inheritable (Gold 1980; Davis-Friedmann 1981; Shirk 1981). The work-unit is like a 'small society' in the sense that it is close to self-sufficient both in terms of reproducing its popula-tion and in terms of the wide range of services which it provides to its members. In most cases, members of this 'small society' share such services and many aspects of their life over long periods.

Within their 'small societies', factory managers are responsible not only for organizing production, but also managing the welfare of workers and their dependants (Walder 1989). They are like paternal heads of extended households who assume diffuse responsibility over the welfare of their members (Yue 1991, quoted in Leung 1992: 6). 'Marriage, divorce, childbearing, education, job assignment, job trans-fer, and the resolution of conflicts all involve the knowledge and, in most cases, approval of these leaders; they are also responsible for the personal well-being of their staff' (Henderson and Cohen 1984: 42). A survey of Guangzhou residents, for example, noticed that '[w]hile one's boss rarely comes into the picture in Hong Kong, seeking help from the *danwei* chiefs is not that unusual in Guangzhou, particularly when one has marital or family problems, when the family encounters financial difficulties, or when one has difficulties in work or career' (Lee 1995: 17). Managerial relations have been described as paternalistic (Henderson and Cohen 1984; Walder 1986) or 'fief-like' (Boisot and Child 1988), and the state-owned organization and management as 'a clan-like structure with a heavy emphasis on informal communication, patriarchal decision-making, guaranteed pay, and egalitarian perform-ance criteria based on the hierarchy' (Baird et al. 1990).

But *danwei* leaders are not just paternalistic figures. Wielding power over the bureaucratic allocation of resources, they are effectively also 'gatekeepers'[10] (Vogel 1989: 409–14) whose decisions have important implications for the life-chances of their subordinates. As they operated with considerable personal discretion over such decisions, 'a competitive effort by subordinates to manipulate personal ties [with them] in order to get their needs met was inevitable' (Whyte 1991: 267).[11] This has led to a proliferation of 'clientelist ties' (Walder 1986) and networks of personal connections, or *guanxi*[12] (Yang 1994), which trade favours and advantages against, irrespective of, or exploiting formal rules and relations. *Guanxi* networks and rampant 'back-door practices' have become the dominant landscape of Chinese organizational life.

Workers' dependence on the *danwei* for satisfying a broad range of their needs, heightened by the lack of alternatives outside and exit from the unit, has another important consequence: it underpins the *danwei*'s control over many aspects of their life. Because the *danwei* is in fact a branch of government and its leaders state and party officials, such control is more than economic; it is also political: it reinforces the state's domination over society.[13] Work-units not only provide many essentials of life; as Whyte (1991: 261–2) notes:

> They supervised the leisure time activity of their members, ran local cleanliness campaigns, organized inoculation drives against diseases, mobilized the flocks to guard against crime dangers, mediated interpersonal and marital disputes, and screened applicants for marriages and divorces (and eventually for childbearing). They regularly organized mandatory political study sessions for employees and required the latter to submit to criticism and self-criticism rituals, and they occasionally extended the activities to dependents of employees as well. The bureaucratic overseers in such urban work units had no clear limits on what activities and thoughts of employees (and family members) they could supervise and control'.

The result was a 'highly intrusive and penetrating system' which 'maximize[d] official control over primary groups at the urban grass roots' (ibid.: 262).

These then are the formidable 'social facts' of *danwei* life. As 'exit' is unlikely and 'voice' difficult when workers are 'facing a reward system that penalizes the voicing of genuine criticisms of conditions and of group demands' (Walder 1986: 247), the only real 'option' for most has been that of 'loyalty' (Hirschman 1970); in other words, of staying on. In the context of the *danwei*, the 'loyalist' response of the Chinese workers has given rise to a distinct set of shared values and attitudes, orientations and habituated behaviour, or 'culture' in the broad sense of the term, which enable them to come to terms with the conditions of *danwei* life and, indeed, 'beat the system' (Walder 1986: 247). This culture consists of, first of all, the value of obedient compliance with the direction and wishes of cadres and leaders; secondly, of passivity, of, indeed, expecting and looking to *danwei* leaders to make all possible decisions; thirdly, the attitude which takes it for granted that workers will be cared for by the *danwei* and which regards it as the *danwei*'s obligation and responsibility to cater to the many needs of its members; and fourthly, the expectation that, in the provision and distribution of welfare, no one should be left out and everyone should have an equal share; the value, in other words, of 'egalitarianism' (*pingjun zhuyi*). What has emerged is, in short, a culture of paternalistic dependence.[14] The culture makes the respective '*carer*' and '*cared for*' roles of the *danwei* and its members obligatory, and stabilizes their reciprocal expectations: while workers can be expected to be co-operative and compliant, the *danwei* is expected to do whatever it can to take 'good' care of its workers. The culture perpetuates dependence, just as it also reinforces paternalism. An important theme discussed in this study is how economic reforms and the rise of the mixed economy have given rise to changes which have upset this culture and forced the *danwei* and its members to adjust to new risks and opportunities. It looks at how their responses and adjustments were shaped by the culture and the extent to which they moved away from its influence.

Chinese occupational welfare is thus much more than a 'fringe' marginal to employment relations and life in the workplace. It is an integral part of life in a state redistributive economy. It underpins the paternalism and particularism that pervades *danwei* relations. It fosters workers' dependence on, and ties them to, their respective work-units. It is at the root of the power–dependence relationship between the *danwei* and its members. It helps to turn the workplace into a *gemeinschaftlich* community which encompasses and controls many aspects of the life of its members. It is also an important means by which the socialist state legitimates its rule.

The economics of Chinese occupational welfare

In economic terms, Chinese occupational welfare is also far from being just a 'fringe'. For the workers, it is what provides them with basic security, various essentials of life and scarce commodities. Throughout the 1960s and 1970s, when wages were low and there were serious shortages of all kinds of consumer goods and services, occupational welfare was the *de facto* life-line for many. As conveyed in one popular expression, 'low wage, high welfare' (*digongzi, gaofuli*), occupational welfare has an importance surpassing that of money wage. It is obvious, also, that in money terms, occupational welfare is an important source of additional income. For instance, 'total work-related insurance and other types of welfare expenditures may be as high as 526.7 yuan (Y) per worker, or 81.7 per cent of the average wage. This does not include the value of access to low-cost housing' (Minami 1994: 217). In the area of housing, rents have been very low, absorbing just under 1.5 per cent of the average family income. A state employee in a 50 square metre flat might have benefited to the tune of nearly 100 yuan per year for maintenance and administration costs alone (ibid.).

It goes without saying that, for the units, occupational welfare is a hefty financial commitment. In 1994, welfare expenses in state enterprises, not including housing subsidies, amounted to Y162.87 billion, or about 32 per cent of the total money wage bill of Y517.74 billion. In 1978, the share was only 14 per cent (Y6.69 billion of Y46.87 billion), as shown in Table 1.2.

Table 1.2   Labour Insurance and Welfare Funds* as Percentages of Total Wage in State-owned Enterprises, 1978–94

	Labor Insurance and Welfare Funds (billion yuan)	*Total Wage Bill (billion yuan)*	*Labor Insurance and Welfare Funds as Percentage of Total Wage (%)*
1978	6.69	46.87	14.3
1980	11.60	62.79	18.5
1984	21.04	87.58	24.0
1985	26.99	106.48	25.3
1986	34.00	128.85	26.4
1987	41.18	145.93	28.2
1988	53.34	180.71	29.5
1989	62.80	205.02	30.6
1990	77.01	232.41	33.1
1991	90.49	259.49	34.9
1992	108.66	309.04	35.2
1993	137.45	381.27	36.1
1994**	162.87	517.74	31.5

Source: State Statistical Bureau (1995: 108, 685).
* *Insurance and Welfare Funds*: Paid by work units to their retired workers and employees on top of their wages and salaries, this includes, for *employees*: medical care allowances, funeral expenses and provisions for family of the deceased, various kinds of subsidies for living expenses, subsidies for such facilities as nursery, kindergarten and barber shops, subsidies for one-child families; and, for *retired workers*: pensions, allowances and subsidies, medical care cost, transportation subsidies, funeral expenses, and so on. Housing subsidies and food allowances are not included.
** As from 1994, subsidies for transportation as well as barber and bath fees are covered by 'wages'.

Table 1.3   Number of Retired Workers (millions) and Labour Insurance and Welfare Funds for Retired Workers (billion yuan), in State-owned Enterprises, 1978–94

	Number of Retired Workers (millions)	Ratio of Employees to Retired Workers	Labor Insurance and Welfare Funds for Retired Workers (billion yuan)
1978	2.84	26.2	1.63
1980	6.38	12.6	4.34
1984	10.62	8.1	8.46
1985	11.65	7.7	11.92
1986	13.03	7.2	16.16
1987	14.24	6.8	20.05
1988	15.44	6.5	25.64
1989	16.29	6.2	30.97
1990	17.42	6.0	38.24
1991	18.33	5.8	45.97
1992	19.72	5.5	57.28
1993	21.43	5.1	75.28
1994	22.49	4.8	102.20

Source: State Statistical Bureau (1995: 688, 690).

A major reason for this staggering growth of welfare expenditures has been the rapid increase of welfare for retired workers. There were eight times as many retired workers in state enterprises in 1994 as in 1978 and, in less than 20 years, expenses on retirement pensions have increased by more than 60 times, from under 2 billion yuan to over 100 billion yuan (see Table 1.3). In 1994, 45 per cent of the Labour Insurance and Welfare Funds in state-owned enterprises were spent on pensions paid to retired workers, as shown in Table 1.4.

Medical care is the next most expensive benefit. In 1994, almost one-third of the Labour Insurance and Welfare Funds were spent on medical care for employees and retired workers. The cost of medical care rose almost six-fold between 1986 and 1994 (State Statistical Bureau 1988, 1995) and is expected to continue to rise at an annual rate of 30 per cent (Li 1996: 66). The increase is partly due to price inflation and a change in the quality of the services (Hussain 1993: 26), and partly due to the ageing of the population[15] and an increase in the number of state-sector employees covered by medical insurance.[16] In 1994, work-units were on average spending as much as 9 per cent of their wage bill on medical care. There were also reports of cases in which work-units were spending more on medical care than on wages.[17]

Table 1.4   Labour Insurance and Welfare Funds for Employees and
Retired Workers in State-owned Enterprises 1994 (billion yuan)

	(billion Y)
For Employees	
Subsidies for public welfare and facilities	12.02
Expenses for cultural and sports activities	2.14
Medical care	30.92
Funeral expenses and pensions for dependants	1.21
Subsidies for living expenses	1.17
Subsidies for family planning	1.68
Subsidies for heating in winter	2.71
Others	8.82
Sub-total	60.67
For Retired Workers	
Pensions*	73.35
Medical care	16.36
Funeral expenses and allowances for dependants	1.45
Transportation subsidies	1.08
Subsidies for heating in winter	0.67
Others	9.29
Sub-total	102.20
Total	162.87

Source: State Statistical Bureau (1995: 686, 688)
* Pensions: This includes pensions for retired workers and cadres.

But housing was the most expensive of all. Housing was heavily subsidized, with workers spending only around 2 per cent of their household income on housing. Rental payment covered but a very small fraction of the total cost of new housing or maintenance and repair. In 1993, housing subsidies were estimated to be about Y130 billion, more than that spent on old age pensions and medical care, and nearly as much as the entire sum spent on Labour Insurance and Welfare Funds (Guojia Jinji Tizhi Gaige Weiyuanhui 1995: 48). With the housing stock more than doubling during the 1980s, subsidy costs also grew very rapidly.

The socialist firm in market transition

Workers' heavy dependence on their work-units for occupational welfare is mirrored at the macro-level by the heavy financial dependence of the work-units on the state.

In the pre-reform days, the state sector was administered by the command economy. The 'socialist firm' depended on the state for everything from output targets to wage funds. In conditions of 'soft budget constraints' (Kornai 1986), it was not required to be sensitive to cost and price considerations and could always rely on the 'paternalistic state' (ibid.: 52–61) to bail it out of trouble. Survival was guaranteed by the state regardless of its performance, and its growth was determined by central planners, who allocated resources on the basis of bureaucratic procedures. As Kornai incisively analyses it:

> Because budget constraints are lax, the firm has little pressure to use resources and investment efficiently. In fact, it often has every incentive to use them inefficiently: rewarded for expansion and physical output, the socialist firm's managers seek to hoard and hide reserves and to maximize the resources and investments allocated to it. For this reason, the firm's demand for resources is theoretically limitless. This perpetual hunger for resources, in turn, gives rise to chronic shortages throughout the economy as firms pump the state for more workers, equipment, raw materials, and investments irrespective of their financial situation or ability to use those resources efficiently. (quoted in Stark and Nee 1989: 9)

As in other socialist economies, China eschewed hard budget constraints. 'The soft budget constraints for industry resulted in inefficiency, low productivity, waste and chronic shortages, especially of consumer goods and foods. All of this cost the state a great deal of money' (Gold 1990: 162). Working under soft-budget conditions,[18] state-sector enterprises could largely disregard the cost and efficiency implications of occupational welfare. They could afford generous welfare provisions to their employees because these were all paid for by the state: 'their benefits are passed directly to the state budget and do not represent a cost to enterprise management, because a fixed proportion of the wage bill is set aside each year for funding these provisions, and the funds cannot legally be used for other purposes' (Walder 1986: 43). Further, their growth and survival had nothing to do with profit; they had more to do with their size and the scale of their production. 'The permanently loss-making enterprises can survive and even expand. The final amount of profit is not decided by the market but through bargaining between the enterprise and its superior authorities' (Kornai 1990: 192). There was therefore little pressure on enterprises to run occupational welfare efficiently, cut costs, or reduce expenditure.

The pressure was rather in the opposite direction: in Kornai's words, to 'pump' the state for ever more allocations. Throughout the period 1949–89, state subsidies to support ailing enterprises and regulate the supply and prices of goods amounted to as much as 20 per cent of state expenditure (Leung 1994). 'It was this type of support, even in the face of inefficiency and low productivity, that provided the metal for the "iron rice bowl" and which enabled people to keep their jobs and feel secure irrespective of their own performance or that of their enterprise' (Westwood and Leung 1996: 383).

The institutional environment for occupational welfare has been radically transformed by the economic reforms introduced since 1979. 'Market transition' (Nee 1989, 1991, 1992) reduces the role of bureaucratic allocation and increases the role of the market. In less than ten years, it has ushered in a 'mixed economy' which 'retain[s] some elements of the traditional Soviet-type economic system along with the adoption of some elements of market socialism' (Dernberger 1989: 21), with a dominant but shrinking state sector coexisting with an expanding non-state sector. The mixed economy is characterized by the 'co-existence of multiple ownership forms' (Nee 1994: 6). It consists not only of state- and collective-owned enterprises, but a growing number of 'private business' (*siying qiye*), shareholding companies and various forms of joint ventures with foreign and overseas Chinese capital. Market transition has also given rise to mixed or 'hybrid organizational forms' at the 'grass-roots level' (i.e., in the firm). 'Within many firms today, the market and planning coexist: some subunits are operated according to the principles of a market economy, while others are still state- or collective-owned and operated according to the principles of a planned economy .... A typical firm is now a hybrid' (Su 1994: 199).

In 1994, there were eight million enterprises in the non-state sector employing 22 million workers. Their output accounted for 25 per cent of the country's gross output value of industry. State-owned enterprises were still the main employer, employing two-thirds (66.4 per cent) of China's urban labour force. But they were producing only one-third (34.1 per cent) of the country's industrial output (see Table 1.5). In Guangzhou, in terms of both number of employees and size of capital asset, the non-state sector now is almost as big as the state sector (*Guangzhou Shi Tongji Ju* 1995: 76–8).

The scaling down if not yet dismantling of the command economy has many implications for both the *danwei* and its workers.

For the *danwei*, the most important implication is that it is now required to be profit-oriented and 'be solely responsible for its profits

Table 1.5   **Number of Enterprises, Number of Employees (millions), and Gross Output Value of Industry by Sector, 1994**

	Number of Enterprises	Number of Employees (in million)	No. of Employees in Percentage	Gross Output Value of Industry (in billion yuan)	Gross Output Value of Industry in Percentage
State-owned Enterprises	102,200	43.69	66.4	2,620.08	34.1
Collective-owned Enterprises	1,863,000	16.04	24.4	3,143.40	40.9
Individual-owned Enterprises	8,007,400	6.07	9.2	885.32	11.5
Other Ownership Enterprises	44,500	–	–	1,042.14	13.5
Total		65.9	100.0	7,690.94	100.0

Source: State Statistical Bureau (1995: 375, 376).

and losses' ('*zifu yingqui*'). It has to work with 'hard-budget constraints' and face the possibility of bankruptcy.[19] Occupational welfare cannot but enter into cost-efficiency considerations. The question now haunting every *danwei* is: Can it still carry on with its welfare responsibilities? The question is a realistic and pressing one. Many state enterprises, especially ones with an ageing workforce or large retired sector, are in very poor shape to compete with enterprises in the non-state sector, which provide fewer welfare benefits to employees, and which usually also have a younger labour force[20] and enjoy tax concessions.[21] Many have, therefore, performed very badly; the number that lost money and their total losses have been increasing since 1985. In 1995, 'officially, 42.2 per cent of SOEs [state-owned enterprises] reported losses. Many unofficial sources indicate that about one-third of SOEs that reported profits were actually in the red' (Lee 1996: 270).

In 1994, state-owned enterprises reported a total loss of 36.6 billion yuan, or 9 per cent of the state's total revenue.

In a large-scale survey of state-owned enterprises, the State Council asked each general manager to identify three main reasons for losses. In descending order the top three reasons reported were the 'heavy burden of social services', 'poor internal organization structure' and 'heavy historical burdens'. The major historical burdens were 'surplus labour', or concealed unemployment, and 'retired workers' (Lee 1996: 270–1). It was obvious that occupational welfare was the main if not the only culprit for the failure of state-owned enterprises.

The attribution of blame was not groundless. The 'heavy burden of social services' has undermined the performance of state-owned enterprises in several important ways. First, it has raised the cost of production. Secondly, it has eaten into funds for capital accumulation and reinvestment. Thirdly, it has led to inflated and inefficient management structures. Fourthly, when welfare is taken for granted and when 'non-wage compensation may be even greater than that of wages' (Hu and Li 1993: 172), it has undermined wage incentives.

The 'burden of social services' has been particularly heavy on 'old' enterprises. Besides having 'ageing facilities' (Lee 1996: 264) and outdated technology, and hence low quality products, these firms are also more likely to have an ageing workforce and large pensioner populations, hence also huge medical and pensions bills. 'Old' enterprises have become trapped in vicious cycles of low productivity, heavy social service burden and swelling debts.

Many state-owned enterprises were also entangled in 'triangular debt'.[22] Before 1985, the financial needs of state enterprises for long-term and infrastructure investment were met by state allocations. The policy of 'converting fund allocation to bank loans' (*tou gai dai*) in 1985 changed the rules of the game on capital budgeting. Instead of obtaining fund allocation from the state, state-owned enterprises had to turn to state banks for loans. However, following the 'cold shower' policy introduced in 1991, bank loans became difficult to obtain. By 1993, many state-owned enterprises were locked in 'triangular debts', which in 1995 amounted to 700 billion yuan (Ming Pao 6 December 1995). It was estimated that 'about one-third of state bank loans may be bad' (Lee 1996: 275) and, as a result, the financial position of many state banks was 'shaky'.[23] 'Most SOEs will not be able to borrow additional capital in open, free financial markets and will face bankruptcy if the creditors have the power to call in their credits and loans' (Lee 1996: 270). Indebted enterprises had got state banks into serious financial troubles.

The state sector was no longer the dominant sector it used to be. In 1994, it was producing only 34 per cent of the country's gross output value of industry, less than half its share in 1962 (State Statistical Bureau 1995). Notwithstanding its declining importance, however, it was still the country's largest employer and produced around 60 per cent of the state's revenue (Li 1996: 64–5). Even more importantly, it was what still stood for socialism and public ownership. The 'haemorrhaging losses' (Lee 1996: 296) of the state enterprises had, therefore, many grave implications. They drained the state of an important source of its revenue. Were these enterprises to go bankrupt, millions of workers would be forced out of their jobs. This would lead to a host of social problems. [24] Also, many state banks would be in trouble if their debtors went bankrupt. It could all add up to a major financial 'crisis'.

The 'crisis' is not simply financial. Because *danwei* welfare has been an important means by which the socialist state legitimates its rule, any failure to continue to deliver and any attempt to roll back such welfare or make the recipients pay for what has hitherto been free or largely free on demand could touch off a 'legitimacy crisis', reminiscent of how some neo-Marxist writers (Castells 1977, O'Connor 1973) describe the fiscal and political problems plaguing the capitalist state.[25] *Danwei* members are bound to ask: Why should we pay for what used to be our entitlements? Is this still the socialism which we have worked all our lives for? What has happened to socialism? In this 'crisis' lurks the danger of the urban state-sector citizenry withdrawing their consent and support of communist rule. The 'crisis' has, therefore, posed a difficult question to the socialist state: How can it strike a balance between the twin goals of socialist legitimacy and economic growth? The 'crisis' has also posed a difficult question to state-owned enterprises: Is there a way out of the dilemma between welfare obligation and productive efficiency?

The rise of the mixed economy, however, has created not just new problems but also new opportunities, for example, the opportunity to charge, if only on a partial basis, for what has hitherto been distributed free or largely free to *danwei* members. There is now the possibility of wedding market and redistribution, or, in other words, of 'going quasi-market': what used to be benefits and welfare can be priced and offered, and not just to the market within but also the market external to the *danwei*. In short, there are now numerous possibilities of combining welfare and business and linking the bureaucracy to the market. These, then, provide the basis of a new *danwei* economy of welfare, a 'mixed economy of welfare'.

For the workers, the mixed economy has created new structures of opportunities centred on the marketplace. There is a growing job market not only for full-time but also part-time jobs, and, which is very unlike state-sector jobs, there are few barriers to mobility (Feng and Xu 1993). In a very important way, therefore, this breaks down the monopoly of the state sector on job opportunities and extends the range of economic opportunities and personal choice. It becomes possible, as in Hungary, for families to 'build lives on two pillars: one in the formal, and another in the informal sector', and 'build into their long-term strategies the stable existence and wide acceptance of the second economy, ... to plan and economize the work and participation of their members, tending to follow an optimal division between the two economies' (Szalai and Orosz 1992: 155–6). The rise of the mixed economy enables workers to move away from their near-complete dependence on the *danwei*. 'Exit' from the *danwei*, partially or totally, is now possible, and, through strategies which often strategically involve their family members, optimize advantages obtainable from both the state sector and the non-state economy – for example, security and welfare from the former and opportunities and profit from the latter. Near-complete dependence on occupational welfare gives way to a distinctive 'mixed economy of welfare' – distinctive with regard to the role of family and the changing relations between work and welfare across the traditional public and the new private sectors.

But while workers enjoy a new sense of freedom and a much wider range of choices and opportunities afforded by a mixed economy, they are also exposed to risks and problems never experienced before. 'To those who have lived within or managed a Soviet-type economy for three decades, these instabilities can be quite alarming' (*Beijing Review* 1990: 20). The prospects of bankruptcy and job layoffs threaten their livelihood. Double-figure inflation erodes their real income.[26] The widening gap between their income and the much higher income earned by workers in the non-state economy also creates a heightened sense of relative deprivation and inequity.[27] The frustration and anguish are vividly expressed in the popular expression, '*Duan qi wan kuai chi rou. Fang xia kuai zi ma liang*' ('Cursing between mouthfuls'). For the first time, security cannot be taken for granted and the *danwei* can be unreliable. For the first time, there are risks in state-sector jobs. The 'iron rice bowl' and the practice of 'eating out of the common pot' are becoming things of the past.

Research questions, concepts and hypotheses

This study describes a unique system of social welfare undergoing a process of social change and, on the basis of empirical evidence and fieldwork data, attempts to reappraise the relevance of a number of key Western concepts and theories to Chinese welfare: for example, the notions of obligations and entitlements, mixed economy of welfare, and the family as the strategic means by which individuals optimize their life-chances and welfare opportunities.

Chinese occupational welfare is unique in that it is a very rare and extreme case of *near-complete dependence*, a situation in which the employer assumes the widest possible range of responsibilities for the welfare of the employees and the employees have the fewest possible alternatives for satisfying their needs. It departs radically from more common situations of *limited dependence* in which the employer assumes obligations over only a limited range of welfare and benefits and the employees have alternatives for satisfying their needs. These two modes of occupational welfare dependence can be regarded as positioned wide apart from each other on a continuum.

In the Chinese context, near-complete occupational welfare dependence of workers on their *danwei* is a defining feature of urban life in a state redistributive economy. In it is embodied the socialist state's obligations to its urban citizenry and the latter's rights and entitlements as state employees. It is constitutive of the *gemeinschftlich danwei* community, which embraces and controls many aspects of the life of its members. It explains socio-cultural features such as paternalism, egalitarianism and particularism which characterize life in the *danwei* community. It provides an important means by which the communist regime gains the consent of its rule from the urban workers. It is a source of legitimation.

The purpose of this study is to explain such a unique system of occupational welfare: how it came about, how it worked, how it coped with market reforms and how it has changed. The focus is on its response to change.

More specifically, the study addresses three sets of questions:

1. How do we explain the origins of the Chinese model of near-complete occupational welfare dependence? How did it come about? In the style of 'new institutionalism', what were the contexts – cultural, institutional, historical, political – within which it was brought about?

2. How is it organized? How does it work? With what sorts of economic and political logic? In terms of what sorts of ideas and values? And with what social, economic, moral, and welfare implications?
3. Market transition has since 1978 shifted the state redistributive economy towards a mixed economy with a dominant but declining state sector and a growing non-state sector. In what ways has this change affected the work-unit, the *danwei* community and the individual workers? What are the problems as well as opportunities which this change has brought about? In what ways has this change reordered and reshaped occupational welfare obligations and entitlements? In what ways has it reconfigured the uses which workers make of welfare and resources available from both the 'traditional' state and the new private sectors? How has the socialist firm responded to the challenge of the market and resolved, if at all, the dilemma between discharging its welfare obligations and ensuring productive efficiency?

On the basis of empirical evidence and field data, it is argued that in the course of economic and social change, Chinese occupational welfare has shifted away from near-complete dependence towards a distinctive pattern of limited dependence which combines in a unique way strategic uses of the mixed economy. Emerging from this change is a hybrid configuration, a mixed economy of welfare which provides new substance and meanings to occupational welfare, reshapes workers' welfare dependence, and creates new opportunities as well as problems for the socialist firm and its members, with far-reaching implications.

2
Research Method

The method of participant observation

This study is mainly based on participant observation and informant interviewing at a state-owned enterprise in the city of Guangzhou in the province of Guangdong in China, over a period of four months between September and December 1994. During this time, I paid several visits to the enterprise, lived in its vicinity and observed it at close range.[1] My role was that of a researcher from Hong Kong interested in how the enterprise ran its occupational welfare. It was in this capacity that I gained access to different kinds of information and conducted informant interviews with the help of two sets of 'guides' constructed before I entered the field, a 'Fieldwork Checklist' (Appendix I), which helped me identify relevant information while talking to people and asking for materials, and an 'Interviewing Schedule' (Appendix II), which structured my interviews with informants. Interviews ranged from formal meetings to informal conversations. I taped most of these and made notes of the rest. Altogether 28 informants were interviewed. Among them were senior cadres, managers, professionals, technicians and workers (Appendix III).[2]

In my other field roles, either as a 'research participant' or as a 'real participant' (Gans 1982: 398–9), I took part in a number of events and functions at the enterprise, joining the activities of cadres, managers, technicians and workers as their guest. These roles enabled me to observe activities and meanings in their natural settings.

The data used consisted of interviews, field-notes and documentary materials given to me at my request, including various publications, organizational charts and a set of in-house newspapers.

Gaining entry to the field was the most difficult part. The socialist firm 'has remained a black box in conventional analyses of state socialism' (Burawoy and Lukacs 1985: 723). Part of the reason must have been the great difficulty Western researchers have in gaining entry and obtaining the trust and co-operation of enterprise cadres and workers. It is difficult to gain entry to the socialist firm because it is not simply an economic organization: it is also a part of the state bureaucracy. Gaining entry to the socialist firm is just as difficult as gaining entry to the state bureaucracy of a communist state. In China, a study such as this one would have been inconceivable in the 1970s when 'politics takes command' and when 'struggles' were in train, at times at fever pitch, against 'class enemies'. Contacts with outsiders, particularly Westerners, were politically risky and had to be avoided. Contacts with the 'Chinese people in Hong Kong and Macao' (*Gangau tongbao*) were as hazardous and shunned. I had been lucky. The study was conducted in one of China's most 'open' cities and during one of the most 'liberal' times in post-Mao China. Being Chinese and speaking the same language, I did not run into cultural barriers that might have separated Western researchers from their field. I was also helped by a useful link with the Guangzhou Academy of Social Science with which I had many years of collaboration. The Academy introduced me to a number of enterprises and asked for their permission for me to do fieldwork in their plants. Some of these requests were rejected, but others responded positively. Lastly, I was helped by my appointment some 18 months before going into the field by the Chinese Government as its Hong Kong Affairs Adviser. The appointment gave me a 'respected' identity and status which helped my acceptance. During the first day in the field, I was given a reception by the *danwei* at which I was formally presented to senior cadres and department chiefs. The occasion *sanctioned* my activity in the plant and smoothed the way ahead. Later on, I also found out that, prior to my visit, plant management had sent notices to all workshops and departments explaining my visit and asking for their co-operation and support. This greatly helped my field activities.

Fieldwork was carried out in two phases. In the first phase, I concentrated on meeting and interviewing the *danwei*'s leaders (including its party secretary) and tried to gather as much factual information as possible on the *danwei*, the operation of its various benefits and services, its problems and how it coped with change. In the second phase, I talked to workers and tried to find out their perceptions and experiences, their 'stories' both of themselves and of their *danwei*. These accounts were inevitably subjective. But to make sure that they were reliable, I cross-checked one account with another on consistencies and factual accuracies. For example, I asked all of them how much they were earning when they first joined the plant, how much they were earning now, how much they were paying for rents and the sizes of their flats, and so on. Also, to make sure that I was not interviewing a biased group of workers, I tried to include in my 'sample' a balanced mix of male and female workers, workers in various age groups and workers with various levels of skills.

Case study

The site was the Dongfang Heavy Machinery Works (DFMW),[3] manufacturer of a wide range of machinery products, including petrochemical equipment, pressure vessels, centrifuges, separators and sugar mills. DFMW is one of the largest of its kind in China and is among the largest state-owned enterprises in Guangzhou.[4] In 1994, it had over 5,200 workers. Its many workshops, buildings and dormitories occupy 550,000 square metres of land along the east bank of the Pearl River in the southwestern part of the city (Figure 2.1). Established in 1948, the enterprise is nearly as old as the Republic. As will be described in Chapter 4, during the last two decades, this 'old' enterprise, just as other state-sector enterprises in China, had been through various reforms and changes which have the overall effect of reducing its dependence on the state, increasing its autonomy and enhancing its orientation as a profit-seeking firm in a socialist economy in market transition. At the time of the fieldwork, the enterprise was in the final phase of a process of enterprise reform which was turning it into a holding company and its various workshops and sub-units into subsidiary companies.

Typical of a large-scale state enterprise, DFMW provides a comprehensive range of benefits, goods and services to its employees and their families. It operates a hospital, a school, a nursery, a day-care centre, a technical school and four canteens. It runs its own security and fire brigades. It provides low-rental housing to over 3,000 families. Typical of an old plant, it has a large and growing retiree population. In 1994, it had over 2,300 retired workers. Just as in other state enterprises, its employees enjoy comprehensive 'cradle to grave' benefits and welfare, including, among others, retirement pensions, medical and health insurance, injury, disability and death benefits, various benefits for women workers, and holiday, sick leave and leave of absence benefits. Also, as in other state enterprises, its employees are paid various subsidies and allowances. (See Table 2.1 for an example of the kind of

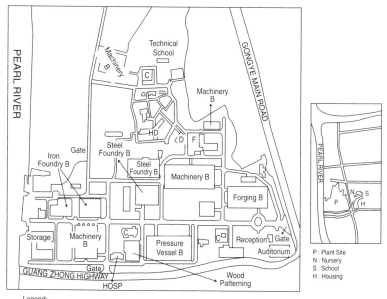

Legend:
C: Canteen B: Branch HD: Headquarter HOSP: Hospital D: Day Care F: Fire Brigade

Figure 2.1   Map of Dongfang Heavy Machinery Works

subsidies and allowances listed on the pay cheque of an ordinary worker.) In these senses the enterprise is 'large and comprehensive'. Hence it has all the features of a *danwei* experiencing the problems commonly shared by state-sector enterprises as they brave market competition: the problem of having to shoulder a welfare 'burden' that has grown heavier and heavier over time and the problem of having to compete with non-state enterprises on unequal grounds.

The city of Guangzhou is close to Hong Kong. Its economic progress since the introduction of economic reforms is one of the fastest among coastal cities.[5] It is therefore not a typical Chinese city. But because it is ahead of many other cities in market transition, in it one can see much more clearly than in other cities the impact of economic reforms on its state-sector enterprises.

This is therefore a case study in the style of participant observation of occupational welfare in a state-owned enterprise within a socialist economy undergoing market transition.

There have been two traditional criticisms of the case study method: 'first, that it is incapable of generalization and therefore not a true

Table 2.1   Itemized Monthly Pay-cheque (Yuan) of an Ordinary Worker[*]

Credits	
Basic wage	144.00
Productivity wage	17.00
Seniority subsidy	5.00
Contribution to superannuable fund	7.20
Water, electricity and vegetable subsidies	11.00
General subsidy	12.00
Non-staple food subsidy	15.44
Transport subsidy	8.00
Coal subsidy	4.00
Single-child allowance	5.00
Debits	
Contribution to superannuable fund	14.40
Insurance premium	14.36
Net pay	199.88

[*] This does not include bonus payments linked to the worker's productivity.

science and, second, that it is inherently "micro" and historical and therefore not true sociology' (Burawoy 1991: 271). These criticisms are not all fair and valid. Geertz's (1973) classic study of Balinese cockfighting, for example, is an elegant example of how the case study is capable of producing general statements about the wider society in which the case is embedded. In studying kinship relations among the Lakeside Tonga of Malawi, Van Velsen (1967) was struck by the extent to which actual marriage patterns *deviated* from the normative ideal. This directed his attention to the broader economic and political forces impinging on the Tonga and led him to question and rethink existing theories on migration. 'By reconstructing existing theories of migration in this way, Van Velsen was able to generalize from his case study' (Burawoy 1991: 279). As these examples show and as Burawoy (ibid.) convincingly argues, case studies can also reflect on the 'macro' and yield generalizations.

This case study of Chinese occupational welfare is intended not only to show what it is like in one particular work-unit and what it might be like in similar work-units, but also, through the case, to reflect on the wider society. It tries to find out how the 'micro' experience of occupational welfare in one particular *danwei* has been shaped by 'macro' forces. From changes observed in such experience it asks questions on social change and relates changes experienced by one *danwei* to changes occurring to the society as a whole.

The advantage of the case study is that it does allow the researcher to pore over the case being studied to gain an in-depth understanding of the 'inside story': people, institutions and environment in interaction; perceptions and experiences; memories; meanings and values; relations and networks; processes at work; and the interplay of subjective experiences and objective forces.

As in other participant-observation studies, I did not go into the field with preconceived concepts and ready-to-test hypotheses. I went into the field mainly oriented by three general questions:

1. How does this *danwei* organize its occupational welfare?
2. Much must have happened since reforms. What specifically has happened to this *danwei*? What has happened to occupational welfare?
3. How do members of the *danwei* perceive and experience the changes that have occurred to their *danwei* and to *danwei* welfare?

I asked these questions and from answers given conceptualized what struck me as interesting and important. These 'concepts' than led me to ask more specific questions, to reconceptualize and formulate the 'hypotheses' to be 'tested' by further field data. In short, I allowed concepts and hypotheses to 'emerge' from the process.

The subjective perspective

Two important insights have been gained in this process. The first is the understanding that welfare consists not only of what is 'dictated' by policies and distributed through formal, institutional arrangements. It consists also of what is 'rooted in the experience of everyday life', in the 'informal, transient, self-organizing networks of relationships' and in 'voluntary association and mutual aid' (Ward 1982: 5). *Danwei* members and their families do not just depend on what is given. They also fend for themselves and 'depend' on their own acts and resources, on their families and on self-organized networks and mutual aid. In other words, there is, besides 'organized welfare', 'self-organized welfare'. In studying occupational welfare, therefore, it is not enough to focus only on the formal and the institutional, on what the *danwei* does for its members. It should also look at what its members are doing for themselves in addition to what the *danwei* is doing for them.

It is important, in other words, not to lose sight of the *subjective perspective*. This perspective directs one's attention to the subjective experience of 'organized welfare', i.e. how people experience the welfare provided through policies and institutions, and also to the experience of 'self-organized welfare', i.e. how they support and provide security for themselves through arrangements and resources based on everyday life experience.

The second insight is that these subjective experiences do interact with and impinge on 'objective' welfare policies and institutions and, as a result, help reshape these policies and institutions. Let me give an example. Allocation of *danwei* housing was based largely on worker seniority. Once it was allocated, the occupants could keep it for the rest of their life. And, when *tingti* (replacement) was practised, *danwei* housing became virtually inheritable. Economic reforms since 1979 and the rise of a mixed economy had broken down barriers against mobility and created many new job opportunities in the non-state economy. Many workers, and particularly young workers, were leaving their state-sector jobs for jobs in the non-state sector. These jobs were usually much better paid, but were typically without the many benefits made available to jobs in the state sector. DFMW, the state enterprise where we did fieldwork, was, just like other state enterprises, losing many skilled workers. To try to stop the outflow of skilled workers and also to make jobs with the enterprise more attractive, DFMW introduced a number of changes to its housing policy. These required quitters to give up their quarters, allowed skilled workers without the necessary seniority to jump the queue, and required workers allocated ownership flats to sign an agreement committing themselves to working for the enterprise until they retired. In short, *danwei* had reshaped its housing policy to make it more flexible and more instrumental.

In this perspective, therefore, policies and institutions change over time not only in response to new socio-economic conditions and 'on the basis of – or in reaction to – previous policy accomplishments' (Weir et al. 1988: 17), but also as a result of their interaction with sub-jective experiences.

This study is therefore very much about the interplay of the 'objec-tive' and the 'subjective' and about how in the process it reshapes dependence and the nature of occupational welfare in a socialist state undergoing market transition.

3
The Origins of Chinese Occupational Welfare

Introduction

Chinese occupational welfare was unique in that the socialist state provided comprehensive welfare to city workers in employment in the state sector. Why did the state feel it necessary to do this? Why this degree of responsibility? Why urban workers? And why not also rural workers?[1]

Explaining the origins of this unique system purely in terms of the ideological traditions of Confucianism, which teaches the values of benevolence and care, and Marxism, which is committed to ending class inequality and exploitation, does not give entirely satisfactory answers. The late Imperial state was steeped in the Confucian traditions,[2] yet its involvement in welfare was very limited.[3] The state relied very much on community initiatives – charitable halls and guilds, among others – to provide welfare and services to its urban population. The former East European communist states had systems of occupational welfare (Deacon 1992: 1–30) reminiscent of the Chinese system, but the welfare which they provided was less comprehensive and their workers were not as dependent on workplace-distributed goods and services as in the Chinese system. 'The greater scarcity of food and consumer goods in China and the administrative role of enterprises in past decades in rationing and distributing a wide array of daily necessities and consumer items have broadened the range of needs met by the enterprises and restricted the alternatives' (Walder 1986: 81). In the Soviet Union, rationing had not been commonly practised since World War II. The steady developments of consumer markets since the 1950s had also provided an alternative to direct workplace distributions.

In seeking to explain the origins of Chinese occupational welfare, we have found three perspectives useful. The first is the perspective shared among 'new institutionalists' (for example, Stark and Nee 1989), which takes the view that state socialism represents a distinct social formation that has its own institutional logic and dynamics of development. In the light of this perspective, Chinese occupational welfare must be studied in its national and historical contexts, and as part of an institutional configuration characteristic of state socialism.

The second is a 'state-centred' perspective, the perspective which 'brings the state back in' (Skocpol 1985) to explain politics and governmental activities. Conceived as organizations claiming control over territories and the people within them,[4] states may formulate and pursue goals that are not simply reflective of the demands or interests of social groups. In this perspective, it will be useful when explaining policies to find out what these have to do with the nature of the state, how these may have followed from the activities of autonomous state actions, and how these may relate to the ways in which the state structures its relations with society.

There are two salient reasons for bringing the state in to explain the origins of Chinese occupational welfare. First, until only recently, the Chinese socialist state was very 'powerful': the extension of state functions was almost unlimited and the state bureaucracy was ubiquitous, displacing or eliminating the market, replacing or pre-empting voluntary associations and secondary groups, and imposing on and intruding into many areas of people's everyday life (Whyte 1991). The Chinese socialist state was more than a 'weighty actor' (Skocpol 1985: 3); it was a heavyweight one.

Secondly, and even more importantly, it was a state whose leaders shared a 'totalist vision' (Tsou 1991; Whyte 1991), the view that the state should totally dominate social life and that there should be no limit to state power. It was a state whose leaders believed that the scale and the seriousness of the problems besetting their country required nothing less than an all-out approach and the total effort of their people, or, in other words, a total if therefore also revolutionary solution. From this vision followed the belief that the state should have all the powers to do all that it needed to do to bring about the desired outcomes and that there should be no limit to the extension of state power.

These two reasons – the state had both the 'might' and the 'will' to rule – together explained the high degree of state autonomy. It makes good sense in explaining the origins of Chinese occupational welfare, therefore, to find out what it had to do with the nature of the Chinese socialist state and with the ways it pursued its goals and actions.

The third perspective that we have found useful is essentially that of the historical perspective. To explain the 'origins' of Chinese occupational welfare, we believe it is important to find out how it came about 'historically', i.e. how it followed from antecedent events and policies and from pre-existing conditions and institutions. As Skocpol made the case in her explanation of the origins of civil war pensions in the United States: 'Analysts typically look for synchronic determinants of policies – for example, in current social interests or in existing political alliances. In addition, however, we must examine patterns unfolding over time (and not only long-term macroscopic processes of social change and polity reorganization)' (Skocpol 1992: 50).

In this study of the origins of Chinese occupational welfare, we submit that the most significant 'patterns unfolding over time' had to do with the formation of the Chinese socialist state:[5] the guerrilla war experiences of its revolutionary leaders, their experiences with a war-devastated economy and their quest for equality and security, the socialist strategy of industrialization, and, in general, what occurred in the early years of the Republic. We intend to argue that the unique experience of the formation of the Chinese socialist state largely explains the unique nature of Chinese occupational welfare.

The welfare role of the imperial state

The involvement of the socialist state in welfare was unprecedented and exceptional in Chinese history: it was not in the tradition of the Chinese state to be directly involved in the provision of welfare services to its urban population.

The late Imperial state, for example, had a very limited role in public welfare. The state's welfare role was largely limited to regulating the supply of grain and disaster relief.

The government regulated grain supply through a system of government granaries. There was an 'ever-normal granary' (*changping cang*) in each province or county, in the charge of a local magistrate:

> These granaries were so called because part of the grain stored in them could be sold to local residents at a price lower than the market price in the spring when the market price was high; in the autumn the granaries could replenish their supplies with the funds obtained from the spring sale. In time of famine the poor families

could borrow grain from these granaries and pay it back after the harvest without interest. Such loans had to be reported to the magistrate's superior officials and approved by them. (Ch'u 1962: 156–7)

Although the system of the ever-normal granary was devised to benefit the poor, it did not always work out to their advantage. Taking advantage of the lower price of the government grain, speculators and profiteers, with the co-operation of the granary clerks, often bought large quantities by using false names, although this was forbidden by law. Moreover, there was frequently a shortage of grain in many of the granaries, largely because of mismanagement and, in some cases, embezzlement.

In addition to the ever-normal granaries, many provinces or counties had 'community granaries' (*she cang*) and/or 'public granaries' (*yi cang*) from which local residents could borrow grain, at or free of interest, depending upon the local harvest condition. These granaries were established in the villages or towns by the local residents, through voluntary donations. But, as in government granaries, there was frequently a shortage of grain and 'in general, the directors were indifferent and the management poor; in many areas the community granaries operated ineffectively or even ceased to operate' (Ch'u 1962: 159).

Disaster relief involved, when calamity struck, besides sending in troops to keep order, 'emergency disbursement of grain from official granaries and, in the most severe cases, with the issuance of daily cash subsidies to the homeless. If the calamity happened in mid-winter, local officials sometimes commissioned the manufacture of winter garments for free distribution to the needy, and, when lingering floodwaters spawned epidemics, they distributed free medical supplies' (Rowe 1989: 93).

But, even as it carried out disaster relief, the role of the administration had tended to be essentially to 'prompt and endorse' (*'quan yu'*), leaving the task of 'financing and implementing' (*'juan ban'*) relief efforts to 'merchants and people'. Hence even in disaster relief, the private sector appeared to have always played the larger role in both emergency and routine efforts to prevent starvation among urban residents.

Beyond its limited role in regulating grain prices and dispensing relief, the Qing administration sponsored a number of agencies involved in the direct provision of welfare services to members of the urban population. Of these the 'poor houses' (*puji tang*) and orphanges (*yuying tang*) were most important. In every district there was a poor house where the aged, disabled and poor were housed and given rations, clothing and medical care. The 'poor houses' were established by local officials. An item in the Qing code charged county magistrates with providing 'sufficient maintenance and protection' to all 'poor destitute widowers and widows, fatherless children, and the helpless and infirm'. Over time, 'poor houses' gradually 'shifted out of official into local societal hands'. As the poor houses usually had limited funds, only a small number of poor people could be admitted. 'For this reason, conscientious magistrates found it necessary to raise funds to meet the need, often through contributions from the magistrates themselves and from the gentry and well-to-do commoners' (Ch'u 1962: 161). The orphanages were established in early Qing as a formal government agency under the direct supervision of the magistrate. With a few exceptions no official funds were provided and, as in the case of the poor houses, 'it was left to the magistrates and/or the gentry to raise money' for the orphanages. Both the poor houses and the orphanages became by and large financed and managed by local elites.

The shift from official to private responsibility had in part to do with the state's continued maintenance of outdated concepts of public welfare needs in the face of population growth and increasing social complexity. Local officials continued to see their responsibilities for public welfare as limited to ad hoc disaster relief, and to prompting and encouraging local elites to come forward to give support. In part this had to do with a rise in community initiatives. The rise of community initiatives was partly in response to the need for increased services, 'when the range of collective services demanded by the community had radically outstripped the growth of state organization', partly to do with the fact that the Qing examinations produced far more degree-holders than the government could absorb into official posts; hence community responsibilities 'provided an outlet for the energy of an elite that could not be wholly employed in the bureaucracy' (Fairbank 1992: 238), and partly inspired by the Confucian moral of benevolence and public-mindedness.

Of these community initiatives, the 'benevolent halls' (*shantang*) and the guilds (*huiguan*) were most important and successful. The benevolent halls were basically neighbourhood self-help institutions initiated, financially supported and managed by merchants. Most served as multifaceted relief agencies providing a wide range of services, including public burial of deceased persons who were either unidentified or whose kin were financially unable to provide coffins or burial plots, disbursement of winter clothing, tea, grain and rice gruel and, increasingly, provision of medical services. By the late nineteenth century, the benevolent halls were everywhere. They had become a 'key (perhaps the key) institution of late nineteenth century urban community' (Rowe 1984: 126). In most cases, the officials had no voice in overseeing their affairs.

The guild was a fraternal association whose members usually engaged in a single economic activity; often, but not necessarily sharing a common geographic origin that was not the city in which the guild was located (Golas 1977: 559). Besides economic and cultural functions (e.g. settling commercial disputes among members and celebrating festivals), the guilds also performed welfare and charitable works for its members (e.g. providing coffins and burial sites, and food and clothing for destitute members) and, increasingly, for the wider community within which the guild was located. One benevolent hall founded in Guangzhou (Canton) in 1871 jointly by the leading guilds in the city, for example, 'provided free outpatient care to the indigent sick, financial support for destitute widows, and free coffins for the poor; it also supported several free primary schools for the children of the poor' (Skinner 1977: 549). In another case, a federation of ten guilds 'operated an orphanage and granary, maintained a militia, and was responsible for fire fighting, the maintenance of roads and bridges, and disaster relief' (Skinner 1977: 550). As these and other examples show, the guilds played an active role in local philanthropy and community services in China's cities.

The conclusion was quite clear: in late Imperial China, many if not most urban services, and most if not all welfare and charitable works, were provided by non-governmental corporate groups. The Qing 'minimalist form of government' (Rankin 1986) relied on local elites to deal with public matters that fell in between the official and the private levels. 'Caring for the ill and for widows and foundlings, maintaining temples, bridges, and ferries, fighting fires, and burying dead were all customary gentry-aided services. They were now coordinated in many localities under omnicompetent welfare agencies headed by prominent local figures and often backed by native-place guilds' (Fairbank 1992: 239). State agents had assumed a less than direct and active role, their parts overshadowed by non-governmental agencies and largely limited to 'selectively extending patronage to projects initiated by local forces, orchestrating these initiatives, and balancing the interests of various social groups' (Rowe 1989: 184). The state's role in welfare was minimal and increasingly in decline, consistent with a 'long-term secular trend from official to private responsibility' (Shiba Yoshinobu, cited in Rowe 1989: 131) throughout the nineteenth century.

Guerrilla war experience

The communist ascendancy to power in 1949 was preceded by nearly a decade (1937–45) of guerrilla warfare fought at and from base areas in the remote, undeveloped and poverty-stricken region in the northwestern border provinces of Shansi-Gansu-Ningxia[6] against the armies of Japanese invasion and the Guomindang Nationalist government. Except during brief and intermittent periods of truce with the Nationalist Government the communists were besieged and blockaded by enemy military forces. There was severe shortage of supplies and great economic hardship for the 'institutional households' (Schran 1976: 96) of armies, cadres and their dependants. During the most difficult times, they had hardly any supplies of 'clothes, cooking oil, paper, vegetable, shoes and stockings, and blankets' (Mao 1976: 184).

The situation was particularly serious after 1939, when the 'united front' with the Guomindang broke down and an economic blockade of the Region was tightened. The shortage of goods and the growing costs of the expanding army and bureaucracy forced the government to increase its demands on the economy. Besides a heavier grain tax which brought even poor peasants within the tax threshold, a number of revenue-raising measures were introduced, 'including a hay tax to provide fodder for government animals, taxes on wool and cattle, lotteries, levies to support the self-defense army and the sale of government bonds' (Watson 1980: 18). This rapid increase of taxation had led to a dampening of peasant enthusiasm to increase production. As the then Chairman of the Party, Mao Zedong, put it:

> When the government is in great difficulty, the people have to bear a heavier burden. This is inevitable, and we must have their understanding ... But even in these difficult periods of time, we must not go too far. The burden on the people must not be so heavy as to break their backs. We must find ways to reduce that burden and let people rest ... Only when they have good rest can they regain the enthusiasm to work hard and increase production. (Mao 1976: 185–7)

Mao also recognized that 'taxation and taxation alone was far from enough to meet the needs of fighting the war and building the country' (ibid.: 189).

The government had to find ways other than collecting taxes from the people to overcome its financial difficulties. The most important of these, and which had profound implications for the Border Region economy was the involvement of troops and public-sector organizations, including government organs and schools, in self-supporting production both to supplement the operating and living costs of their units and also to provide for their own subsistence. The practice began with trying to make up for shortages and improve the living conditions of the troops. But its potential was soon recognized and the Party began to consider the possibility of achieving self-sufficiency and of supplying some of the needs of the war. The system was then extended to all organizations and schools. Thereafter self-supporting production became a major feature of the Border Region economy both in terms of its contribution to the government's budget and in terms of its agricultural and industrial importance. By 1943, all military units, government organs and schools were engaged in production. They concentrated primarily on agriculture, but in most cases they were also operating and managing commercial and small-scale industrial enterprises. As a result of self-supporting production, the schools, for example, became self-sufficient in meat and vegetables; they produced 15–25 per cent of their grain; made their own uniform, shoes, wooden furniture, porcelain ware and other necessities; the revenue from commercial activities also contributed 48 per cent of their running costs (Mao 1976: 317–30).

Emerging from these activities was increasingly a 'mixed economy' with a growing public sector. In 1942, the public sector was generating more revenue for the government than were various kinds of taxes (Mao 1976: 260). Even more importantly, as Mao said, 'We have gained experience in running economic enterprises. This is a priceless treasure that cannot be reckoned in figures' (ibid.: 331). The experience proved to be of immense relevance and importance when in less than 20 years the socialist state began its ambitious programme to nationalise the Chinese economy.

But what is even more important from the point of view of this study was the genesis of the prototype of what was later to become the predominant organizational form in socialist China: the work-unit. The 'institutional households' of the army, government organs and schools were not just military, administrative and educational organizations; they were 'multi-functional' structures, having taken on the additional economic functions of production and collective consumption. They were also to some extent self-sufficient. Their members depended on them not just for their jobs, but for supplies of daily necessities of various kinds.

An important feature of the public sector economy was the practice of a 'supply system' (*gongji zhi*), i.e. the payment of most salaries in kind rather than in cash. The 'supply system' assured soldiers and cadres supplies of basic necessities and protected them from wartime inflation, which was drastically cutting into their purchasing power and destroying the morale of officials in Guomindang China. The supply system was largely egalitarian. Closely pegged to subsistence needs, it provided more or less the same for everyone, with only slight variations on the basis of rank or office:

> The major component of cadre income was a food allotment usually provided directly in grain. The daily grain allowance for all government cadres, regardless of rank, as well as for students on government subsidy, was one and two-thirds pounds of millet or the equivalent. All soldiers regardless of rank received one and three-quarters pounds of grain, and men in combat were allotted two pounds. Clothing and a small cash allowance for vegetables and oil completed the subsistence income for all cadres. (Selden 1971: 173)

Supplies to cadres and soldiers were pegged at levels comparable to those of factory workers. The government insisted on the egalitarian principle that 'cadre and military salaries would never exceed those of ordinary workers in the border region' (ibid.: 153). This was important because 'rations of food, clothing and housing which are comparable to those of the people not only serve to support surprisingly large numbers of them but also tend to associate them with the people' (Schran 1976: 7–8).

The 'supply system' applied not only to soldiers and cadres, but also to their dependants. 'The government assumed the additional burden of feeding and clothing cadre and soldier families' (Selden 1971: 154). But its responsibility was not limited to providing for their basic needs. Besides basic necessities, 'institutional households' also provided many cultural, educational, health care and other services collectively for their members (Schran 1976: 215). In other words, they assumed a wider range of responsibilities than just catering to the physical needs of their members.

The policy, however, was to be concerned with the needs and well-being not only of members of the 'institutional households'. The 'mass line' – the Party's political methodology – required the government and its cadres to build close relations with the people, to listen to them and be concerned with their problems and needs. As Chairman Mao put it:

> If we can only mobilize the people to carry on the war and do nothing else, can we succeed in defeating the enemy? Of course not. If we want to win, we must do a great deal more. We must lead the peasants' struggle for land and distribute land to them, heighten their enthusiasm and increase agriculture production, safeguard the interests of the workers, establish co-operatives, develop trade with outside areas, and solve the problems facing the masses – food, shelter and clothing, fuel, rice, cooking oil and salt, sickness and hygiene, and marriage. In short, all the practical problems in the masses' everyday life should claim our attention. If we attend to these problems, solve them and satisfy the needs of the masses, we shall really become organizers of the well-being of the masses, and they will truly rally round us and give us their warm support. (Mao 1953: 147–8)

The mass line was reflected by greater concern for the people's economic welfare and by involving their active participation in production movement. 'Their labor was channeled into rationalized and cooperative ventures. Much of the initial impetus and direction in the production movement were provided by the party and government, but the financing, adaptation to diverse conditions, and subsequent development depended heavily upon local resources, above all on the active participation of the entire population' (Selden 1976: 265). This approach was, in essence, Mao's model of economic development, one which grew out of the unique historical conditions and experiences of guerrilla warfare. This unique approach saw government and party cadres playing active leadership and organizational roles in economic development, mobilizing the people and involving them in an active way in economic activities.

If the co-operative movement started modestly with the aim of increasing agriculture production, in time it became an integral part of the revolutionary struggle. Peasants were recruited into the armies; work and battle teams composed of young peasants were organized; young village leaders were taken into the Party and made new cadres; and, as the war progressed, 'villages were turned into military bastions, and, accordingly, the various social forms of cooperation were linked with military forms of organization' (Schurmann 1968: 427). As a result, war, organization and work were linked and the village became militarized. The communists had created a form of organization that enabled the Party to penetrate into the village and mobilized its members to fight in war and engage in production activities.

Mao's experience in running the guerrilla economy continued to influence and shape his approach to economic development and political leadership years after the guerrilla war ended. The Great Leap Forward (1958–9) and the Cultural Revolution (1967–76) were archetypal examples of the approach applied to the country nation-wide. There are, however, five important points in this experience which are of particular interest to this study. First, the Border Region saw the genesis of the prototype of what was later to become the predominant organizational form in urban China: the work-units. The 'institutional households' of army, government organs and schools possessed features which had much in common with the socialist work units. They were multifunctional structures performing a wide range of functions and assuming a wide range of responsibilities. They 'looked after' not just public-sector employees but also their dependants, and not only their physical but also other needs. Secondly, largely because there were severe shortages of basic necessities and in order to protect soldiers and their families from wartime inflation, the public sector practised a 'supply system' which paid salaries in kind rather than in cash. Thirdly, there was a high degree of egalitarianism both between cadres and ordinary workers and between cadres and soldiers. Fourthly, the 'political methodology' of the 'mass line' required that the Party and government care for the people and consider their problems and needs. Fifthly, the Party found an effective means to organize peasants for war and production, by militarizing and mobilizing the areas under its control.

Wartime experience, in this case that of a guerrilla war fought in the unique context of revolutionary China, had a lasting impact on subsequent policy and institutional developments. The spirit of egalitarianism and the welfare value implied in the 'mass line' had become integral parts of the ideology of the socialist state. Various modified forms of the 'supply system' had continued ever since although, as a formal wage policy, the 'supply system' was discontinued in 1955. The *danwei* was the 'institutional household' writ large, the 'institutional household' within the bureaucracy of the redistributive state. The experience of mobilizing and organizing peasants for war and production taught the communists the way to organize a socialist economy.

Rehabilitation of the economy

Two most difficult economic problems faced China's revolutionary government on achieving state power in 1949. These were chronic hyperinflation and widespread urban unemployment.

Inflation started with the Japanese seizure of the most productive areas of the country and the chief sources of the Nationalist Government's revenue. It continued with the failure of the government to generate public revenue and its resorting to printing more money to finance war expenditures. It culminated in hyperinflation. By the beginning of August 1948, Shanghai wholesale prices had reached a level 4.7 million times that of early 1937 (Riskin 1987: 33).

The government brought hyperinflation under control by a combination of administrative, monetary, fiscal and economic measures. These included taking over the entire banking system to gain control of credit; requiring all enterprises, public offices and military units to deposit their holdings of all but petty cash in the People's Bank of China; and enforcing stringent economies in government spending. Two measures were, from the point of view of this study, particularly significant. (1), The government paid public employees in subsistence goods with a small money supplement, a system which had been practised in guerrilla base areas and which was to continue well unto the 1970s in the form of a system of urban rationing. (2), The government set up nationwide trading associations in each major commodity to gain control of goods. By early 1950 the inflationary spiral had been broken and inflation was reduced to about 15 per cent a year (Fairbank 1992: 348).

What was significant beyond the immediate issue of inflation, however, was that, as a result of these measures, the state gained near-complete control over foreign trade and banking, control of over half of total industrial product, and control of about one-sixth to one-quarter of wholesale and retail trade (Riskin 1987: 43). In nationalizing the economy, the state had got more than a foot in the door.

Urban unemployment was the next difficult problem. The new regime spent many years trying to solve it but with no real success. Between 4 and 12.5 million urban residents were estimated to be out of work in 1950. These numbers periodically swelled as a result of state pressures on the private sector, such as during the 'five-antis' (*wufan*) campaign, which resulted in the closing down of many businesses.

The first step taken to limit unemployment was to re-engage *en bloc* Guomindang officials. These government personnel, totalling some two million (Fairbank 1992: 348), were allowed to keep their jobs and salaries and continue to perform their functions. Besides these government officials, there were also about one million (Zhou 1993) Guomindang soldiers. They were also allowed to stay. The concept underlying the policy was *'bao'* or *'bao xia lai'*, or 'take on all and be responsible for all' of them. Premier Zhou En-lai explained in a speech given in December 1949 why the government had to assume this responsibility:

> As you know, since last year but especially this year, we have taken the large majority of the Guomindang soldiers captured by us. After we liberated Beijing, we sent several hundreds of the captured soldiers home. When we liberated Suiyuan, we ran into them again. This time there was nowhere else to send them. If we did not keep them, there could be social problems. We had to *'bao xia lai'*. Besides the soldiers, we have also *'bao'* all government personnel. Not too long ago we tried to streamline the Shanghai government. This has caused a great deal of anxieties. We reckon that it is important for people to be employed. What we have tried to do is to 'share the rice for three among five persons' (*san ge ren di fan wu ge ren chi*). And then we must explain it very clearly to the people that the several million officials and soldiers so taken on by the government are not useless. They will become a useful force in production. (Zhou 1993: 23)

What was significant beyond the immediate issue of re-engaging officials and soldiers of the ousted government was that the government assumed responsibility for providing jobs to people who would otherwise be unemployed. It was a significant step in the direction of the state assuming the responsibility of providing jobs for all.

The next step taken to limit unemployment was directed at private enterprises. The aim was to prevent these enterprises adding to the ranks of the unemployed by discharging their workers. The government required private enterprises to apply for permission either to hire or discharge any workers on the payroll or a significantly large number of temporary workers (Yuan 1991: 78).

In 1952, government regulations further stipulated that all public and private enterprises had to assume *'bao xia lai'* responsibilities for employees displaced from their jobs by new production technologies. They had to give these employees retraining and, while on retraining, their previous salaries. In 1957, this requirement, that surplus labour should not be out of work, was extended to cover government personnel and public-sector employees.

At the same time as steps were taken to limit unemployment, measures were also introduced to help unemployed workers get back to work. 'Job-introduction Offices' (*laodong jieshao suo*) under government Labour Bureaux were set up in 1950 to register and match jobs to unemployed workers. The government soon made it compulsory for all public and private sector enterprises to apply to the Labour Bureaux for the workers they wanted and for these offices to coordinate job placements. In 1955, it further stipulated that 'recruitment of new workers must be approved by state labour agencies according to a unified plan' and that 'no workplaces should recruit workers without approval' (He et al. 1990: 7). In other words, there was to be centralized job allocation. What had started as a system of job introduction had grown into a system for centrally planned placement (Bian 1994: 52). In his memoir written 40 years later, Bo Yi-bo, one of China's leading economic officials at the time, commented on what had happened:

> The economy was in a very bad shape and many people were unemployed. The Party and the government took this very seriously. They regarded helping these people and putting them back to work a big task. Chairman Mao, President Liu Shao-qi and Premier Zhou En-lai were all personally involved. The Party Centre issued directives in April, June and November 1950 on how to provide help and assistance to unemployed workers. In retrospect, there were both positive and negative aspects in what we had done. On the positive side, we did help the unemployed and as a result gain their support and trust in the new government. The negative side of this was that from then on the government took on the heavy responsibility of providing jobs and looking after the livelihood of all unemployed people. This had evolved into a system in which the state assumed '*bao xia lai*' responsibility for allocating people to jobs. (Bo 1991: 107)

By 1957, the policy of '*bao xia lai*' had been extended to cover all graduates from universities, technical colleges and vocational schools. The government assumed the responsibility to place each and every one of them in a job.

As a result of these and related measures, by 1957, 16.7 million jobs had been created and the unemployment rate was reduced to 5.9 per cent (Bian 1994: 52–3). But what were even more important than these figures were the far-reaching implications of the various measures that had been put in place to bring about these results. The first and most important was that, as a result of these measures, the state had come to assume an all-important role and responsibility in urban employment. Urban residents looked to and depended on the state rather than the market for work. The second important implication was that jobs became more or less permanent. There was no such thing as 'dismissal' or 'firing', and, once assigned to a work-unit, and unless there were job transfers, which happened only very rarely, a worker could expect to stay in the same work-unit for the rest of his or her working life. The third important implication was that the system that had been set up gave both enterprises and individual workers little autonomy or choice. It was a system that prevented enterprises from choosing their workers and workers from choosing their jobs and employers.

Socialist industrialization strategy

On the eve of the communists' victory over the Nationalist Government, Mao outlined in a speech delivered at the Seventh Plenary Session of the Party Central Committee the overall strategy to build the country as soon as the guerrilla war was over. He said:

> From 1927 to the present the centre of gravity of our work has been in the villages ... The period for this method of work has now ended. The period of 'from the city to the village' and of the city leading the village has now begun. The centre of gravity of the Party's work has shifted from the village to the city. We must revive and develop production in the cities. And we must turn the cities around, changing them from 'consumer' to 'producer' cities. Only then can we consolidate the power of the people. All our work must now focus on and serve this very central objective: develop production in the cities. (Mao 1967: 364–5)

This emphasis on the cities and on industrialization was to dominate the agenda of the Party's work in the early years of the socialist state.

According to official ideology, rural–urban relations in the period of socialist transition would have two main characteristics: first, the cities would lead the countryside, with 'industry leading agriculture' economically and 'workers leading peasants' politically; secondly, rural urban relations would change from exploitative to mutually supportive as the cities changed from centres of consumption and extraction to centres of production. In the words of Premier Zhou En-lai:

In China, rural–urban relations are very important. On one hand, China's revolution has to be led by the working class. On the other hand, to gain revolutionary victory, we must rely on the support of the peasant and the countryside ... On the question of who is to lead whom, we have now decided on the policy of the cities leading the countryside and of industry leading agriculture ... Urban demand for food and raw materials will stimulate agricultural production. The supply of consumption and producer goods by the cities will help to develop agricultural production (Zhou En-lai 1993: 28).

The stress on the cities on the one hand, and the decision to make cities centres of production rather than centres of consumption on the other, reflected the coexistence of both an 'urban bias' and an 'anti-urban bias' in the Chinese approach to the cities.

The 'urban bias' was, first of all, ideological. The Chinese communist *Weltanschauung* was, in effect, the Marxist materialist conception of history and historical change. In this conception, the driving force of both world and national history was class conflict; the inevitable resolutions of class conflict propelled history in a unilinear direction. The proletariat, according to this view, was the revolutionary class, the class to lead the struggle for socialism. The Chinese Communist Party saw itself as representing China's proletariat and in this capacity the revolutionary force leading China's socialist transformation. The cities were the home of the proletariat.

As Marxist-Leninists, the leaders of the Chinese Communist Party looked to China's cities as potential revolutionary centres. Shanghai, for example, had a glorious revolutionary history which 'dated from the May Fourth Movement and included not only the ill-fated labour movement of the 1930s and 1940s. Underground organizations loyal to the CCP were active in many spheres of Shanghai society' (Gaulton 1981: 39).

There was also an economic reason in the 'bias'. In Mao's words, the 'centre of gravity of the Party's work has shifted from the village to the city'. Now that it had won the war, the goal was to achieve industrialization nationwide. In achieving this goal the roles of cities and their industrial workers were strategic. Shanghai, in particular, was expected to play a strategic part in leading China's industrialization. As China's largest and wealthiest city, with nearly half the country's modern industry, Shanghai was a major potential source of strength for the economic reconstruction and modernization of China. The goal of the communist leaders was to raise industrial production from 10 per cent to 30 per cent or 40 per cent of total production within 10–15 years (Gaulton 1981: 39). They had to rely heavily on Shanghai and cities like Shanghai to achieve this goal.

As for the 'anti-urban bias', this was not just a Chinese proclivity. The neglect of the cities was common among socialist countries. 'Industrialization strategy in almost all socialist countries has included the desire to achieve industrialization with minimum urbanization cost' (Naughton 1995: 62). Urbanization was viewed primarily as a cost incurred in the process of industrialization; cities were costly because urban infrastructures and services – housing, hospitals, schools, sewerage and road building – were expensive. While the cost of providing for these facilities and services was unavoidable, the objective was nevertheless to try to keep it to the minimum.

In China, anti-urban attitudes might have been readily accepted because the large cities (e.g. Shanghai and Tientsin) were usually also treaty ports which had developed under foreign aegis. They were 'accompanied by the aura of corruption that came from excessive foreign influence and cooperation with the imperialists' (Naughton 1995: 64). Anti-urban attitudes were readily accepted also because the communist revolution was based in the countryside and relied on peasant support. Its leaders disliked the 'vicious and lavish' lifestyles of city life and had a 'peasant-inspired and Puritanical distrust of the cities' (Steiner 1950: 62), the centre of capitalist avarice and exploitation, arsenals producing 'sugar-coated bullets' which could destroy unwary comrades, and the power base of the ousted Nationalist Government. Politically banished to the countryside, the triumphant revolutionaries returned to the cities with anti-urban attitudes.

In an important way these two antithetical tendencies – 'urban bias' and 'anti-urban bias' – shaped and underpinned China's industrialization strategy, which on the one hand recognized the strategic roles and importance of cities and urban workers in industrialization, but which, on the other, was prepared to achieve 'industrialization without urbanization' (Kirby 1985; Naughton 1995), i.e. stressing the contributions that cities had to make to industrialization yet reluctant to pay for the cost of urbanization. The cities were to be 'producer' rather than 'consumer' cities. From these two 'dialectical' tendencies several important policy emphases in China's industrialization strategy followed.

1. Emphasis on labour welfare

It meant, first of all, a commitment to providing for the basic needs and security of the industrial workers. This included, most importantly, the promulgation in 1951 of the 'Labour Insurance Regulations of the People's Republic of China.'[7] The social security system covered all employees in state-owned enterprises and their dependants, giving them maternity and birth benefits and support in old age, accidents, illness and death of breadwinners. By 1958, this system covered 13.7 million workers and staff (State Statistical Bureau 1960: 218).

Insurance funds were borne in full by the employers. Enterprises participating in the programme each contributed a sum equivalent to 3 per cent of its payroll to a labour insurance fund. 'The fund, set up within individual enterprises, was partly managed by the enterprises and partly by the trade unions, which would transfer about 30 per cent of the contributions to a higher level of trade union organization so that a certain degree of redistribution could be effected between enterprises of varying financial commitments' (Chow 1988: 40).

Though 'comprehensive in coverage, generous in the level of benefits, non-contributory in finance' (Leung 1992: 3), the system was highly exclusive: it covered only a very small fraction of China's economically active population. Peasants were excluded altogether. The criterion of coverage was basically to include those enterprises wherein the majority of China's industrial workers were employed and those industrial fields central to the industrialization efforts of the Party. In other words, it mainly covered workers in large-scale and state-owned enterprises in transport, construction and heavy industry. 'Between the announcement and the effective date of enforcement of the 1951 regulations, banks were dropped from coverage on the ground that their employees did not face as difficult economic conditions as others. Cadres and soldiers who were being paid by the "fixed supply" system were not initially included, and the majority of state employees (for example, teachers) did not receive labor insurance benefits at this time' (Kallgren 1969: 546).

It was clear that the coverage of the social security system was strategic and intended to induce productivity and discipline from workers expected to be making strategic contributions to China's industrialization: the urban, heavy industrial, and elite sectors of the society.[8]

Besides social security, the government also introduced a range of welfare and benefits aimed at, in the words of the then President, Liu Shao-qi, 'gradually improving workers' livelihood so as to promote their production enthusiasm'. The 'People's Republic of China Trade Union Ordinance' promulgated in 1950 committed the government to providing trade unions at various levels with premises and facilities for welfare functions and activities. In 1952, workers began to receive winter heating subsidies and hardship allowances. The 'Amended Draft Operation Guidelines for Labour Insurance' promulgated in 1953 required enterprises to set up, independently or together with other enterprises, canteens and nurseries for their workers. The 'Instructions on Certain Questions Relating to Workers' Livelihood' issued by the State Council in 1957 gave specific guidelines on how to provide benefits and subsidies to workers for housing, transport to work, medical care, basic necessities and in cases of hardship. In 1962, the State Council required enterprises to pay for the home leave passage of their workers.

Funds in support of these benefits and subsidies were to come from five sources: (1), for the construction of housing, from 'non-production-related construction and investment' (*fei shengchanxing jianshe touji*) funds directly allocated by the government; (2), as supplements to the above, from an enterprise 'bonus fund' (*jiangli jijin*); (3), for paying hardship subsidies and for covering the recurrent expenses of such facilities as canteens, nurseries, bathing facilities, and barbershops, from an enterprise 'welfare fund' (*fuli jijin*);[9] (4), for various kinds of subsidies and allowances, from the 'management expenditure' (*guanli fei*) of the enterprise; and (5), for supporting the welfare activities undertaken by trade unions, from their 'employee welfare' (*jigong fuli*) expenditures.

Because the enterprise in fact did not retain any profits – all profits were returned to the state – and because expenditures on benefits and welfare were all part of its production costs and covered by allocations from the state, it was the state which was actually and eventually paying for all these expenses.

2. Emphasis on industry

It meant, secondly, an emphasis on industry, particularly heavy industry, at the expense of agriculture and light industry.[10] The development of heavy industry was strategic both because this would prepare the industrial base for the technological transformation of agriculture and for the development of light industry, and also because the Chinese leaders wanted to build the state's military power as rapidly as possible and be economically independent of the rest of the world, including the Soviet Union (Perkins 1966: 205–6).

The emphasis on heavy industry had several important implications. The stress on 'massive, capital-intensive projects called for highly centralized control, an exalted role for scarce experts and technicians, and unambiguous lines of managerial authority' (Riskin 1987: 59). The result, as in the Soviet Union which China was turning to for models, assistance and advice in the early 1950s, was a highly centralized mode of command planning and a highly bureaucratized system of management.

One aspect of this bureaucratized system was a nationally unified wage system copied from the Soviet central planning system. The traditional principle of this system was the socialist orthodoxy of 'distribution to each according to one's work' (*anlau fenpei*). Based on this principle, enterprises paid urban workers according to wage grades defined in a state-designed set of wage grade tables in which wage levels and differentials were stipulated for different regions, sectors, enterprises and occupations (Takahara 1992: 2). There were two important points about this wage system. First, unlike in a capitalist economy, where distribution is largely determined by market mechanisms, the Chinese system of distribution – not only in wage levels and the structure of wage differentials but also the distributional principle itself and specific criteria for wage allocation – was determined by government policies. Secondly, it followed from a system of 'redistribution': state enterprises handed all profits to the state and paid their workers with wages redistributed by the state (Bian 1994: 148). How much an enterprise paid its workers was unrelated to its profitability or performance. Enterprises had no incentives to produce for the state and the workers had no incentives to produce for the profits of their enterprises. This had two important implications: it was bound to result in low productivity, and, increasingly, enterprises had to resort to various non-wage means to achieve labour productivity and discipline. Non-wage benefits and subsidies assumed increasing importance as work incentives.

Emphasis on heavy industry at the expense of agriculture and light industry had also caused the supply of grain and consumer goods to fall short of demand. There was critical shortage of grain, meat and most kinds of consumer goods. To ensure that there was equitable distribution of items in short supply, the government resorted to bureaucratic allocation procedures. The most important of these was rationing and bureaucratized distribution.

Rationing and bureaucratized distribution were also made necessary by the implementation in 1953 of a wage restriction policy. To maintain a high level of capital formation, labor costs had to be kept to a minimum. Practically all of society's incremental output had to be reinvested to sustain economic growth, leaving little or nothing to increase personal incomes. 'Because an increasing share of national income was going into accumulation to sustain this growth (an average rate of 4–6 per cent in real terms or 2–4 per cent per capita), real wages and peasant incomes languished from the late fifties' (Howe 1981: 153). Wages were kept low and effectively frozen for two decades after 1957. The real wage index (1952 = 100) fell from 126.5 to 106.7 during the period 1956–76 (Table 3.1). Within the state sector, the general wage freeze after 1957 and the entry of new workers onto the lowest rungs of the wage ladder thereafter caused the average wage in real terms to fall by 17 per cent between 1957 and 1977 (Riskin 1988: 263). Increasingly, workers had to be given basic necessities to tide them over difficulties.

From the 1950s, therefore, a system of socialized distribution was applied which at various points encompassed grain, basic necessities and consumer durables. Grain, pork and cooking oil were staple food items that were rationed in most cities from the 1950s onwards. Major consumer durables like sewing machines and bicycles, and daily necessities such as cloth and coal, were also rationed.

Table 3.1   Average Annual Wage for Employees in State and Collective Enterprises, 1952–88

Year	Average Nominal Wage (Yuan)	Money Wage (1952 = 100)	Real Wage (1952 = 100)
1952	445	100.0	100.0
1956	601	135.1	126.5
1960	511	114.8	102.9
1966	583	131.0	110.1
1970	561	126.1	105.6
1976	575	129.2	106.7
1977	576	129.4	104.0
1978	615	138.2	110.3
1979	665	150.1	117.8
1980	762	171.2	124.7
1981	772	173.5	123.4
1982	798	179.3	124.9
1983	826	185.6	126.7
1984	974	218.9	145.6
1985	1,148	258.0	153.5
1986	1,329	298.7	166.1
1987	1,459	327.9	167.7
1988	1 747	392.6	182.8

Source: State Statistical Bureau (1989: 21).

The system of socialized distribution had both positive and negative features. On the positive side, rationing assured equality in the distribution of consumer goods. 'Except at the very highest levels of the administrative hierarchy, everyone shared the same rations of these controlled-price goods' (Parish 1981: 45). The negative side was that the system was plagued by problems which also 'plague socialist distribution systems everywhere – rigidity, low quality goods, poor service, frustrated consumer demands, red tape' (Whyte and Parish 1984: 106).

The workplace was a central point in the urban distribution system. Workplaces were points of distribution for ration coupons not only for highly sought after industrial goods – sewing machines, bicycles, radios, watches and furniture – but also for additional coupons for grain and other foodstuffs above the basic rationed amounts.

> By law, state enterprises obtain rationed coupons for these items from state commercial agencies and distribute them to employees according to a method of their own determination. But in practice, enterprises regularly engage in 'outside the plan' deals with these same agencies or with other enterprises in which they traded products and spare parts in return for goods, which may include ration coupons for, or actual deliveries of, television sets, furniture, or watches. (Walder 1986: 63)

These were distributed to workers.

State enterprises also regularly engaged in similar exercises to procure for their workers supplies of cured meat, vegetables and fresh fruits. These came in addition to rationed amounts and were made available to workers either free, as at major festivals, or at subsidized prices.

Besides rations, workers in state enterprises were also given, in cash or in kind, various kinds of supplements and allowances which added to their real incomes, improving their living standards in no small way. These included, for instance, a winter heating supplement, 'cool drink fees' in summer, transportation fees to compensate workers for tram or bus fare or for the physical energy expended in bicycling the extra distance to work, travel supplements to cover train fares and living expenses en route while on annual leave, wage supplements for working in hazardous or difficult lines of work, and so on.

It is clear that the living standards of state workers depended importantly on direct distributions and subsidies. Walder (1986: 61) estimated that these were responsible for more than half of the state workers' living standards.

3. De-emphasizing Services and Consumption

Anti-urbanism disposed the Party against first, 'the demand for ever-greater *non-productive* urban expenditures (in housing, roads, recreation, public transport facilities, drains, electricity supply, shops, and so on) occasioned by industrial growth' (Kirby 1985: 15); secondly, 'consumerism' and high life-styles; and thirdly, occupations associated with consumption and 'bourgeois' life-styles perceived as not contributing significantly to production.

Soon after it came to power, the Party took actions against 'unbecoming' business activities and occupations. Targeted businesses had to wind up and their employees find new jobs. Prostitutes, fortune-tellers, Buddhist monks and nuns and Taoist priests had to give up their 'trades'. 'Transportation, food and drink, retailing, and other activities with the taint of bourgeois production for exchange rather than material production for use were sharply reduced relative to other occupations. Work as maids, barbers, and other service type jobs were reduced to a small fraction of former levels' (Whyte and Parish 1984: 34). The 'five-antis' (*wufan*) campaign between 1951 and 1952 dealt service-related activities and businesses another heavy blow. The campaign was directed at the capitalist class. Under charges of 'bribery, tax evasion, theft of state assets, cheating in labour or materials, and stealing of state economic intelligence', nearly every employer could be brought to trial. In an atmosphere of terror many businessmen and their businesses were eliminated. As a result of the campaign, service-type businesses were reduced to an even lower level and 'the greater part of the capitalist sector was directed into the orbit of the state plan under the leadership of the state sector' (Xue et al. 1960: 53). Between 1956 (the 'high tide of socialist transformation') and 1980, the sometimes lenient but more often harsh policies (Solinger 1984) of the government also led to a sharp decline in retail trade and self-employment. Small family businesses were effectively eliminated, and, along with the disappearance of these small businesses, a variety of small but important goods and services. The urban economy was becoming increasingly one without a service sector of a scale and diversity which matched the needs of its fast-growing population. Living in the cities became, for the average Chinese, very inconvenient: 'It became almost impossible to find someone to fix a bicycle or repair a pair a shoes' (Shirk 1993: 42) and:

> Residents in many large and medium-size cities find it difficult to get clothing made, have their hair cut or styled, eat out in restaurants,

buy nonstaple foodstuffs, buy furniture, or get repairs done. But the state and collective enterprises are unable to solve these problems for the time being. (Fang 1982: 179)

Because cities were centres of industrial production and because the government maintained low prices for agricultural products and high prices for manufactured goods, Chinese cities were also the primary collection points for state revenues. They became 'cash cows' for the government. 'Cities were milked for revenues and output, while the minimum possible investment went into them' (Naughton 1995: 70). As a result, urban infrastructure was allowed to deteriorate. The consequence was the neglect, atrophy and underprovision of various urban services and facilities. Investment in 'non-productive' services (e.g. construction of residential housing, hospitals, schools and office buildings) made up one-third of total capital construction investment between 1950 and 1952, but fell to between 12 and 15 per cent during 1958–62 and remained at that level through to 1976. The largest item in this category was residential housing. The annual average rate of investment in housing construction fell steadily from Y1 billion between 1953 and 1957 to Y740 million between 1966 and 1970 (Riskin 1988: 273). Already cramped housing space of 4.3 square metres per urban inhabitant in 1952 fell to 3.6 square metres in 1977 (Walder 1984: 24).

To help 'solve real problems in the daily life of urban workers' and in order also to 'reduce tardiness, absences, and poor performance, and to promote labor discipline' (Kallgren 1969: 564), various facilities and services which were in short supply and which workers had difficulty obtaining for themselves from either the public or the market, like housing, schooling, nurseries, barber shops, dining facilities and bathing facilities, were increasingly made available to workers at their workplaces.

The result, increasingly, was that workplaces became centres of collective consumption. They became 'small societies' each equipped with a wide range of facilities and services. Giant industrial enterprises, in particular, became 'large and comprehensive', complete with facilities and services of all kinds. The scale and comprehensiveness of these facilities and services was particularly extraordinary in the huge factories built between 1965 and 1971, when Mao's Third Front industrialization strategy sent industry into the far hinterland in massive proportions. 'Industrial projects were dispersed in mountainous terrain, and workers' dormitories were built alongside the factories' (Naughton 1995: 67). In geographic isolation these huge establishments could not but turn themselves into self-contained communities.

4.   Restricting Rural–Urban Migration

The government had to impose strict control on the growth of population in the cities because such population increases necessitated provision by the government not just of jobs but also of welfare and heavily subsidized provisions of basic goods and services to urban workers. An important way to achieve this was strict migration controls. This was done through a system of household registration implemented since 1958. Each household had a 'residence booklet' (*hukou bu*) and the head of household had to register the number of people residing with him with the public security office in his district. When he or any member of the household planned to move, he had to apply to the household registration office for a change-of-residence permit and cancel his residence registration. A would-be migrant to the cities could only leave the village with a police permit. However, the possibility of obtaining a permit for such move was very slim. Moving from the countryside to a large city was all but impossible.

To the ordinary residents, household registration was the single most important registration. It defined their identity and in many ways shaped their life-chances. The residence booklet was needed for food rations, purchase of travel documents, job hunting and change of domicile. A 'black household' (*hei hu*), one without proper registration, would be left to languish in the city. Its members would have little chance of enrolling in a school, getting a job, obtaining access to various publicly provided services and obtaining rationed food and other basic necessities.

The registration system divided the entire population between those with 'urban residence' (*chengshi hukou*) and those with 'rural residence' (*nongcun hukou*), anchoring people to where they were and limiting their movements in either directions. The trouble of going through an irksome process to obtain permission to change one's domicile also discouraged intra-city mobility.

The system reinforced the tendency of socialist firms to 'hoard labour', discouraged job mobility and encouraged workers to stay in their jobs. Workers became permanent members of their work-units upon which they were dependent for social services, rationed food and a wide range of distributed goods and necessities. These dependencies further enhanced their immobility and kept them where they were.

Changes and developments through the 1960s and 1970s

By the mid-1950s, China had in place a system of occupational welfare which had all the essential features of what was known in the 1970s. In a nutshell, these features were: a comprehensive labour insurance system that provided old age pensions and a range of benefits covering maternity and birth, illness, accidents and death of the breadwinner of a family; a system of distribution through the workplaces of various daily necessities, food, consumer durables, both by ration coupons and in kind, and various kinds of supplements and allowances both in cash and in kind; and the provision by the workplace of a comprehensive range of facilities and services which catered to the many daily needs of their members.

This system of occupational welfare was part and parcel of an urban political economy in which the state assumed an all-important role and responsibility in providing employment and allocating people to jobs; jobs were more or less permanent; and wages were kept low. It was an integral part of a 'low wage, high employment, high welfare' (*di gongzi, gao jiuyie, gao fuli*) package.

The basic features of this system had remained unchanged ever since. There had been, however, some modifications and developments in some of its more specific features. The most important of these had to do with the administration and financing of the labour insurance scheme. This happened during the Great Cultural Revolution (1966–76). The Great Cultural Revolution threw the entire country into chaos and disorder. The labour insurance scheme, like many social and political institutions and policies, was also in turmoil. Trade unions, which had been under political criticism since the 1950s, were disbanded in 1967. 'As a result, the enterprises were left to decide for themselves whether or not to provide the necessary benefits as stipulated in the Labour Insurance Regulations; only those less affected by the Revolution observed the practice' (Chow 1988: 24). In 1969, the Ministry of Finance issued an order which, in effect, stopped the labour insurance funds, formally put an end to the involvement of trade unions in the administration of the scheme, and made enterprises responsible for both the administration and financing of labour insurance. In other words, labour insurance became, from then on, the responsibility of the enterprises.

Conclusion

Chinese occupational welfare was unique in that the state provided through the workplaces comprehensive welfare and benefits to urban workers in employment in the state sector.

We have seen in this chapter that the origins of such a system of welfare had to do with the unique 'state formation' experience of the Chinese socialist state. The chapter discussed the impact and implications of three important historical experiences in the formation of the Chinese socialist state: guerrilla war experience, experience in rehabilitating a war-devastated economy, and China's socialist industrialization strategy. It showed that these experiences had in important ways shaped the formation of policies and institutions which made up Chinese occupational welfare.

More specifically, the chapter showed: (1) The 'institutional households' of armies, government organs and schools in the guerrilla base areas could have been the organizational prototype of the *danwei*, the socialist work-unit which became more or less a *gemeinschaftlich* community looking after many aspects of the life of its members. (2) The distribution of basic necessities and goods through the workplace can be traced back to the 'supply system' among soldiers and government personnel in the guerrilla base areas as well as the system of rationing and bureaucratized distribution introduced in China's cities since the 1950s. (3) Measures used to bring hyperinflation under control in the early years of the socialist regime had extended the state's control over the economy in general and over the distribution of goods in particular. (4) Measures to limit urban unemployment had committed the state to 'taking on all and being responsible for all' (*bao xia lai*) employment and paved the way for permanent employment. (5) The industrialization strategy of the socialist regime accounted for its emphasis on (urban) labour welfare. (6) The emphasis of this strategy on heavy industry at the expense of agriculture and light industry had led to low wages and severe shortages and under-supplies of basic necessities, food and all kinds of consumer goods. A system of socialized distribution had to be introduced to close the gap between supply and demand. The work-unit became the centrepoint for the rationing and distribution of a wide range of goods and benefits. (7) The neglect of 'unproductive' trade and services and the continuous decline in the quantity and quality of urban facilities and services had greatly inconvenienced average city dwellers. For their members' convenience, workplaces equipped themselves with a wide range of these facilities and services. (8) Measures against rural–urban migration also discouraged intra-city and job mobility, enhancing immobility and reinforcing workers' dependency on their workplaces.

In short, the chapter has shown how it can be useful to explain the origins of Chinese occupational welfare in terms of the unique historical experiences of the Chinese socialist state and, more specifically, in terms of its experience in state formation: war experience, the experience of rebuilding a war-devastated economy, and the experience of socialist industrialization.

The chapter highlights three important themes in these experiences: first, the extension of the state's power over an increasing range of activities and functions (e.g. distribution of goods, allocation of jobs); secondly, the assumption by the state of an increasing range of responsibilities (e.g. 'taking on all and being responsible for all' employment); and thirdly, following from these two themes, individuals coming increasingly under the control of and becoming increasingly dependent on the state. The history of Chinese occupational welfare is very much a history of extending state power and responsibility, and declining personal autonomy.

4
The Changing Contexts of Chinese Occupational Welfare

Introduction

Chinese occupational welfare was part and parcel of a distinct 'low wage, high employment, high welfare' (*di gongzi, gao jiuyie, gao fuli*) package given to urban workers in employment in the state sector. The package was made up of three interrelated parts: (1) an 'iron rice bowl' employment system with lifetime employment in one work-unit; (2) a low wage; and (3) a wide range of benefits and services provided through the workplace.

This distinct pattern of wage, employment and welfare was embedded in a socialist 'redistributive' (Szelenyi 1983; Kornai 1984; Nee 1989, 1990) economy, characterized by the allocation of resources and distribution of goods through central planning and bureaucracy. In this kind of economy, state-owned enterprises receive their plan quotas from and remit their profits to the government. The government exercises control over labour, setting enterprise labour quotas and assigning workers to enterprises. Enterprises have neither a choice over what and how much to produce nor how many and which workers to hire (and fire) and how much and what to pay them.

The shortcomings of such an economy are now common knowledge (Kornai 1984, 1986, 1989). First, plans once made and commands once given are hard to change. Any significant change in one part of the plan has spillover effects on other parts of the plan and many adjustments have to be made. 'Planners understandably are not fond of such extra work. As a consequence, response to unexpected shifts in supply, demand, or technology is slow and incomplete' (Kornai 1989: 38). The system is inherently rigid.

Secondly, enterprises do not produce for profit and are not held responsible for losses. Working under 'soft-budget constraint' conditions, they are not required to be sensitive to cost and price considerations and there is little incentive to use resources and investment efficiently. Rewarded for physical output and size, the incentive is rather in the opposite direction: to use these resources inefficiently and, in practice, to hoard and conceal reserves so as to cushion themselves against unanticipated changes in the bureaucratic environment, and ask the state for more allocations. This results in chronic 'shortage', wastage and inefficiency.

Thirdly, workers, similarly, have no incentive to work hard because their pay is unrelated to their personal performance or to the performance of their enterprises, and their jobs are secure. 'The income of a worker ... did not increase if he worked harder than others. Nor would he lose his job if he worked less hard' (Yeh 1993: 15).

All these problems impinged adversely on the Chinese economy. By 1978, the economy was plagued by institutional rigidities, economic inefficiencies, slow growth, massive unemployment and shortages of food and consumer goods and all kinds of basic necessities and services. After three decades of socialism, China remained a low-income economy by World Bank standards and its per capita GNP was the lowest among the centrally planned economies (Yeh 1993: 13).

The opportunity to reform the economy came with the downfall of the Gang of Four and the official end of the Cultural Revolution. The Third Plenum of the Eleventh Central Committee, which met in December 1978, officially declared a change in direction of China's economic policy and the launching of the 'Four Modernizations' Programme in industry, agriculture, science and technology. Reform, though 'open-ended' (Lin 1989) and approached pragmatically and incrementally, began to move China steadily in the direction of market transition.

The main objective of the reform was to modernize the economy by bringing the market back in: by increasing the role of market forces in influencing allocation and distribution decisions. This implied, on the one hand, reducing the role of the state and of central planning and bureaucracy and, on the other hand, attaching more importance to competition, profit and wage incentives, price signals and the forces of supply and demand.

The first stage of China's reform programme began in the countryside, home to some 80 per cent of China's one billion inhabitants. The centrepiece of rural reforms involved the daring measures of doing away with collectivized agriculture and the introduction of a 'household responsibility system' which 'contracted out' production responsibilities to individual peasant households. After fulfilling their quota and tax obligations and paying local organizations for collective services, farm households were free to dispose of their output as they saw fit. The contract period was later extended from a few years to 15 years to give farm producers more incentive to increase output and invest in capital improvements (Koo et al. 1993: 34).

The introduction of the 'household responsibility system' radically altered the organization of production and the distribution of output in the countryside. Essentially the 'functional equivalent of family farming' (Davis and Vogel 1990: 4), it proved so popular that by 1983 98 per cent of farmland had been contracted to households (Cheng 1986: 91).

Alongside this radical policy the government had also introduced a number of other agrarian policies to reduce the degree of central control and provide more incentives to producers. The most important of these included raising quota procurement prices for major agricultural products and liberalizing sideline production and rural marketing.

These policies were very successful. From 1978 to 1982 grain output grew by 2.4 per cent per annum and output of key commercial crops such as cotton and edible oil grew by 13.5 per cent and 22.7 per cent respectively. The state's grain procurement increased from 46.5 million tons in 1978 to 54.55 tons in 1981. And, from 1978 to 1981, real per capita rural income grew at an annual rate of 11.4 per cent (Davis and Vogel 1990: 10–11).

The second stage of the reform was directed at the urban economy and had therefore a direct impact on and many implications for occupational welfare. It is to these urban reforms that we must now turn.

Ownership reform

Urban reforms were at once more difficult because they involved very complex and sensitive issues of public and private ownership, of property rights, of defining the claims different parties have on the income generated from state owned and collectively-owned enterprises, of control and autonomy, and of ideological and material incentives.

The urban reform programme consisted of two main parts. The first aimed at reforming the existing ownership structure to bring about a mixed ownership system in which alternative forms of non-state ownership were allowed to operate alongside the state sector. The second part of the programme was directed at the state sector itself. The aim here was to revitalize state-owned enterprises by increasing their managerial autonomy and making them responsible for their own profits and losses. Let us take these in turn.

Instead of privatizing state-owned enterprises, the reform in ownership opted to legalize and expand the non-state, or 'second', economy by a combination of strategies. These included, first, encouraging collective enterprises, 'individual firms' (*geti hu*) and 'private firms' (*siying qiye*) to develop;[1] secondly, accepting foreign investment and the setting up of Chinese–foreign joint ventures and joint ventures with overseas, including Hong Kong and Macao, Chinese capital; [2] and thirdly, giving state managers the right to diversify ownership forms within state firms, by channelling some of their retained funds into collectively or privately owned subsidiaries, merging with collective or private firms, or leasing existing facilities to groups or individuals (Shirk 1993: 44). The government supported these non-state enterprises with various preferential measures, including, for urban collectives and private enterprises, low tax rates, the retention of all their profits and no restrictions on employees' salaries, and, for joint ventures, concessionary customs and tax treatment. These preferential measures gave non-state enterprises advantages over their state-sector competitors.

By 1994 the number of employees in urban collective enterprises had grown to 32 million (from 20 million in 1978) and those in private businesses to 6.4 million (from 150,000 in 1978). An additional seven million were employed by Chinese–foreign joint ventures, state–collective joint enterprises, or state–private joint enterprises (China Statistical Yearbook 1995: 94–8). From 1978 to 1994 the share of total industrial output produced by non-state firms trebled, from 22 per cent to 66 per cent. In 1994, only 34 per cent of China's total industrial output was produced by the state sector (ibid.: 377).

Without dismantling the state sector, ownership reform had ushered in a mixed economy with a still dominant but declining state sector coexisting with a fast growing non-state, second economy characterized by a mix of ownership forms.

The rise of the mixed economy had meant, for state enterprises, a whole new ball game. Protected from competition in the past, they were now forced for the first time to compete with private and collective enterprises. They suffered from several serious disadvantages in this competition. First, their competitors enjoyed generous profit retention ratios and concessionary tax rates. Secondly, moreover, their competitors were different and more dynamic kinds of firms: producing for profits, financially independent and enjoying managerial autonomy. Thirdly, state enterprises were usually 'older' and saddled with ageing facilities and outdated technology. Fourthly, their workers were usually also 'older', which meant, in many cases, a growing retired population and a hefty budget for retirement benefits and medical care. Fifthly, their competitors, in general, were not as generous with occupational welfare.[3] They could produce at lower production costs. State enterprises were therefore losing out to non-state enterprises in the competition. They were losing not just business, but also skilled workers.

For workers in the state sector, the emergence of the non-state sector was a mixed blessing. The positive side was that the second economy created many openings for both full-time and part-time jobs. Workers, particularly those who were young and skilled, now had the opportunity either to quit their jobs for jobs in the non-state sector, which usually paid two to three times more, or take on second jobs in the second economy to supplement their incomes. There was a growing labour market, and mobility, undreamed of in the past, was now possible. Workers were no longer as tied to or as dependent on their work-units as before.

The negative side was that they discovered, much to their frustration, that their jobs were no longer the 'good' jobs which they had been for the last 30 years. They were earning several times less than their counterparts in the non-state sector and the prospect of their jobs did not look good when state enterprises were losing their business to private and collective enterprises and suffering heavy losses.

At their workplaces, reforms were also underway, changing the ways state enterprises were managed and the ways they hired, managed and paid their workers. It is to these changes that we now turn.

Enterprise reform

1. The contract responsibility system

At the enterprise three sets of interrelated changes were underway: (1) enterprise reform, (2) wage reform, and (3) employment reform. The main aim of enterprise reform was to make state enterprises more independent and enable them to become responsible for their management, profits and losses. The instruments used to achieve this aim involved the application of some variant of the 'contract responsibility system' (Koo et al. 1993: 34) whereby an enterprise director entered into a contract with the state which held him responsible for a specified level of performance, gave him a freer hand to run the enterprise, and rewarded him and his staff for above-level performance. The purpose of the contract was to link profit to enterprise performance and give directors and workers the incentives to work hard for their enterprises.

The 'contract responsibility system' had evolved and changed over time. Briefly, what happened was as follows. In 1978, state enterprises were allowed to set aside, on top of a fixed percentage, an additional 5 per cent of their wage bills to fund bonus payments. As long as enterprises completed specified targets set by the state plan, they could distribute the bonus funds as they saw fit. The scheme was, however, rather rigid. It did not allow enterprises to withdraw additional bonus funds even if they had over-fulfilled specified targets. The breakthrough came in 1979. In that year, all state enterprises were permitted to retain a 'normal' profit equivalent to 10–12 per cent of basic wages to fund basic bonus payments. They were allowed to keep additional earnings if they made extra profits; out of their retained earnings they could fund additional bonus payments and welfare expenses. By 1983, most industrial state enterprises had adopted some form of a payment scheme which linked the increases in wages, bonuses and welfare expenditures with increases in enterprise profits.

From the end of 1983 to the end of 1985, the government gradually replaced this 'profit retention' scheme by a 'Substitution of Tax for Profits Programme'. Under this new programme, state enterprises were to pay taxes instead of remitting profits to the state. All state enterprises had to pay a basic corporate tax rate of 55 per cent and, in addition to this, a number of other taxes. After paying these taxes, state managers could allocate up to 30 per cent of retained earnings for increases in wages and bonus payments, and up to 20 per cent for increases in welfare spending.

By linking profits to performance and allowing enterprises to pay additional bonus and welfare expenditures out of retained or after-tax profits, the profit retention scheme and the Substitution of Tax for Profit Programme which replaced it had made it much easier for enterprises to increase bonus payments and welfare spending. This had the unintended consequence of raising the expectations – and demands – of workers not only in high-profit enterprises but also enterprises that were making little profit or no profit at all. When high-profit enterprises increased their bonus payments and welfare spending, there was pressure on enterprises which were performing less well also to increase their bonus payments and welfare spending. 'As a result workers employed in state enterprises that earned little or no profits demanded and received increases in bonuses comparable to that of workers employed in high-profit enterprises' (Hu and Li 1993: 156). In no time it became common practice for enterprises to increase their bonus payments regularly irrespective of whether or not and how much profits they had.[4]

Between 1977 and 1984, the average money wage for state enterprise employees increased by 69 per cent (Y576 in 1977 vs. Y974 in 1984); bonuses also increased from 2.3 per cent of the total wage bill in 1978 to 14.4 per cent in 1984 (Koo 1993: 41). However, even as wages and bonuses in state enterprises were rising, they were not rising as rapidly as those in the non-state sector. In 1985, for example, the average state worker earned Y1,213; his non-state counterpart earned 1.18 times as much (Y1,436). In 1994, the average state worker earned Y4,797; his non-state counterpart earned 1.3 times as much (Y6,303) (Table 4.1). Workers' demand to close the non-state–state sector income gap put pressure on state enterprises, forcing them to look for ways to increase the income of their workers. They could do this rather conveniently by increasing what they gave their workers via bonus payments and welfare spending. The former was, however, relatively 'costly' because there was a 30 per cent bonus tax on bonus payments that exceeded four months' basic wage. The bonus tax rate increased progressively to 300 per cent when the average bonus payment exceeded nine months of enterprise basic wage. To avoid paying this tax, many enterprises simply gave their workers more benefits and subsidies instead of giving them bonuses (Guo et al. 1990: 17).

Table 4.1   Average Annual Wage of Employees, 1985–94, in Yuan

	1985	1991	1992	1993	1994
State-owned Enterprises	1,213	2,477	2,878	3,532	4,797
Urban Collectively Owned Enterprises	967	1,866	2,109	2,692	3,245
Other Ownership Types	1,435	3,468	3,966	4,966	6,303
Jointly Owned	1,269	1,789	3,336	3,741	4,982
Shareholding	–	–	–	5,171	6,383
Foreign-funded	1,847	3,918	4,347	5,315	6,533
Overseas Chinese	2,143	4,071	4,740	5,147	6,476
Others	1,000	2,622	3,371	3,279	4,954

Source: State Statistical Bureau (1995: 118–22).

Table 4.2   Composition of Aggregate Wage Bill in State Enterprises
1978–88 (percentage of total)

Year	Total	Basic Wage	Piece Rate	Bonuses	Subsidies	Overtime	Others
1978	100	85.0	0.8	2.3	6.5	2.0	3.4
1979	100	75.0	2.5	7.5	8.8	2.0	3.7
1980	100	69.8	3.2	9.1	14.1	1.6	2.2
1981	100	67.2	5.5	10.2	14.0	1.6	1.5
1982	100	64.4	7.6	10.9	14.1	1.5	1.5
1983	100	63.5	8.5	11.1	14.1	1.3	1.5
1984	100	58.5	9.5	14.4	14.5	1.5	1.6
1985	100	57.2	9.5	12.4	18.5	1.6	0.8
1986	100	56.3	8.7	12.8	18.8	1.8	1.6
1987	100	54.3	9.2	14.7	18.9	1.9	1.0
1988	100	49.0	9.4	17.2	21.2	1.9	1.1

Source: State Statistical Bureau (1988: 179); State Statistical Bureau (1989: 217).

The pay package of the average state-sector worker had always consisted of a wage component made up of basic wage and bonus, and a non-wage component made up of various in cash and in kind benefits and subsidies. As a result of what was often done to enable workers to earn more, bonus was becoming an increasingly important part of wage income and non-wage income was becoming an increasingly important part of a worker's total pay package[5] (Table 4.2).

2.   Internal subcontracting

The 'contract responsibility system' had also been a popular intra-enterprise practice. Many enterprises, especially large-scale ones, signed responsibility contracts with their sub-units which, in ways similar to enterprise contracts with the state, required these sub-units to perform economic obligations for the enterprises and, in return, gave them the autonomy to run their own business and the right to dispose of retainable profits. In many cases, these sub-units also signed contracts with their own sub-units.

The implication, as this happened, was that an enterprise became subdivided into many sub-units, each with its own distinct interest and identity. The whole became disaggregated into many smaller parts. For the average worker in an enterprise with many internal subcontracts, what mattered for him or her as a result was no longer the performance of the enterprise as a whole, but rather the performance of the particular sub-unit to which he or she belonged. In an unintended way the practice of internal subcontracting was reshaping workers' organizational identity.

3. Bankruptcy Law and enterprise Law

Bolder measures to make enterprises more independent and responsible for their own profits and losses came in the forms of the Bankcruptcy Law (1986), the Enterprise Law (1988) and, on the basis of these two laws, Regulations Governing State Industrial Enterprises Changing Their Management Structures (1992).

According to these laws and regulations, state enterprises were to become 'self-managing (*ziwo jingying*), self-responsible for profits and losses (*zifu yingkui*), self-developing (*ziwo fa zhan*), and self-regulating (*ziwo yaoshu*)' firms. They were to have the rights and powers to decide on employment and wage policies, including the power to hire and fire, and the power to decide on how and what to pay their workers. For the first time, it was also made clear that firms unable to pay their debts had to go bankrupt.

By 1992, therefore, state enterprises had largely become firms which, though owned by the state, were allowed to conduct themselves more or less like capitalist firms. Unlike their capitalist counterparts, however, they had inherited from their earlier history what had been the responsibility of the socialist state to urban workers in employment in the state sector, the responsibility of having to provide their employees with a wide range of non-wage benefits and services through the workplaces. This was a responsibility that had now proved to be a heavy burden, a burden that had become increasingly difficult to bear when state enterprises were losing out in market competition and when financing welfare was becoming increasingly costly.

Wage reform

Prior to 1978, state enterprises paid their workers according to a centrally determined wage-scale. They could grant wage increases to their employees only when the central government approved and set aside additional funds to finance these increases. Between 1959 and 1976, there had only been three rounds of such increases. The rigidity of the wage system coupled with low wage and the *de facto* freeze on wage increases for nearly 20 years had been an important reason for the lack of work incentives.

Wage reforms began with the restoration of piece rates and bonus payments that had been banned during the Cultural Revolution. More radical reforms followed between 1984 and 1986. Following pilot experiments carried out between 1981 and 1984, the government encouraged state enterprises to adopt either a fully floating or a semi-floating wage system linking the size of their wage bill and other components of labour compensation (bonuses and benefits) to an index of performance such as increases in average labour productivity, remitted profits and taxes, or retained earnings. By 1989, most large industrial enterprises had adopted some form of a fully floating wage system.

Following the adoption of the fully floating wage system, an increasing number of state enterprises also began experimenting with changes in their internal wage systems, changes like adding additional levels or points to the wage scales. Some enterprises also assigned internal 'responsibility contracts' to sub-sets of employees linking labour compensations to required levels of performance.

As a result of these reforms, state enterprises were no longer stuck with a centrally determined and standardized wage system. They had a much freer hand to decide on how and how much to pay their workers. This had a number of important implications. First, it had made it much easier for enterprises to increase their wage bills. Secondly, this had also given rise to a great diversity in the ways different enterprises paid their workers. Thirdly, there were increasing inter- and intra-enterprise wage differences, hence income disparity, among enterprise workers.

Employment reforms

Prior to reform, China had a nationally unified labour allocation system. Prospective employees were assigned to different industries by the labour bureaux according to the needs of the state plans. Neither the enterprises nor the workers were given much choice in the matching. For the workers, there was little if any mobility at all: most of them practically worked for the same unit until they retired. Their jobs were more or less for life.

In 1980, the government proposed an end to the system of unilateral, top down, job assignment. In its place the government recommended a system of 'bilateral choice' (*shuangxian xuanze*) in which local labour bureaux continued to recommend candidates to state enterprises but enterprises could decide whether or not to take these candidates. They could also recruit on their own.

The next step was more radical: to put an end to permanent employment. In 1983, the Ministry of Labour announced the implementation of a 'contract employment system' (*laodong hetung zhi*) and required all state enterprises to offer fixed-term contracts to their employees after 1986.

In 1986, the government passed four provisional regulations[6] aimed both to consolidate these changes and to introduce related changes. These regulations (1) required all new recruits to be employed on fixed -term contracts; (2) allowed open recruitment and competitive examinations for posts and put an end to the practice of *ding ti* which allowed an adult child to inherit the job of his or her retiring parent; (3) gave enterprises the right to dismiss employees repeatedly disobeying orders; and (4) announced the setting up of unemployment insurance. During the period of redundancy, an allowance equivalent to 50–75 per cent of the workers' previous basic wage would be paid, up to a maximum of two years (*Renmin Ribao*, 10 September 1986).

These regulations were to have profound implications. First, they were to marketize wage and employment arrangements in the state sector. Increasingly an employment relation in the state sector was to be like a market one, 'a specific contractual exchange of efforts and skills for money and other compensations' (Walder 1986: 16). Secondly, they were doing away with the 'iron rice bowl'. As a result of these regulations, state-sector jobs were no longer permanent. Employees on contract could lose their jobs and they could be dismissed. Thirdly, they were to induce mobility into and out of state-sector jobs and, in the process, foster the growth of an urban labour market. Fourthly, the growth of this labour market would be putting pressure on state enterprises. To be competitive in this labour market, they would have to make their jobs more attractive or they could lose out in the competition to other state enterprises and to non-state sector firms. Perforce they had to create their own internal labour markets and, among others, make strategic use of occupational welfare as means to attract and retain labour. Fifthly, as wage and employment arrangements became marketized and urban labour mobilized, benefits and services hitherto available only to state workers would need to be 'universalized', to be provided also to workers in other sectors of the mixed economy. A 'particularistic' system of benefits and services inhibited labour mobility: state workers who otherwise could have left the state sector for 'better' jobs in the non-state sector might have stayed because they could not take these benefits and services with them. It was also unfair to workers in the non-state sector.

Employment reforms 'must be accompanied by housing, social insurance, and unemployment insurance reform, throughout every level of the economy and society' (Hu and Li 1993: 173).

Although all state enterprises were supposed to offer fixed-term employment contracts to their employees after 1986, these regulations were not strictly enforced. In 1987, for example, only 5 per cent (5.2 million) and, as late as 1994, only 26 per cent (28 million) of state-sector employees were on fixed-term contracts (Table 4.3). There were reports of cases in which these contracts became life employment in disguise. Although the central government regulations recommended a contract term of 5–10 years, some enterprises offered their workers contracts of 30–50 years (Hu and Li 1993: 175). Many enterprises adopted the so-called 'new workers new method, old workers old method' (*xin ren xin banfa, jiu ren jiu ban fa*) (Dai and Li 1991: 95) policy and managed to give fixed-term contracts to just the newly hired (Hu and Li 1993: 158).

This slow progress was understandable. Employment reforms had not been accompanied by the extension of occupational welfare to cover also non-state-sector workers, or the development of unemployment insurance to cover all urban workers. State workers were reluctant to accept contracts because in doing so they could be giving up job security and a wide range of benefits and services, most of which were beyond the reach of contract and non-state workers. Moreover, if

Table 4.3   **State-sector Employees on Fixed-term Contracts**

	Number on Contracts (in 10,000)	*Percentage of All State-sector Employees (%)*
1984	174	2.0
1985	332	3.7
1986	524	5.6
1987	735	7.6
1988	1,008	10.1
1989	1,190	11.8
1990	1,372	13.3
1991	1,589	14.9
1992	2,058	18.9
1993	2,396	21.9
1994	2,853	26.2

Source: State Statistical Bureau (1995: 99).

they were to lose their jobs, there was no guarantee of unemployment insurance. In 1995, half of all urban employees were not covered by unemployment insurance (Feng 1996: 277).

The social consequences of reform

Economic reforms changed not just economic institutions. They also led to many social consequences and had some major impact on the cultural and social contexts of occupational welfare.

First, market reforms led to shifts in popular attitudes from Maoist values of collectivism and asceticism to values sanctioning individual and materialistic aspirations (as vividly captured by the popular expression, *'xiang qian kan'* or 'money orientation') and 'massive cravings for personal possessions and strong preferences for privacy and individual choice' (Davis and Vogel 1990: 4). In the contexts of work and occupational welfare, these shifts in attitudes and values had several important implications: they undermined the appeals of normative and ideological incentives, encouraged workers' calculative involvement in work and defections from altruism, loyalty and commitment, and they encouraged workers to regard calculatively their rights and entitlements to occupational welfare. Changing popular attitudes were reflected in changing values and relations in the workplace.

Secondly, economic reforms had produced a new and increasingly unequal distribution of wealth and income in favour of private entrepreneurs and workers in employment in the non-state economy and against workers in employment in the state sector (Nee 1989, 1991; see also Szelenyi 1978). In 1990, non-state sector workers were earning 31 per cent more than their counterparts in the state sector. By 1995, they were leading by a difference of 33 per cent (Li 1996: 61) (See also Table 4.4). Entrepreneurs of 'individual firms' (*geti hu*) represented just 4 per cent of the country's working population, but owned 26 per cent of the savings in the country's banks. The Gini coefficient of income distribution among urban residents increased from 0.16 in 1978 to 0.23 in 1990 (Zheng and Zhang 1993: 37). Private entrepreneurs were earning many times more than state-sector workers (Zhu 1996: 152). Among urban households, in 1978 the top 20 percentile were earning 1.8 times as much as the bottom 20 percentile. In 1994, they were earning three times as much (Zhu 1995: 197).

Hence although state-sector workers were earning seven times as much in 1994 (Y4,797) as they earned in 1978 (Y644) (China Statistical Yearbook 1995: 113), there was among them a widely felt sense of

Table 4.4   Average Annual Wage of Employees in State and Non-state Units, 1978–94, in Yuan

	Employees in State-owned Units	Employees in Non-state Units[*]
1978	644	–
1980	803	–
1984	1,034	1,048
1985	1,213	1,136
1986	1,414	1,629
1987	1,546	1,879
1988	1,853	2,382
1989	2,055	2,707
1990	2,284	2,987
1991	2,477	3,468
1992	2,878	3,966
1993	3,532	4,966
1994	4,797	6,303

Source: State Statistical Bureau (1995: 113).
[*] These include 'jointly owned', 'share-holding', 'foreign-funded', 'overseas Chinese from Hong Kong, Macao and Taiwan-funded', and 'others' units.

inequity and relative deprivation (Wang 1993: 176). The frustration and anguish in these feelings was vividly expressed in the popular saying, '*Duan qi wankuai chi rou. Fang xia kuaizi ma liang*' ('Cursing between mouthfuls'). This sense of frustration and anguish was accentuated by the fact that, since the mid-1980s, there had been a persistent double figure level inflation.[7]

To improve their lot many state-sector workers resorted to one or a combination of the following methods: seeking second jobs; demanding increases in their pay; and quitting for non-state jobs (Wang 1993: 177).

These had a negative impact of one kind or another on state enterprises. Second jobs undermined workers' commitment to their full-time jobs. Meeting workers' demands for increases in pay by increasing bonus payments and welfare expenses undermined wage incentives and reduced funds available for capital investment and development. Outflows of workers to jobs in the non-state economy drained state enterprises of a skilled workforce.

Thirdly, state enterprises were in a difficult situation. In 1995, about 40 per cent of all state enterprises were in the red and over 40,000 enterprises with more than seven million employees were either 'stopping or half-stopping production' (*tingchan ban tingchan*) (Feng 1996:

271). In many of these enterprises workers had not been paid their wages and benefits, and retired workers their pensions, in full and on time (Feng 1996: 271). Many workers became 'surplus workers' (*fu yu jigong*) and asked to 'leave their posts' (*xia gang*) either to 'wait for a posting' (*dai gang*) or be retrained for other posts, or find new jobs. In 1995, of the 30 million 'surplus workers' in the country most were state-sector workers (Zhu 1996: 153). Most '*xia gang*' workers lost their jobs and became unemployed.

Understandably, there was increasing tension between management and workers in state enterprises. There were increasing instances of industrial disputes, strikes and '*shang fang*' activities in which disgruntled workers and pensioners marched to government offices to express their grievances and demands (Feng 1996: 276–9).

Economic reform had brought workers not just higher wages, better supplies of goods and more opportunities and individual choice, but also more inequality, insecurity and industrial conflicts. Our focus in the next chapter will be on how workers in one state enterprise experienced change in their ordinary everyday life, how they coped with its many exigencies and how their dependence on occupational welfare was reshaped as a result.

The changing organizational context

The Dongfang Heavy Machinery Works was, by China's standard, a large-scale industrial enterprise. In 1994 it had over 5,200 employees. Since the 1950s it had been under the various leaderships of the central First Ministry of Machine Building, the provincial Office of Industry and the city's Bureau of Machine and Electric Power and since 1984, its Economic Commission. Before reform, it was, as were all state enterprises, a cog in the machine of a state redistributive economy.

Like all state enterprises, DFMW had been through the various stages of enterprise reforms and had, by December 1994, metamorphosed into a state-owned corporation consisting of a holding company with 42 subsidiary companies (*zi gongsi*). The first important step in this process was taken in 1985 when the enterprise 'upgraded' its 15 'workshops' (*chejian*) into 'sub-units' or 'branches' (*fenchang*), and arranged with each of them some form of the 'contract responsibility system'. It gave these sub-units a greater degree of autonomy and with each of them it signed a contract specifying expected performance targets. More radical steps were taken in 1987–8. In June 1987, the manager of the enterprise signed a contract with the government agreeing to remit a specified level of profits to the state during the next four years.[8] In December of the same year, the enterprise invited applications from its cadres and workers to bid for internal contracts for the plant's 15 sub-units. Successful bidders became sub-unit managers.[9] Instead of their old salaries, they were paid new salaries linked to performance.[10] The next step, after appointing sub-unit managers and their deputies, was to give contracts to units – sections or teams – further down. These 'sub-units' were allowed to 'prioritize their workforce composition' (*youhua laodong zuhe*), which basically enabled these 'sub-units' to reshuffle their membership and, most importantly, to get rid of slow and un-cooperative workers.[11] These bold measures culminated in the introduction in 1988 of a 'fully floating piece rate' (*quane jijian*) wage system which linked the entire 'wage bundle' – consisting of a basic wage, bonus and some subsidies – of a worker to his or her productivity.

Progress in employment reform was much slower. All state enterprises were supposed to give fixed-term employment contracts to their employees after 1986. At DFMW, however, as of 1994 only 10 per cent of its 5,225 employees were on these contracts. As in other state enterprises, the policy was to apply 'new method to new workers, old method to old workers' and limit contract employment to only the new recruits.

Enterprise reform had proceeded at a much faster pace. In December 1994, DFMW was incorporated as a holding company (*Dongfang Qiye Jituan Gongsi*) with 42 subsidiary companies. The organizational chart of the enterprise immediately before and after this change are as shown in Figure 4.1 and Figure 4.2.

By 1994, therefore, each former sub-unit or workshop of the enterprise was technically independent, a company responsible for its own profits and losses and enjoying a high degree of autonomy. This had several important implications. First, it meant that, for workers, their pay was no longer related to either the performance of the holding company or the performance of subsidiary companies other than the one they belonged to. Secondly, because of the differential performance of these subsidiary companies, it meant also that there were bound to be differences in the wages paid to workers in different subsidiary companies. Hence income inequality between workers who were paid more or less the same wages in the past.

The decentralization of economic responsibility had not been accompanied, however, by a corresponding decentralization of welfare responsibility. The hospital and the school remained the responsibility of the holding company, as did housing (see Figure 4.2). What had

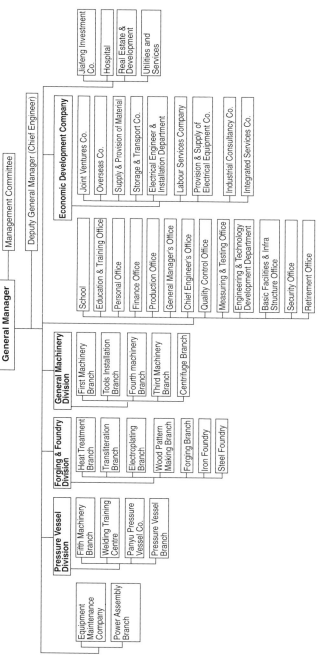

Figure 4.1 Organizational Chart of Dongfang Heavy Machinery Works, 1993

78

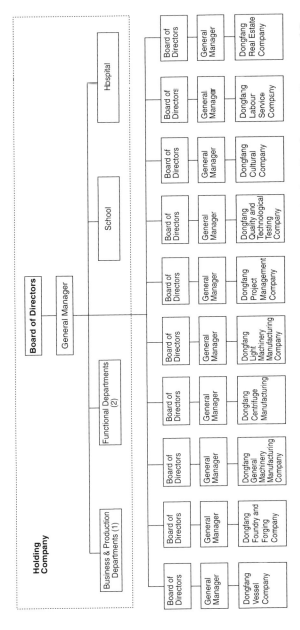

Notes: (1) *Business and Production Departments*: These include: Import and Export, Product Development, Storage and Transport, Supply and Provision of Materials, Electroplating, Iron casting.

(2) *Functional Departments*: These include: Discipline and Supervision, Political Work, Retirement, Security, Real Estate and Management, Power Supply, Development, Personnel, Finance, General Affairs.

Figure 4.2   Organizational Chart of the Holding Company and Main Subsidiary Companies, December 1994

been passed to subsidiary companies were retirement benefits and 'domestic' ('*houqin*') services. Subsidiary companies were each respons-ible for their share of the enterprise's contribution to a city-wide pool of pension funds. Each contributed a share equivalent to 24.5 per cent of its total wage bill. 'Domestic' services consisted of such services as nurseries, kindergarten, pest control, sanitation and the delivery of bottled gas. These used to be under the enterprise's 'general service unit' (*xingzheng chu*). In 1985, the economic responsibility for these services was 'contracted out' to the unit. The 'contract' held the unit responsible for the wages and bonuses of its employees and allowed it to dispose of its profits in ways it saw fit. In 1994, the unit was incorpor-ated as a subsidiary company ('*Dongfang Laodong Fuwu Gongsi*') of the holding company. It became responsible for its own profits and losses.

What had happened had, in other words, redistributed the welfare responsibility of the enterprise, reducing to some extent the overall responsibility of the holding company and giving some of the redis-tributed responsibility to subsidiary companies. As a result, housing, the hospital and the school had become largely the responsibility of the holding company, retirement benefits the responsibility of all sub-sidiary companies, and '*houqin*' services, that of the *Dongfang Laodong Fuwu Gongsi*.

Conclusion

Economic reforms since 1978 have transformed the institutional and social contexts of occupational welfare. This chapter has surveyed the changes that have occurred and discussed their implications for occu-pational welfare. The most important of these changes are: (1) the emergence of a mixed economy; (2) in the state sector, the extension of marketized employment relations and systems of wages linked to productivity; (3) the growth of an urban labour market and increasing job mobility; (4) socialist firms becoming increasingly like their capital-ist counterparts: they had to produce for profits and be responsible for their own profits and losses; (5) shifts in popular attitudes from Maoist values of collectivism and asceticism to values sanctioning individual-ism and materialistic aspirations; and (6) increasing inequality in the distribution of wealth and income.

These changes exposed state enterprises and their employees to new problems and risks. State enterprises were outmatched in market com-petition. They were losing both business and skilled workers to non-state competitors. Many of them were suffering heavy losses. That they were 'independent' meant, however, that they could no longer turn to the state for help. Under the new Bankruptcy Law, they might have to go bankrupt.

State employees were exposed to the risks of their enterprises closing down and of losing their jobs amidst widespread unemployment. Job security was no longer to be taken for granted. What was also upsetting them was that their incomes were lagging far behind those earned by private entrepreneurs and non-state workers. Both in terms of money income and occupational status they were becoming worse off. There was among them a widely shared sense of agony and frustration in reaction to what had happened to them.

The exigencies of these situations compelled state enterprises and their employees to reshape their approaches to occupational welfare.

In the pre-reform days, occupational welfare was all paid for by the state. It hardly bothered the enterprises that it was run inefficiently or that it was costly. This no longer could be the case. Now that they had to be responsible for their own profits and losses, occupational welfare could not but enter into cost-efficiency considerations. Perforce they had to find ways to make it less a heavy financial burden. Based on a case study, Chapter 6 looks at how a state enterprise tried to reduce this burden without giving up its responsibility to its employees, how it acted on the dilemma between obligation and efficiency, and how the *danwei* welfare economy was reshaped as a result.

State employees, on the other hand, were keen not to lose what they already had. Welfare was what gave state sector jobs an edge over non-state-sector jobs. It was also what in no small way topped up their relatively low wage income and closed the gap between their wages and the wages earned by non-state sector workers. It was what made state-sector jobs still attractive. The question, however, was not just to hold on to what they already had:

> People have two diametrically opposite sets of attitudes. On one hand they want the freedom and autonomy of the new system. On the other hand they are not willing to give up the security of the old system. On one hand they criticize the 'iron rice bowl'. On the other hand they are afraid of losing the 'iron rice bowl'. Some private entrepreneurs, for example, are on no-pay leave from their state-sector jobs. This arrangement allows them to return to the state-sector if things go wrong. People criticize the fact that there are 'too many people around for too little work'. Yet they cannot take it when there is unemployment. They want absolute economic secu-

rity. They do not want to lose 'from cradle to grave' social security. They love yet hate what is happening. (Dai and Li 1991: 96)

Economic reform and the rise of the mixed economy had created opportunities and risks in both the old state sector and the new non-state sector. The question was how to maximize gains and minimize risks: how to have the best of both worlds. Based on the case study of a *danwei*, Chapter 5 looks at how workers worked out ways which enabled them to gain from both the security and welfare of state-sector jobs and the flexibility and profit of non-state-sector jobs and how as a result this had given rise to a distinct pattern of dependence on occupational welfare. It is to this case study that we now turn.

5
Reshaping Dependence

Introduction

In the pre-reform days, Chinese workers were highly dependent on their work-units to satisfy a wide range of their needs, from job security to all kinds of non-wage benefits and welfare services. Membership in the work-unit guaranteed an 'iron rice bowl' and entitled workers to a 'life-long voucher' giving access to different welfare packages.

Economic reforms since 1978 and the rise of the mixed economy have created a radically different environment for occupational welfare, introducing new parameters and forcing work units and their members alike to reorder their commitments and attempt strategic responses.

Most importantly, for the workers, the mixed economy has created new structures of opportunities centred on the marketplace, eliminating the monopoly of the state sector and extending the range of personal choice and economic opportunities. It is now possible to quit a state-sector job for a non-state-sector one, or seek an income supplement from part-time jobs in the latter while holding on to a job in the former. It is now possible to 'build lives on two pillars: one in the formal, and another in the informal sector' (Szalai and Orosz 1992) and for families to strategically involve their members in both to minimize risks and maximize opportunities and advantages.

There are now also many more alternatives to what used to be distributed through one's *danwei*. The increased supplies of food and consumer goods, the gradual easing of rationing and the opening up of a private trade and services sector in cities have provided alternative sources for the satisfaction of many needs. Workers are no longer completely dependent on their enterprises for the direct delivery of many foodstuffs and consumer goods as in the pre-reform days.

The rise of the mixed economy has enabled workers to move away from their near-complete dependence on the *danwei*. But at the same time as it opens up opportunities and options, it has also created for the workers many new problems.

Layoffs and bankruptcy, hitherto unimaginable, are now real possibilities. *Danwei* benefits are no longer free, as readily available or as cheap as before (see Chapter 6). The 'iron rice bowl' and the practice of 'eating from the common pot' are becoming things of the past. In addition to these is the hard fact of a persistent two-double-figure inflation which reduces their real income and quality of life. The widening gap between their incomes and the much higher incomes earned by workers in the non-state sector[1] has furthermore accentuated a sense of frustration, inequity and relative deprivation.

There is a growing income disparity not only between workers in the state and the non-state sector, but also among workers in the state sector, within the same industry, and even among workers in the same work-unit (Bian 1994). The *danwei* community has become increasingly differentiated and stratified by economic interests (Fung and Hsu 1992). It is becoming less and less like the highly homogeneous and equalitarian community of the pre-reform days.

The *danwei* community is also becoming divided from within by new values that compete with what used to characterize the *gemeinschaftlich* community in the past. The rise of an ethos characteristic of the market, with values placed on profit, individual interest and competition instead of on egalitarianism, solidarity and altruism, upsets pre-existing values, reduces members' taken-for-granted commitment to their community and induces conflict.

In summary, economic reforms have shifted the basis of state occupational welfare and transformed the ethos of the community. While opening up new opportunities and options, these changes have also exposed workers to new risks and problems and increased the financial burden on the family of sickness, disability and other misfortunes in life. Based on field data, what follows describes how workers at one *danwei*, the Dongfang Heavy Machinery Works (DFMW), perceived and acted on these changes and in so doing reshaped their dependence on welfare.

Using the mixed economy

The rise of the mixed economy has created many new opportunities outside the state sector. Part-time job opportunities with private enterprises are particularly attractive ways to supplement income.

'Moonlighting', or *chaogang*, enables workers to gain from an arrangement straddling two economies and systems of opportunities, the state and the non-state, the public and the private, and the formal and the informal sectors. The strategy combines the benefits and security of the former and the flexibility and opportunities of the latter.

In China, 'moonlighting has become a way of life' (Han 1990). It is particularly widespread in port cities. In Guangzhou, around 30 per cent of workers have second jobs. the main reason for the upsurge in second jobs has in part to do with the rapid growth of industry in the market sector. This increased demands for technicians, engineers and other skilled workers. 'In 1987, for example, China had 1.5 million "township" enterprises and 1 million private enterprises. With fewer than 2.5 million technicians to serve them, these firms provided a vast market for "Sunday engineers"' (Han 1990). People take second jobs partly also because of rapid inflation. They have been forced to search for supplementary sources of income to maintain their standard of living. Also, in many state-owned enterprises where there are not enough assignments for everyone, workers prefer second jobs to sitting idle.

At DFMW, *chaogang* has been a popular practice especially among young workers. Mr Deng, the director of one of DFMW's 12 subsidiary companies, was tolerant towards *chaogang*:

> In the past, *chaogang* was not allowed. This is now tacitly permitted. Workers, you see, can make more money from *chaogang* than from their wages and bonuses. So they really do not care too much about how much they earn from the plant. What they do care is its security and benefits. Young workers, in particular, are actively involved in *chaogang*. As director, I do not mind if workers are not here all the time, as long as they get their jobs done.

Why were young workers in particular so actively involved in moonlighting? Mr Tao, a 24-year-old driver and formerly a skilled worker in one of the workshops, explained why:

> In my old workshop, business was so bad you just spent the day idling around. Every day you went in, got roll-called, and after that, there was nothing for you to do. And then, at the end of the month, you got so little pay you simply could not make ends meet. I had to ask my parents to send me money. I then got into *chaogang*, working from 4 p.m. till 10 p.m. It was very tough. Many workers like myself were engaged in *chaogang*. It was no secret. You did not

let your chiefs know. But they knew of course and well, they just pretended that they didn't know. It was all right if you *chaogang* after work. But occasionally you also took a few days off to work on a well-paid project. For example, it could be a project which paid two workers 4,000–5,000 yuan for seven days' work. Each worker could make over 2,000 yuan in just a week. Some workers would take leave from the plant to work on the project. For, you see, you could work so hard in the plant and be paid just around 400–500 yuan. You make so much more in just seven days. So even if it means forfeiting some bonus, we don't mind. In short, everything depends on how well you are paid. Old workers are generally less actively involved in part-time jobs. However, if the pay is attractive, they will still do it, but not for a long period, usually around two to three days. And, if you have the right *guanxi*, you can even be off on sick leave for outside practice.

The average wage at DFMW was around Y700. This amount included a 'basic wage', about Y200, some 10–12 kinds of subsidies ('*butei*') ('productivity wage', 'seniority subsidy', plant's contribution to superannuable fund, water, electricity and vegetable subsidies, general subsidy, auxiliary food subsidy, transport subsidy, coal subsidy and single-child allowance) adding up to around Y50, and a bonus. The bonus varied with one's productivity during the month. In some exceptional cases, the bonus could go up to between Y1,500 and Y2,000. But this was extremely rare. For the average worker the bonus was around Y300 to Y400. There were also many cases in which the workers did not get any bonus at all, because their workshops did not have enough work for everyone. They just had their basic wage and subsidies. When the iron-casting shop closed down not too long before this researcher visited DFMW, its workers were sent home to 'rest and wait' (*daigang*) and paid a uniform *daigang* wage of Y250. Workers like Mr Tao and those who earned not much more than their basic or *daigang* wage had no choice but take up additional jobs through *chaogang* to tide over their difficulties. As in other socialist societies undergoing economic reforms, they 'attempt[ed] to mitigate the uncertainty of earnings by taking their skills into an auxilliary market sector' (Stark 1986).

But it was not just *daigang* workers or workers like Mr Tao who had second jobs. Workers who earned twice or even three times the *daigang* wage had found it difficult to catch up with inflation. Commodity prices had risen by 17 per cent in the first nine months of 1994 (*Wen Hui Bao* 19 October 1994). Ms Feng, an unskilled worker married with a

daughter, told the researcher how difficult it had been for her to make
ends meet:

> Workers like me are earning about Y500 to Y600. This includes
> everything: bonus, basic wage and all kinds of subsidies. But prices
> have been going up. This month's water fee has gone up by as much
> as 20 cents. Sending the kid to school is also expensive. Just tuition
> fee alone costs you over Y100 a month. On top of this you also have
> to pay for her lunch and all kinds of fees, including after-school
> tutorial fees and various miscellaneous fees. The school is always
> asking you to pay this and that kind of fees. But can you not pay?
> Prices are going up. Our pay, instead of going up, has gone down.
> That's why whenever fellow workers meet, their topic is on prices
> going up. It is very tough. Take for example, my husband and
> myself, together we make Y1,200. Nearly half of this amount is
> spent on the kid and her education. But this is not all. You have to
> buy her dresses too. And then all of a sudden the school asks you to
> pay several hundred yuan for her school uniform. It's hard. And
> then prices of all basic necessities are going up rapidly. They are dif-
> ferent every month. That's why we have been eating very simple
> food. Nevertheless, the expenditure on food comes to over 1,000
> yuan a month. Pork, for example, is 9–10 yuan a catty [0.5 kg]. But
> you can't just have pork. That is why we workers find it very tough
> this year. Every one overspends every month. Every family manages
> to have some savings. We are kidding you if we tell you we do not
> have any savings. But it isn't really that much, and it won't last too
> long when you continuously dip into it. And to be frank with you,
> we rarely go out to eat, not even once a month. A very simple meal
> for three of us is easily over 100 yuan. We cannot afford it. We can
> only occasionally have breakfast outside and spend around Y30.
> Eating out is very much beyond us.

Workers like Ms Feng were obviously under pressure to seek second
jobs to supplement their income. Mr Wen, principal of the plant's
school, explained that, in his school, young teachers took second jobs
for an additional important reason: like most urban youth in the
country, they had to 'save their income to meet their own marital
expenses' (Stacey 1983: 236):

> Getting married is now becoming very expensive. On the average, a
> young man has to spend around Y20,000 to Y30,000 on wedding gifts

and the wedding banquet. You cannot rely on kin and relatives to give much assistance. And in fact among this generation of young men there are not that many relatives whom they can turn to anyway. For they do not have brothers or sisters: they are a single child.

Chaogang is apparently a common practice among workers, particularly young workers, and not just among workers, but also among professionals. But *chaogang* was not strictly an after-work activity. As reported by Ms Ma, a 'National Model Worker' in her forties, it was not uncommon for workers to take their part-time jobs back to work and, indeed, 'moonlight on the job':

> It is not uncommon for workers to take home small tools and materials for private use. Also, it is common for people to be working on their private jobs while on duty. It is held that one advantage of working in a big plant is that it is possible for one to be doing one's private jobs: the tools and machinery are all there, very handy, and, moreover, no one knows whether you are working for the plant or doing your own private work. It is the view of some that when people do such a thing, it is because they feel that they have not been given the worth of their labour by the plant.

Chaogang on the job showed how pervasive and widespread part-time activities had become. But what was even more striking was that workers did not seem to disapprove of what was strictly speaking an illegitimate practice.[2]

Pervasive though it was, not everyone was engaged in moonlighting, and it seemed that the practice was more prevalent among male than among female workers. Ms Cao, 43, Ms Zhou, 41, and Ms Feng, 42, all married, did not *chaogang*. They explained why:

> You need to have the skill and the opportunity to get into *chaogang*. It is mostly men who do it. Women seldom do it. Also, it depends on the type of work that people do. Some workers *chaogang* after work. (Ms Cao)

> No I don't *chaogang*. I'm happy that I have been able to look after my family after work. For, you see, I have to go to the market and prepare dinner. I don't have much free time. (Ms. Zhou)

> If you have the skill, you can go *chaogang*. But even if you don't, you can also do such things as hawking, mending bicycle tyres or,

among female workers, working on some take-home jobs. I would say two to three out of ten workers are involved. I myself am not. My husband used to do it before his recent posting to the production office, where he has to work all day, for the full eight hours. He does not have any time for *chaogang* now. If you *chaogang* in the evening and go to work the next day, you'll get so tired. He used to earn around Y300 from his second job, serving as an open-air market-trader. That was not much really. (Ms Feng)

There were then, it seems, gender differences in moonlighting. Female workers were less involved in part because of their 'double burden': in addition to their full-time jobs, they were also doing the bulk of the household chores. And because household electrical appliances and equipment which would ease that workload were not as readily available to the ordinary families as in other more industrialized countries, the double burden for women in China is probably more onerous than in many parts of the world (Whyte and Parish 1984: 204). 'The toll this double burden of full-time work and full-time housework takes on women physically is serious' (Wolf 1985: 73). It leaves them little time and energy for yet another shift. Female workers were less active in *chaogang* secondly because, compared with male workers, they generally had fewer years of education (Chang 1995) and fewer of them had the skills in demand in the market.[3] Jobs which did not require these skills, jobs like shop assistants and car-park attendants, were, however, not so well paid.

Ms Ma herself had not engaged in *chaogang* activities. At the age of 43, she was planning to retire in two years' time: 'If they want my service, I can come back. Otherwise I will get a job elsewhere. It will pay better.' Ms Ma obtained her *danwei* flat in 1992. If she retired, she would continue to live there and, in addition, collect her monthly pension. She would also continue to enjoy medical care and other *danwei*-provided benefits. And if she did return to her job on a new contract, she would be 'earning' almost twice as much. Like *chaogang*, her strategy was to optimize her advantages and opportunities by combining the security and benefits of the state sector with the flexibility of the non-state sector.

In 1994, DFMW had around 2,300 retired workers and around 700 who, like Ms Ma, would be joining the retired population in the next five years. Male workers retired at the age of 60 and female workers 50. Workers in high-temperature and hazardous working environment retired at an earlier age: 55 for male and 45 for female workers. Upon retirement, they were entitled to a monthly pension of around Y250. Besides pensions, they were also given various 'subsidies' (*butei*), including rent, water and electricity charges, and 'seniority' (*gongling*), which together amounted to Y70. In 1994, following a directive from the Guangzhou Municipal Government, pensioners were each paid an additional Y100 to help alleviate their 'hardship'. Adding all these together, the 'package' a pensioner received came to around Y400 a month.

To survive on this amount was not easy. Many pensioners had taken jobs in the non-state sector, jobs such as car-park assistants, shop attendants, and hawkers. According to Mr Deng:

> There are two retired workers in my workshop. One of them has got relatives and friends in Hong Kong and Macao. He has been receiving support from them and is living rather comfortably. The other has to get himself a job. The retirement pension, you see, is barely enough to keep one alive.

Ms Feng described the situation of retired workers as follows:

> Retired workers who have got several children are all right. They can depend on their children each to give them Y30 to Y40 a month. Very few children do not support their parents. There may of course be cases in which the children themselves are in financial difficulties, in which case they may even have to turn to their parents for assistance. Workers of my generation will face a rather different situation: we have got only one child to turn to in our old age. Either he or she has the means to support you, or he or she hasn't. In the latter case you may have to help him or her instead. I do hope my daughter can be good to me when I am old. That's why I've been telling her all the time how much I have done for her and hope that she takes this to heart.

Mr Zhu, a 37-year-old skilled worker, lived with his retired parents. Had he not lived with them, he would still support them, he maintained:

> Even if you do not live with your parents, you will still give them some money if you know they have difficulties. You try to spend less on other things. It won't be too difficult. Childless people are in a more difficult situation, you see, when in their old age they have

this kind or that kind of illness and problem, and when they do not have that much pension. They are a pitiful lot.

Many families in the Pearl River Delta area have external linkages with friends and relatives in Hong Kong, Macao and other overseas Chinese communities with dense Chinese immigrant settlements (Johnson 1993) Some are even 'Dependants of Overseas Chinese' (*qiaojuan*). Among the *qiaojuan* households there are those whose kinsmen abroad are distant and others who have kinsmen with a direct relationship either through marriage or descent. The closeness of relationships will determine the kind and amount of support that the relatives abroad will provide. This can be regular remittances, as was the case with one of Mr Leung's workers, or the 'likelihood of obtaining an immigration visa and the possibility of joining kinsmen abroad' (Johnson 1993: 127).

Support from children is both more common and more important than support from external connections. The Marriage Law of the People's Republic of China, in both its 1950 and 1981 versions, requires children to support their elderly parents.[4] In general, however, children support their parents not so much because this is required by law,[5] but more because of their commitment to the Confucian value of reciprocity: 'Children provide for elderly parents, and parents turn to adult children without guilt, because both generations believe that the creation of the children's physical existence and the care given them in childhood require children to reciprocate in their parents' old age' (Davis-Friedmann 1983: 53). Interdependence and reciprocal obligations characterize their close relationship. The urban elderly 'expect and receive support from all their children and are almost as likely to live with an adult daughter as with a son' (Stacey 1983: 236). Because of housing shortages, young men cannot always establish a separate household even after marriage.[6] In the periods of high unemployment that have prevailed since the mid-1960s, many men must also rely on their parents' connections to secure jobs.[7] Their dependence on their parents for housing and employment draws them closer to parents, further obliging them to give support to their parents in their old age.[8] What they commonly do includes 'caring for parents when they are sick; giving them money and, if there are brothers and sisters, each giving a share; helping with some household chores; and talking to them and giving them psychological and emotional support' (Wei 1990: 46).

Ms Feng herself would be retiring in three years' time. Upon retirement, she planned to take a job in the non-state sector. Her husband, a co-worker, would in a year or two quit his job too. She explained their plan: 'We can afford to do so because as a retiree I am entitled to keeping the flat and the benefits which we now have. My husband will spend the first year or two learning a new trade, then he will try to have his own business. And by the time when I retire, I can be his assistant.'

The plan was exemplary: it strategically positioned members of a family in both the state and the non-state sectors and enabled the family to optimize its opportunities and advantages through, in short, a 'one family, two systems' (*yijia liangzhi*) (Dai and Li 1991) arrangement. In many cases it was the wife who stayed on, maintaining the family's link with the *danwei*, and the husband who gave up *danwei* membership and ventured into the unknown and excitement of the non-state economy. Beside 'husbands go, wives stay' (*nancho nuliu*) cases, there were also cases in which it was the son or the daughter who gave up his or her job and the parents who stayed on. Miss He, a young computer programmer, for example, quit her job at DFMW and, in partnership with a friend, set up a private computer consultancy company. Miss He's father, a worker, and her brother, an engineer, stayed on in their jobs. Miss He explained why she decided to quit:

I got a diploma in computer studies. After finishing the course, I received on-the-job training at DFMW and gained from the experience. Because I had some savings, I felt bold enough to leave the job at DFMW. You see, in the later period of my appointment at DFMW, we did not have much work to do. We were wasting our time. It was hard to give up welfare and *danwei* benefits. But if you didn't take the risk, at the end of the day you might lose everything.

In both cases, it is clear that there was a 'family strategy' in action. Family members did not act individually but as members of a 'corporate entity'[9] (Johnson 1993: 103) and in line with some collective strategy designed to advance the interest of the group as a whole. The main point of the strategy was to position family members strategically in the mixed economy so that the family could minimize risk and maximize gains from the arrangement.

The risk would be too great were family members collectively to give up their state-sector jobs. Non-state-sector jobs generally paid higher wages. On the other hand there was no guarantee of job security. Employment was entirely on a contract basis and workers, unlike in the state sector, could be sacked. Furthermore, such jobs came with few benefits and welfare. Many of these jobs were also with 'village and township enterprises' located in rural areas far away from the city. Were the whole family to move to where these jobs were located, they could lose their 'home-base' in the city and all the economic and cultural advantages of city living.

Foreign-owned enterprises paid better. The government fixed the minimum wage of their employees at a level at least 120 per cent above the average national wage. But the working conditions of these enterprises, especially those in small and medium-sized ones, were not always desirable. For example, there had been allegations of a lack of facilities for basic hygiene in work and living places, frequent industrial accidents, forced overtime, extremely high output norms and even human rights abuses (Zhu 1995: 46). And, were workers to move without the approval of their work units, they were 'penalized by loss of their seniority, and skilled workers are required to compensate the enterprises for on-the-job training if they attempt to move before their contract term is up' (Hu and Li 1993: 173).

Quitters from state-sector jobs could also set themselves up as 'private entrepreneurs' if they had the capital and skills. This would be no less risky for, besides risk of a business and financial nature, they would also be running certain political risk. In an officially socialist society and 'after several decades both of intense criticism of private business as a "tail of capitalism" and of policies aimed at eliminating it and preventing its emergence' (Gold 1990: 162–3), there was always the possibility that in the next swing of the political pendulum the regime might again reverse its present policies and crack down on private business.[10]

But if family members were to remain together and stay in their state-sector jobs, they would be running a risk of yet another kind, the risk that they might all 'sink with the ship' and lose all they had, welfare, security and permanent jobs, were their poorly performing state-owned enterprises to give up and go bankrupt.

The risk was greater when family members were all in the same *danwei*. According to Mr Liao, the plant's office manager, there were many cases of both husband and wife and even their children working for the same plant:

> Being a large-scale enterprise, it has got many *guanxi* among its employees and these *guanxi* are also highly complex. There are husband–wife *guanxi*. There are also father–son *guanxi*. In the days of planned economy, many *lingdao* (cadres and managers) got their

children and relatives into the plant and created for them jobs which did not have much work to do. Since reforms, the plant has undertaken many exercises to streamline and cut unnecessary manpower, regardless of whether it is related to *guanxi* or not. This has caused many disputes and much unhappiness. Interpersonal relations have become very complex. They are very difficult to handle.

Dr Mao, director of the plant's hospital, confirmed what Mr Liao described. The plant was densely overlain with 'networks of kin' (*qinshu wang*) (Pan and Lin 1992: 80):

> The entire *danwei* is embedded in complex and inter-related networks of *guanxi*. People are all somehow linked directly or indirectly to one another. It is like a string of pumpkins. You pull one pumpkin and discover to your amazement that it is connected to a whole string of pumpkins. The *guanxi* network goes far beyond husband and wife. It includes also their brothers and sisters, the husbands and wives of their brothers and sisters, the in-laws of the husbands and wives of their brothers and sisters and their relatives and so on. The network goes on and on and sees no limit.

The strategy of the pre-reform days had turned against itself. What used to serve the interests of an extensive network of kin was now a major disadvantage when it exposed the entire group to the danger of 'sinking with the ship'.

To limit these various kinds of risks and also to maximize gains, the family strategy was to engage family members strategically in the state and the non-state sectors. In the case of Ms Feng, the wife stayed, keeping the family's link with the state sector; the husband ventured into the unknown world of market competition, risk and profit. In the case of Miss He, it was the elderly parents who stayed and the unmarried daughter who gave up her job to try her luck in the world of private business. In both cases, it was the family member who had the best potential and the most to gain from a successful non-state-sector career who embarked on the adventurous journey to the alien land of market competition, the male breadwinner in one case and the unmarried child in the other case.

In the 'husbands go, wives stay' strategy, it was usually the wives who stayed first, because female workers, particularly female workers aged over 30, were less in demand in the non-state-sector job market than male workers (Tan 1994; Liu 1995: 51; *Beijing* Federation of

Women et al. 1990), hence it was more difficult for them to find jobs; and secondly, because they were in fact enjoying more *danwei* benefits than male workers.[11] For example, they were entitled to more leave.[12] Health-care of female workers was on the whole more expensive than that of male workers. And because female workers retired at 50 instead of at 60, they received a pension much earlier than male workers. 'Husbands go, wives stay' was in many ways a 'least to lose, most to gain' arrangement.

Workers unconnected to any *guanxi* in the plant had fewer options than workers well connected to *guanxi*. Their options were either to give up everything and quit, or stay. Young workers like Mr Tao were prepared to stay. Mr Tao was not yet married:

> It depends on the conditions outside and your own ability. What can I do if I quit? I really do not want to go back to my old trade. I can work as a taxi driver, but it is not easy to make money. I have got many friends who are drivers. They are able to make a lot of money, but have to work really hard. That's why I do not fancy leaving my job. It's stable and secure here after all. In time I will be old enough and get married. With my marriage certificate I can apply for housing and wait for allocation. This is life. Honestly speaking, I do not want to return to my village. I have no choice.

Many others were not as patient as Mr Tao. They simply gave up and left for jobs in the non-state sector. In the first six months of 1994, around 100 had resigned.

To stay or not to stay? A key factor in the consideration was housing. Workers would normally have to serve the *danwei* for over eight years and be occupying not more than 5 square metres of living space in their present accommodation to be qualified for *danwei* housing, for which, depending on size, they paid a rent between Y6 to Y15 a month. There were, however, long queues for *danwei* housing. According to Mr Tang, the work-unit's senior accountant, around one-fifth of the plant's 4,842 employees were on the queue and at least 500 of the lot were 'hardship' cases deserving priority treatment. It took workers many years to get into the queue and many years after they were on the queue to be housed. According to Ms Feng:

> It very much depends on whether there are flats available. Many workers got their flats not until both husbands and wives were retired. In our workshop, there is one 'old young man' ('*da qingnian*') who is

now in his forties. He wants to get married but cannot because he is still on the housing queue. And, without a flat, the couple would not be able to live together. They would be living in separate places. He is getting very desperate. He told us he was losing patience and would quit the *danwei* if he was not allocated a flat soon. We also have many cases in which young married couples live in separate places, the husbands in dormitories for single men and the wives in dormitories for single women.

For many young workers, the waiting time and the uncertainty of getting *danwei* housing was just too much for them.

There was also a second reason why young workers such as Mr Tao were not eager to quit. Mr Tao came from a village in a remote part of the countryside in the province. He joined the plant in 1987 as a student in its vocational school. To enable him to stay and work in Guangzhou, the plant had acquired a temporary city *hukou*, or urban residency status certificate, for him by paying the municipal government an 'additional population fee' (*zheng rong fei*). Were Mr Tao to quit his job at DFMW, not only would he have to repay his tuition fees to the vocational school, but he would also lose his residency status. Mr Tao explained his decision to stay:

> There would not be much for me to do back in the village. My parents have retired and all my brothers and sisters have gone elsewhere to work. There is not much point for me to go back. Because I have got this job here, it's better for me to be contented and carry on, and hope that in time I may be allocated housing and have my own family. And, you see, our *hukou* is in the hands of the plant. You are allowed to have it in your own name only when you are married: it is now a collective *hukou*. And if I quit this job, I will have to pay back my tuition fees and lose my city *hukou* too. Quitting is not really that difficult, but you have to think it over very carefully. It is all right if everything goes well. But if things do not work out, I will lose my *hukou*. To me, unless I am eighty per cent sure of the outcome, I will not take the risk.

Housing was less of a problem to older and retired workers. By the time they were about to retire, their seniority would have qualified them for housing. The problem which many of them had was of a different kind, that of finding enough money to buy the flats. *Danwei* flats became available for sale to workers in 1989. To qualify, workers had to have worked in the plant for at least 30 years. As Mr Wu and Ms Feng described their problem:

> Most retired workers have now been housed. However, very few of them have got enough personal savings to buy the flats recently offered to them. They have to seek help from children, or borrow from friends and relatives. Also, they have been asking the plant to give them special treatment, for example, in allowing them to defer some payments, or giving them certain exemptions. (Mr Wu)
>
> Managerial staff who have been in the plant for more than five years can apply to buy these flats. Ordinary workers, like us, are not qualified unless we have been here for at least 30 years. Many retired workers have bought these flats. To pay for these flats they either have to borrow from friends and relatives or get their children to help. But you see these flats are getting more and more expensive. The first batch of these flats were sold at around Y5,000 to Y6,000. The more expensive ones were only about Y9,000. The second batch were sold at almost four times these prices. They could be even more expensive by the time I become qualified. Saving Y20,000 is very very difficult for ordinary workers like us. Any amount more than that will simply be beyond us. And mind you, I have got only one child. (Ms Feng)

As described by Mr Wu and Ms Feng, their problem was of an order different from that of young workers. And although there were those who, like Ms Feng, found it difficult to raise the required amounts, there obviously were many others who successfully mobilized the required financial resources from their children and social networks.

Middle-aged workers were in a situation different from both old and young workers. They were not 'old' enough for retirement benefits, yet, were they to quit, they would have more to give up than young workers. Mr Peng, a skilled worker of 40, described his plight and dilemma:

> Some co-workers of mine quit the plant not too long ago to work in joint-venture companies. They are all doing very well, getting much better pay than what I am getting. They have moved into company flats much bigger than my present flat, around 60 sq. metres. Mine is just 24 sq. metres. I was so stupid not to have foreseen all these and quit as they did. It is now too late. I am too old for these jobs: they want workers in their thirties. The quitters have sort of got out

of water and landed on the shores already. As for workers like myself, we are stranded: in no way can we move, but see no future if we stay. The quitters have got everything in just a matter of a few years. We've been here for nearly 20 years and what have we got? Nothing. Also, compared to friends and relatives working in joint-venture and foreign-capital companies, I am lagging behind. Even a shop assistant makes over Y1,000 a month. Workers of my generation do not have a future. (Mr Peng)

Mr. Deng's situation is not dissimilar to Mr Peng's. Asked whether he had given any thought to leaving the *danwei* for a better job, he said, 'Well, you see, I am already 50 and no longer have the strength and energy of a young man. Also, when I bought my flat from the *danwei* last year, I have signed an agreement which requires that I stay on the job for ten more years, until I retire. I'll have to give up the flat if I quit.'

There were then, it seems, both gender and generational differences in workers' responses to the rise of the mixed economy. Moonlighting in the second economy was more popular among young than among old workers, and more preferred by male than by female workers. Many retired workers were economically active. In addition to the retirement benefits obtained through the *danwei*, and in addition to the financial support and care given them by their children and social networks, many retired workers had been working and earning incomes from paid jobs. They made innovative use of an arrangement that enabled them to draw upon support and resources from both the state and the non-state, the public and the private, and the formal and the informal sectors. Like their counterparts in Hungary, 'The overwhelming majority of pensioners (both those who retired earlier, and those who did so at the "ordinary" retirement age) work hard either in various "branches" of the informal economy or in part-time employment in the formal economy to supplement their pensions, but usually ... with much more flexibility and much better working conditions than they had before' (Szalai and Orosz 1992: 155). Young workers were in a very different situation from that of the old workers. Because they were junior, they were not yet eligible for such benefits as housing. Because they were less dependent on the *danwei*, they had fewer stakes and less to lose were they to give up their jobs. Middle-aged workers were caught in the middle. They were not yet in line for retirement benefits. Unlike young workers, however, they were enjoying more benefits, hence also more dependent on the *danwei*. They had more at stake and more to lose were they to quit their jobs. They were, as Mr Peng described them, the 'stranded generation'. Gender and generational differences among workers shaped their differential dependence on *danwei* welfare and explained their differential response to change.

It is clear that the family was performing a very strategic role. It was important both in providing resources and support to its members and in co-ordinating strategic arrangements aimed at protecting and advancing the collective interests of the family as a whole. Workers without family support were less resourceful. They had fewer strategic options. Workers who had the support of their families were more resourceful and more adaptable to change. But, as pointed out by several informants, the family may become less able to give support to its members when in due course the 'one child policy' deprives parents of more than one child and their child of his or her siblings. This policy 'flies in the face of a long tradition of values calling for many children (especially sons), a welfare program in which children form the major bulwark against the hazards of old age' (Kallgren 1985: 131).

Calculative uses of *danwei* welfare

The life-chances of workers were no longer entirely dependent on the *danwei* and its welfare. The mixed economy opened up exit and second job opportunities which many workers exploited to their advantages. In the course of fieldwork, the researcher discovered also that workers were making calculative and selective uses of *danwei* welfare instead of just receiving and consuming whatever was made available to them through the *danwei* bureaucracy.

The *danwei*'s school, for example, was not as popular among workers as one might imagine, although it was conveniently located in the plant's residential areas. Few workers interviewed by the researcher were positive about the school. Ms Cao and Ms Ma explained why they did not think the school was good:

> People outside do not have much regard for the school. They believe its teachers are not well qualified. I have doubts too about whether they have the right qualifications. Many colleagues also think that they may be all right as primary school teachers, but as secondary school teachers they cannot compare with teachers of other schools. (Ms Cao)

> Yes, it is true that workers prefer schools outside the plant. You get an idea of what the school is up to by reading the public examina-

tion results of its students published in the *Dongfang Bao* [the plant's monthly newsletters] and by following the performance of its students participating in competitions in the city. The standard of its primary school is all right. It is, however, not so good at its secondary school. Graduates from the secondary school do not stand much chance getting admission into the university. (Ms Ma)

The plant's accountant, Mr Tang, was even more critical. Bluntly, he said:

The standard of the school is rather low. Because it is not government-funded, the education department is not supervising it in the same way as it does with other schools. Parents who care and who can afford it send their children to schools in other parts of the city. To get their children into these schools they need only to give some donations in the form of sponsorship fees. Many parents did.

Mr Zhu placed his six-year-old daughter in a private nursery outside the plant:

It's simple. You don't need to fill out different kinds of forms and go through troublesome procedures. You just pay and she's in. The nursery is good. Of course, it is also more expensive.

Asked whether he would let her attend the plant's school, Mr Zhu flatly said no:

I don't think I'd like her to go to the plant's school. There are two other schools in the neighbourhood. I'd rather she go to either one of these instead. If this does not work out, I'll see what I can do. She may end up with the plant's school, but this is unlikely. You see, if only you are prepared to spend some money, you can sort things out. How much? It's not a small amount: around Y2,000 to Y3,000. (Mr Zhu)

It was obvious that workers would rather place their children in some other schools if they could afford the tuition fees. Mr Wen the principal had a much more difficult decision to make. His daughter, aged 6, would be ready to go to school in a year's time:

It would be a boost to the morale of teachers if my daughter goes to the plant's school. However, this would not be without any problem. Teachers do not feel comfortable teaching the daughter of the school's principal. It could cause all sorts of problems. It is sensitive.

The hospital was in a situation similar to that of the school. Workers and their families could see doctors at the hospital's out-patient department and could also seek referrals to other hospitals in the city. In both cases, following a policy just introduced, workers had to pay 20 per cent and their family members 50 per cent of the bills. The rest of the bills and any expense over Y350 were covered by the plant. Workers' opinion of the hospital and the quality of its service was, however, very negative. In the view of Mr Tang the accountant, for example, the hospital was a 'sub-standard and filthy facility where patients hated to go' and where 'doctors and nurses outnumber their patients'. Ms Feng and Ms Cao described their dissatisfaction:

> I am, of course, dissatisfied. The doctors there are not up to stan-dard. Yet you have to pay the 20 per cent. And the medicine that they give you is no good. Some has even passed the expiry dates. Some is so outdated it's no longer sold in pharmacies. Anyway, they prescribe whatever medicine you ask for. They have such easy jobs. But then they just give you outdated medicine. They won't let you have new drugs. That's why it's cheap and you need only to pay 4–5 yuan to take home a lot of medicine. Not so in other hospitals where they give you better drugs. Of course you pay many times more. They can, of course, refer you to outside hospitals. They'll ask you which hospital you like. If they agree, they can let you go. It is usually like that. For example, just last month I strained my leg. I told the doctor I liked to be treated by traditional Chinese medicine. He agreed and let me go. On that occasion I paid Y100 but claimed Y80 back from the plant. (Ms Feng)

> For minor problems it is all right. The doctors are not really that reliable. I seldom go to see doctors outside, for you'll need referral letters. Moreover, you also spend much more time, queuing for reg-istration, waiting to see the doctor, queuing for drugs on one floor and queuing to pay your fees at another and so on. But if there are emergencies, or when you have a high temperature, they let you go. Otherwise you'll have to pay yourselves. In any case, if doctors here can't cure you, they won't kill you either. (Ms Cao)

Dr Mao became director of the plant's hospital in 1993. She confirmed their accounts:

> It is true. This hospital is very unlike the public hospital where I used to work. There everyone was so busy, working so hard, and the pace of work was so very fast. Here people have got so little work to do. I was bored to death. You see, the hospital looks after minor illnesses and cuts and wounds. Patients with more serious problems are referred to other hospitals. At first, I tried to be strict with referrals. This caused an uproar among workers. They complained to *lingdao*. *Lingdao* told me I should not be so strict. I had to give in. And it was like opening the flood-gate. You lost all controls. Doctors, you see, don't care. After all, it is not their money. It is public money, the state's money. And why not, when they can use the power to sign referral letters exchanging favours with *guanxi*. I had such a tough time then, besieged and attacked from all sides. It is so very difficult to try to introduce change.

Workers like Ms Cao abided by the rules. They seldom went to see doctors at other hospitals. However, as described by Dr Mao, there were apparently many others who were able to use their *guanxi* with doctors to obtain for themselves the advantage of using medical facilities and services external to the *danwei*.

Unlike the school and the hospital, *danwei* housing was highly treasured. Guangzhou was overcrowded. Almost no new housing was constructed between 1949 and 1979, and most of the housing stock had badly deteriorated by the 1980s. 'Since the population had doubled in the meantime, there was an acute shortage of space' (Vogel 1989: 197). Workers in state enterprises looked to their *danwei* to provide them with housing. Once allocated, it was for life and they had to pay only a tiny fraction of their monthly income on rent. In the late 1970s and early 1980s, when *tingti* (replacement of parents' jobs by their children) was practised, *danwei* housing became virtually inheritable. Since 1988, workers could also buy their flats from the *danwei* at well below market prices.

> The market price is around several thousand yuan per sq. metre. With our meagre earnings, this is simply beyond us. The price of some housing estate flats of very average quality comes to Y3,900 per sq. metre. For a mere 30 sq. metre flat, you have to pay Y120,000! By the time we have this amount of saving, the price

would have gone up even higher up. There is no way we can catch up. Moreover, unlike in Hong Kong, there is no such financial facility as mortgage: we can't pay by installment. There is little hope we can buy a property from the market. (Ms Cao)

There were nevertheless cases in which workers turned down the *danwei's* offers because they did not like the flats allocated to them:

I didn't apply for *danwei* housing. You see, being a worker, I am entitled to no more than 24 sq. metres. Managers and cadres are entitled to bigger and better flats. In my workshop, three colleagues have recently been offered *danwei* flats. None took up the offer. Why? Because the flats offered them were so very small. The kitchens were dark too. You couldn't believe how small these kitchens were. There was one flat in which the kitchen was located not within but outside the flat! Can you imagine this? Isn't this ridiculous? I am living in a flat with two bedrooms and one sitting room. It is over 30 sq. metres and I pay not more than Y20 on rent. I have no intention of moving. And, you see, the building is very old and is due for redevelopment. We are expecting the government to give us compensation to move out of the building. So we are waiting. Let's see what will happen. (Ms Cao)

From the examples of the school, the hospital and housing, it is clear that workers were no longer entirely dependent on the *danwei* for all its facilities and services. They were moving away from near-complete dependence and were no longer passive recipients who just took whatever was available. They had more individual choices and, exercising their preferences, were using *danwei* benefits more selectively and calculatively. They made greater use of, and hence were more dependent on, some *danwei* benefits, but used more discreetly, and hence were less dependent on, other benefits.

Reshaping identity and commitment

In 1983, DFMW had 6,421 employees. By 1995, the figure had dropped to 4,503 – the plant had lost 30 per cent (1,918) of its employees in 13 years. During the three-year period 1993–5 as many as 999 employees left the plant for jobs elsewhere. Many of those who left were young workers aged between 18 and 35 (Table 5.1).

Table 5.1   Number of Permanent and Contract Workers, and Number of
Workers Who Quit in 1993, 1994, 1995

	1993	1994	1995
Permanent and Contract Workers*	5,081	4,842	4,503
Workers aged between 18 and 35	1,799	1,518	1,239
Workers aged 45 and above	1,375	1,346	1,296
Male workers	3,445	3,279	3,019
Female workers	1,636	1,563	1,484
Quitters	267	432	300

Source: DFMW Annual Report on Labour Statistics 1995.
* Temporary workers not included.

The 'exodus' of young workers highlighted the radically changed
'cultural landscape' of the *danwei*: it was no longer the basis of one's
identity and the subject of lifelong commitment. Ms Feng remembered
the days when in 1970 as a youngster of 17 she joined DFMW:

You were so proud and happy to be a worker in such a big factory.
You even wore your uniform when you went shopping and when
you met friends from secondary school. Even if you were to die for
work, it was worth it, you thought. At that time, you could work
very long hours, until nine or ten o'clock at night, without overtime
pay. All that they gave you was a rice dumpling for midnight
supper. But we did not have any complaint. People then earned
more or less the same pay. There was a good deal of equality. It was
like water in your bowl – we were all at the same level.

Mr Chen, senior cadre in charge of DFMW's propaganda department,
confirmed what Ms Feng said:

In those days, workers did not just work for pay. They worked all
day and night and got up at three or four o'clock in the morning to
continue. It was like that in the early years after Liberation and
through the 1960s and 1970s. There was no such thing as overtime
pay. Since reforms, things have changed, because people do care
about pay. Life was very tough, though, in the pre-reform days and
all that the *danwei* could give to a worker at the end of a long day of
work was a food-coupon for two tails [around 225 g] of food from

the canteen. Everybody was treated in the same way, be they managers or *lingdao* or workers.

While Ms Feng and Mr Chen missed the altruism, egalitarianism and commitment of the *danwei* in the past, Ms Ma lamented the passing of the days when workers shared a much stronger sense of the 'whole':

> The spirit of co-operation is much weaker now. There is no longer a strong sense of the whole. People these days care much more about their own little units and much less the *danwei* as a whole. What they care most is getting their jobs done and getting good bonuses.

Mr Zhu, a skilled worker in his late thirties, had been with the plant for over 15 years. According to him, there was not a strong sense of belongingness among workers:

> Well, the plant is for the time being still dependable. But you do not know what will happen to it in the future. It may of course change for the worse. And when that happens, I may leave. But for the moment you can still depend on it. You see, people are no longer as idealistic as in the past. They all talk about economic outcomes. In the past, people were proud of belonging to a big factory. They no longer are. There is no longer a sense of belongingness. They regard it as just a job.

What had made the difference? Ms Feng suggested that it was the widening difference in earnings and life-styles among people and the new values on material gain and economic achievement:

> It is now a very different situation. While there are people who have not got enough to eat, there are those who have plenty of meat and fish for every meal. There are such big differences in people's incomes. Moreover, people now like to compare with each other: how much their husbands earn and so on. I do feel a sense of inferiority and try to avoid going to gatherings of old friends and alumni. There is not much you can share with them. And people look at you strangely. Friends are now more difficult to make. They care much more about money and status. Also, in the plant, *lingdao* were not as approachable as in the past. They seldom come to see the workers and do not seem to care about their difficulties. I think Mao's times were better times.

Mr Deng explained what he experienced in terms of, first of all, 'enterprise reforms', which turned the plant into a series of companies each with its own profit targets and, secondly, market values that changed people's attitudes towards work and work relations:

> In the past, the entire plant was just like one big assembly-line: work flowed from one workshop to another and workshops could depend on each other to get their jobs done. This is no longer the case. Sister companies need to pay each other for what used to be taken-for-granted services. Because there are cheaper providers for such services from outside the plant, sister companies have turned to these instead of to each other. These are usually township enterprises which can afford much lower labour cost because they provide very little welfare and benefits to their workers. As a result, sister companies are not helping each other out. Some have got into difficulties and do not have enough jobs for their workers. The old co-operative spirit is gone. Sister companies are no different from heartless capitalist competitors. Some are on the verge of bankruptcy and have sent many of their workers home on *daigan* (rest and wait). I have heard some of these workers wondering aloud, 'I love *Dongfang* (DFMW), but does *Dongfang* (DFMW) love me too?'
>
> Income differences have also widened bigger among workers in sister companies. Because not all sister companies are making the same profits, some are able to give greater bonuses to their workers than the others. For example, it is quite possible that a cleaning woman in a profitable company takes home a fatter bonus than a senior engineer in a non-profitable company.
>
> Just as sister companies have turned into competitors, so has the relationship between co-workers. Co-workers are not as prepared to give a hand to each other. For example, they may hold an attitude such as the following when a fellow colleague runs into some technical problems: 'Well, if he does not know how to do his job, it is just too bad for him. I am not going to teach him how to do it. After all, I must mind my own rice-bowl.'
>
> My job as director is also getting more and more difficult. In the past, you could work on people's thought and make them understand the importance of their duties. And if this did not work, you could always resort to administrative power. These no longer work now. Few care to listen to high-sounding words. All that they want from you is an answer to the question, 'How much?' All they care are immediate gain. To get them to co-operate, you have to speak in

a low voice, hold down your temper and ask them to give you some 'face'. You can of course curry favour with them from time to time also. The trouble is: you cannot do this all the time. There are side effects too. You are bound to make some unhappy if you do not curry favour evenly.

As the *danwei* became increasingly differentiated in structure and interest, workers had also come to identify less with the enterprise as a whole than with its sub-units. Ms Cao and Mr Tao described the change they saw, as follows:

Yes, in the past, Dongfang was big and you feel proud of being a member of a large-scale enterprise. People don't feel the same now. They look at the economic performance of the units. They feel proud of being members of units which make good profits. (Ms Cao)

With the setting up of companies, things are now quite different. For instance, when some friend of mine told me it was not bad for me to have got the job in my present company, I really felt flattered. I think I feel a stronger sense of belonging to my company than to Dongfang. (Mr Tao)

Unlike in the past, workers were much more calculatively involved and, as Mr Tao put it, 'most people nowadays are money-oriented':

When I first came to Guangzhou seven years ago, I found a pair of shoes priced at Y200 to Y300 very expensive. Today, I wouldn't mind paying Y1,000 or even more for a pair of shoes that I like as long as I can afford it. You see, as the economy develops, people's values change too. If I like something, I will work hard for it. I do not care if they give me a promotion or get me into the Party, as long as I can make money. This is really the most important thing ... Even friends, you see, are very instrumental. What they really care is their own interests and what you can do for them. Friends who are true to you are now so rare.

At 42, Ms Feng was no longer the enthusiastic young worker ready to work 'until nine or ten o'clock at night, without overtime pay'. Calculative and resigned to the fact that hers was a low-paid job, she was not prepared to put too much effort into her job. She was also unhappy that other workers were earning more.

Why should we work so hard? They want us to work hard, of course. Our answer to them is to work less hard. There is little else that we can do. There is no better way to ventilate our feelings. Some piece-rate workers do work very hard because the more they get done, the more they earn. We try not to co-operate with them. We deliberately go slow to make them earn less. (Ms Feng)

The Party and what it stood for had also fallen casualties to the changes transforming the ethos of the *danwei* community. Ms Feng, in reply to whether she had to be a Party member to be involved in birth control activities, told the researcher:

No, you don't have to be a Party member to be involved in these activities. In fact, of the three managers in our company, only one is a Party member. Ability counts more than Party membership now. And it is entirely up to you to decide whether or not to join the Party. Very few workers care to join. Of the more than 100 workers in my section, only two to three workers are Party members. No one wants to be a Party member. It is now rather easy to become one. In the past, you had to go through a very strict process to get in. And Party members were good people. They were models whom you looked up to. They no longer are. Some Party members are more backward than myself. Among workers there is the view that one must be nuts to want to join the Party. Moreover, it is not free: you have to pay membership fees. It is not much – around 1 to 2 yuan. Workers just wonder why one should want to join the Party.

This was a far cry from how things used to be: when the Chinese Communist Party was difficult to get into, when Party membership was a respected status and when CCP members were admired as social-ist role models. The status of being a CCP member was once a 'political resource' (Bian 1994: 47). It brought one closer to where power was and where decisions were made. In subtle ways it also gave one an advantage over non-Party members in job promotion and access to scarce resources (Walder 1986: 148, 163).

Ms Feng 'used' the Party, nevertheless, to promote her familial inter-ests. She so described her instrumental approach to the Party: 'I have been applying to switch to a bigger flat. I asked the Party Secretary at my company for help. I explained to him why I needed a bigger flat and expected him to speak up on my behalf.' Mr Deng, himself a Party member, bluntly explained why the Party was in decline in the *danwei*:

'Managers are in charge; the Party is only supposed to oversee their work. There are bound to be differences in their views and approaches. Yes, there is still a formal position for the Party in the plant, but it is finding it increasingly difficult to wield influence. For, you see, all that people care now is whether they can make more money.'

Party secretaries used to be the most powerful people in the enterprise. However, with the implementation since 1984 of the 'factory director responsibility system' (*changzhang fuzezhi*), giving factory directors the power to manage and holding them responsible for the economic performance of their enterprises, Party Secretaries had increasingly been sidelined (Chevrier 1990). Mr Dong, DFMW's Deputy Party Secretary, described what had happened:

> Yes, our roles have changed. We are no longer directly involved in management. And, frankly, we are no longer in power. The power over money and people is not in our hands now. It is in the hands of the General Manager. The enterprise is still under the Party and if I've got something to say, he'll listen. He won't just ignore me. But, you see, I must take care not to say things which fall within his responsibilities. For, after all, there should only be one person who calls the shots. Otherwise there will be chaos.

The rise of an ethos that placed a value on profit, individual interest and material gain had upset pre-existing values and relations in what used to be a highly stable, egalitarian and homogeneous community. It spelt differentiation and division, undermined identity and commitment, and weakened the hold of the Party and its ideological appeals.[13] Most importantly, it had changed the community's welfare ethos and encouraged workers to regard their welfare rights and entitlements calculatively: to bargain for welfare and make their commitment to the *danwei* conditional upon what they could get out of *danwei* benefits and welfare. Mr Tao stated the case of housing:

> Housing is what keeps people in their jobs. It is as simple as that. If you have got someone in your family working in the *danwei*, well, it's simple: you just quit and let this someone, your wife for example, hold on to the flat. If you haven't got this someone and if you quit, you will lose your flat. It's tough, but you can't help it.

Housing was not only instrumental in obtaining the conditional commitment of workers to the *danwei*, it was also the cause of much dissatisfaction among workers and many disputes both among workers and between workers and management. The annual housing allocation exercise was invariably tension-ridden, generating allegations of favouritism and inequity, and making many unhappy. As Mr Deng described it, 'There was an earthquake every time.' Mr Dong, Deputy Party Secretary, reflected on the differences between the 'old days' and the present time:

> The Party's job is now much more difficult. In the past, people did not know much about the market and ideological incentives could be effective. For example, if there was just one flat and if three workers wanted to have it, they were somehow more ready to give in and gracefully tell the other guys, 'You take it. I can wait.' They were more altruistic. And although the two workers who gave in did not get their flats, they nevertheless enjoyed some kind of spiritual satisfaction. The worker who got the flat was also happy. He felt the warmth of comradely care. This is no longer the case now. People just will not give in. They argue fiercely using all kinds of reasons. They care only for their own interests.

The eight-year rule for young workers to get on to the housing queue as well as the even longer years-of-service requirement, i.e., 30 years, to qualify ordinary workers to purchase their flat were also divisive, alienating many in the rank and file. Grudges against the policy were widely shared among workers. On their grudges Ms Cao and Ms Feng were outspoken:

> Workers are of course very upset. You see, the first lot of the ownership flats were sold at just 6,000 to 7,000 yuan per flat. If we had been allowed to buy these flats, we would have bought them, borrowing from friends and relatives. But these flats were exclusively for managers and cadres. We were not allowed to buy these flats just because we were workers. Just think of this: for the *lingdao*, a family of three have a flat with three rooms and one sitting room all to themselves. And we workers have to crowd our families into tiny cubicles between 18 and 21 sq. metres instead. Some even have to put up with cubicles not larger than 14 sq. metres. Is this fair? (Ms Cao)

> Yes, we do have many grudges. Take myself as an example. I have been a worker for many years, yet I do not have a flat of my own.

> Managers and cadres have advantages over us. They are allowed to 'jump the queue' even though their length of service is as short as just five years. You see, we workers are working very hard. Yet we do not have a decent place to rest after work. The cadres and managers do not work as hard. Yet they can have comfortable places to live in. (Ms Feng)

Workers clearly perceived inequities in the allocation of housing. Cadres and managers had advantages over ordinary workers. But it was not just ordinary workers who were unhappy. More recently, the plant had introduced a policy which gave preferential treatment to capable administrative personnel and young graduates as a means to attract and retain skilled manpower. As it advantaged these young executives and professionals, it disadvantaged old cadres and managers, many of whom wanted to switch to a bigger flat. Mr Chen, a senior cadre in charge of DFMW's propaganda department, was outraged by the policy: 'I have been with this plant for over 30 years. Why should workers like myself not be entitled to a flat, at the least a flat with one bedroom and sitting room or two bedrooms and one sitting room? We deserve it after all these years of service for the *danwei*.'

Mr Chen's remarks carried an important 'moral' message: that old workers had a just and rightful claim for their entitlements and that it would be wrong for the *danwei* to deprive them of what they deserved. Old workers believed they had a legitimate claim to what should be their entitlements, a claim based on the assumption that there should be fair exchange. Exchange was not fair if what one party gave to the other party was not eventually balanced by what the other party gave back in return. The 'legitimacy' issue was not just confined to housing, however. Mr Deng also raised the issue when he discussed the impact of the *danwei*'s recent policy to re-engage all permanent workers on contract:

> From government documents we have learnt that all permanent workers are to become re-engaged as contract workers next year. Workers in their forties and fifties have a lot of anxiety over this. They have, you see, given their best years to the plant. What they have given to the plant far exceeds what the plant has given back to them in return. And in their old age, the plant is going to abandon them. Also, you see, the planned economy has not been able to really put into practice the principle of 'from each according to his ability and to each according to his work'. The rewards to workers have not been in accordance with their contributions.

Mr. Tao also made reference to the issue when he discussed workers' reaction to a recent policy which required patients to pay 20 per cent of their medical bills:

> Old workers were particularly unhappy. They had worked so hard for the plant for so many years and yet they have to pay the twenty percent. I do not know the view of *lingdao* on this. But I do know that many people were very dissatisfied. I am all right because I am young and seldom get sick. I see the doctor not even once a year.

The issue raised by Mr Chen, Mr Deng and Mr Tao was not just the issue of one *danwei*. It had a much wider and far-reaching significance. In the context of state socialist occupational welfare, this was at once an issue about the reciprocal responsibilities and obligations between the socialist state and its urban citizenry. The workers had 'worked so hard for' and given their 'best years' to not just their work-unit, but to the state in the cause of socialism. And it was in terms of the state's reciprocal obligations that the workers were justifying their claim to security in their old age. Any attempt by the *danwei* to give less than workers regard as its obligations was at once a legitimacy issue of a much wider import and raised questions about whether or not the socialist state was abdicating its responsibilities.

In the new mode of orientation towards welfare, workers had become much more conscious of and calculative about their welfare rights and entitlements, and much more ready to address these as their legitimate claims. This had made the *danwei*'s tasks of reshaping its welfare obligations much more complex and difficult, complex because what to one group was their legitimate claim might not be similarly regarded by another group, and difficult because what to the *danwei* was right and justified might to its members be wrong and illegitimate. The *danwei* had a very difficult balancing act to do, and it was left with little room to manoevre.

Conclusion

This chapter has examined the impact of social and economic change on the *danwei* community and observed that the rise of the mixed economy has reshaped workers' dependence by opening them up to new opportunities and options. Using a combination of strategies that often strategically involved their families in both the state and the non-state economies, and drawing upon the support of family and social networks, workers had shifted from the kind of near-complete dependence of the pre-reform days towards a new pattern of dependence which was at once more diverse and pluralistic, combining the state and the non-state sectors, the public and the private, the formal and the informal, and integrating at once both market and traditional values. The resulting pattern of dependence was a 'mixed economy of welfare' of a very unique kind, one grown out of a 'mixed economy' dominated by a state sector inherited from a socialist command economy coexisting with an expanding non-state economy.

The chapter observed also that market reforms and the rise of an ethos characteristic of the market had upset pre-existing relations and values in what used to be a highly stable, homogeneous and egalitarian community, undermined identity and commitment, changed workers' values and attitudes towards welfare, and encouraged them to regard calculatively their rights and entitlements and addressing these as their legitimate claims.

In short, what social change and economic reforms had ushered in was a 'mixed economy of welfare' which, while offering more diversity and choice, was also more tension-ridden and more conducive to conflict.

The next chapter focuses on a state-owned enterprise and examines how, in response to the challenge of the market, it tried to resolve the difficult dilemma between efficiency and obligation.

6
Reshaping the *Danwei* Welfare Economy

Introduction

In the pre-reform days, the *danwei* welfare economy was essentially a monolithic and closed system.[1] Benefits and services were provided by and distributed through the bureaucracy to its members. These were all paid for by the state, 'passed directly to the state budget and [did] not represent a cost to enterprise management' (Walder 1986: 43). There was little pressure on the enterprise to run these services efficiently and cost-effectively. Quality was generally poor and choice by users and consumers very limited. 'It was a very inefficient system. There was a lot of waste. It was in a mess' (Liu 1995: 135).

Economic reforms since 1979 have brought these problems to the fore. The enterprise has to be profit-oriented and 'be responsible for its own profits and losses' (*'zifu yingqui'*). Welfare cannot but enter into cost-efficiency consideration. For many enterprises for which welfare has become a growing burden, it is all too clear that things must change.

Change has been mainly in the direction of 'dissociating the enterprise from its welfare functions' (*'fenli qiyie ban shehui zhineng'*). 'Dissociation' has occurred mainly through 'socializing' (*'shehui hua'*) the functions, i.e. returning the functions to 'society', or, more specifically, the government,[2] or through either contracting the responsibility of managing the services to be dissociated to sub-units concerned,[3] or setting up these sub-units as subsidiary companies responsible for their own profits and losses.[4]

In the cases of contracting the welfare responsibility to a sub-unit or devolving the responsibility to a subsidiary company, 'dissociation' entails either fully or partially 'commodifying' (*'shangpin hua'*) welfare

(Liu 1995: 136), i.e., pricing welfare and 'selling' it for profit to consumers at markets either internal or external to the enterprise. Housing, for example, is increasingly sold as a commodity to *danwei* members at below (external) market prices.

There is no single model or unified approach for the change. The government made it clear that 'enterprises should be free to take their own steps and do it their own ways' (Zhang 1995: 6). 'Dissociation' has occurred therefore in many different ways. There are variations not only between enterprises, but often also within the same enterprise between its various services. Within one enterprise, therefore, it is not uncommon for there to be services still run according to pre-reform principles, for some services to have been hived off and taken over by financially independent subsidiary companies, and for still others to be on responsibility contracts. The typical *danwei* welfare economy becomes a hybrid, a mixture of different ways of running welfare.

While the government encouraged enterprises to try out different ways of 'dissociating' themselves from welfare, it also warned that as they do this they 'must protect the proper rights of their employees', and 'must try not to dampen their enthusiasm' (Zhang 1995: 5). They were told that 'social stability should be the uppermost concern' (Liu 1995: 34) and that they should try to avoid upsetting that stability. In other words, in reforming welfare, they had to be careful not to create 'social problems'. Workers should not suffer and it would still be the responsibility of enterprises to look after their welfare. 'Dissociation' applies, therefore, more to 'functions' than to 'responsibility' and enterprises are not supposed to abdicate that responsibility. In other words, for the enterprises, the challenge was how to reduce their welfare burden without giving up their welfare responsibilities.

In this chapter, based on the case study of DFMW, we look at how this state-owned enterprise faced this challenge in the face of its many problems and difficulties.

What the enterprise had done was, strategically, to combine welfare with business and to link the bureaucracy to the market. The strategy, in other words, was to 'go quasi-market'. The strategy enabled the enterprise to provide welfare and do business at the same time. Hence at the same time as it provided 'free' benefits and services, it also tried to 'market' these benefits and services to make profit.

The *danwei* economy of welfare emerging from the changes introduced was increasingly a *mixed* economy of welfare, a hybrid system, one characterized by greater openness, diversity and, for users and consumers, a wider range of choice.

The cost of welfare

The term '*xiaoyi*', meaning profitability or the ability to realize economic gain, was frequently referred to when workers and managers talked about their *danwei*. DFMW was reckoned to be an enterprise with poor or low '*xiaoyi*'. In 1993, DFMW earned Y372.9 million from the sales of its machines but made an after-tax profit of only Y500,000. For the first eight months of 1994, its sales amounted to Y327 million and its net profit only Y380,000.

Mr Dong, Deputy Party Secretary, explained why the *danwei* performed so badly:

> For several decades under the planned economy, we had made a lot of contributions. We used to be very profitable. In one of our best years in the 1970s, our profit was over Y20 million. During all these years we have also trained and produced a large number of skilled workers, management personnel and cadres. However, since reforms, we have run into many difficulties. There are three important reasons why we are doing not so well now. First, we have not developed new products. Our products are not in demand in the market. Secondly, our technology is outdated. Although we have over 1,000 pieces of machine tools, very few of these are really modern and advanced. And thirdly, we have been over-burdened by welfare. The burden of welfare is getting heavier and heavier and becoming impossible to bear. We are spending so much on welfare there is very little left for development and reinvestment.

Mr Wu, Deputy Director of the plant's Political Work Department, explained how welfare had become the plant's economic burden:

> It is no small achievement that we have been able to feed so many mouths and keep our machines running. Mind you, we have to look after the welfare of our people too. What a heavy burden this is! We shouldn't have this burden in the first place. Township enterprises and joint venture companies do not have this burden. This explains why we have higher production costs and why our products are not as competitive as theirs.

The plant did have a hefty welfare budget. In 1994, the plant budgeted Y70 million for wages and bonuses and one-third as much, Y23 million, for welfare. About one-quarter of the plant's recurrent cost expenditure of the year was spent on the wages and bonuses and welfare of its workers.

Before 1 July 1993, state enterprises were allowed to retain 75 per cent of their after-tax profit for two purposes: 'reinvestment and development' and 'welfare and bonus', 60 per cent for the former and 40 per cent for the latter. However, very few enterprises stuck to the 60:40 rule. Instead of keeping the larger part of after-tax profit for 'reinvestment and development', many enterprises simply siphoned it into the 'welfare and bonus fund'. In other words, much of the 'retained profit' of an enterprise was used to supplement the income and provide for the welfare of its workers.

In July 1993, the government lowered the profit tax rate from 55 per cent to 33 per cent, abolished the 60:40 rule and allowed state enterprises to make welfare and bonus part of recurrent cost expenditures. The new policy enabled enterprises to 'normalize' the bonus, making it a regular part of a worker's pay package. Because how much an enterprise spent on bonus and welfare was no longer capped by the size of its profit, the policy encouraged the enterprise to spend more on bonus and welfare and discouraged spending less on these so as to increase the size of profit. And because there was no longer the 60 per cent requirement, it became even less certain that an enterprise would reinvest its profit in capital and development.

Retirement pensions were given a large slice of DFMW's hefty welfare budget. DFMW participated in a pooling scheme which required it to devote 24.5 per cent of its wage bill to pensions. Since it was not the pool but enterprises which disbursed pensions, the pooling arrangement worked by *ex post* redistribution. Enterprises spending more than the percentage claimed the difference and, conversely, those spending less paid the difference into the pool. In the case of DFMW, because it was spending less than the percentage, on top of the pensions for 2,107 retired workers it also had to pay the difference of Y1.56 million into the pool. In 1994, its net expenditure on pensions amounted to Y12 million. 'Retirement pensions,' said Mr Li, director of personnel department, 'have become our heaviest welfare burden.'

The cost of pensions was expected to increase steeply in the next five years as more workers became pensioners. According to Mr Dong:

The number of retired workers increases by around 150 each year. About 2,000 workers joined the plant in 1958. Most of them are now in their fifties and sixties. In five years' time, there will be more

than 3,000 retired workers. We will be in big trouble if the government does not do something about it.

Mr Liao, head of the General Affairs Office, described the problem:

We have taken over what should have been the responsibility of
society. This is affecting our '*xiaoyi*'. You see, retirement benefits are
eating away funds for the maintenance and upkeep of machines and
building. The interest of workers has also been affected when they
have to share what they have with the retirees.

The plant had an after-tax profit of Y2.13 million for the first eight
months of 1994. This was reduced to just Y380,000 after it paid retired
workers Y1.75 million to cover their cost-of-living adjustment and
'hardship' allowance.

Financing the plant's soaring health-care costs was no less tricky.

Employees and retired employees in state-owned enterprises are
covered by Labour Insurance (*laobao yiliao*). Labour Insurance provides
comprehensive insurance benefits, including primary health care and
hospital treatment, surgery, maternity services and also drugs. Benefits
include pay during sickness and maternity leave on full pay for
100 days. Medical benefits can also extend to the immediate dependants of the employees, if they are not already covered by health insurance. Unlike with old age pensions, health care costs are not pooled
and each unit is responsible for the cost of its employees. At DFMW,
this consisted of first, the cost involved in the provision of direct
medical services through its in-house hospital, and secondly, the cost
of reimbursing workers for their referrals to doctors or hospitals outside
the unit.

In 1994, the health care budget amounted to 7 per cent of the plant's
wage bill, or Y4.9 million. Users bore a small part of the cost. User
charges took the form of cost-sharing and a small registration fee for
visits to the hospital. Cost-sharing applied to both medical care and
drugs. The cost-sharing formula required employees to pay 20 per cent
of their medical bills, but only as long as their total contributions
during the year were not more than Y500.[5] In other words, the formula
limited their contributions to a 'protection point' ('*baohu xian*').
Beyond that, the plant took over.

Actual expenditure in the year amounted to Y6.4 million, over-
shooting the budget by 30 per cent. Dr Mao, Director of the Hospital,
explained what had happened:

Rising costs largely explain [the situation]. Drugs are becoming more and more expensive. The fact that we have an ageing labour force and an increasing number of pensioners also explains it. Elderly people are more likely to be more seriously ill and hospital-ized. Last year, for example, we spent Y1,057 on each retiree but only Y407 on each worker. But most importantly, it has to do with the 'protection point' policy. I was against the policy from the very beginning. But management was too cautious; they cared too much about workers' reactions. They just wouldn't listen to me. The 'pro-tection point', you see, was so easy to over-shoot. Workers all want to see doctors in other hospitals. And these hospitals all want to make money. For, the more money they make, the more bonus they can give their staff. Unlike government departments, we have not entered into any contract with any hospitals. So there isn't any control at all on how much they charge our workers. They just perform all kinds of medical checks on them and prescribe lots of drugs. Our workers, of course, don't mind, for, you see, once their contributions go over the 'protection point', they don't have to pay any further amount. Bills for hospitalization are rarely less than 7,000–8,000 yuan and easily between 10,000–20,000 yuan in each case. Maternity used to cost just 40–50 yuan. It is now 700–800 yuan. It was the management who decided on the policy. But when things went wrong, they all blamed it on me.

Dr Mao's account revealed the deep-rooted nature of the problem. There was serious under-utilization of the plant's in-house hospital and heavy use of outside services. Workers rejected the plant's hospital because of its poor facilities and services. Outside services were much more expensive than in-house services. Heavy use of outside services over-spent the plant's health care budget. An over-spent budget left little for medical equipment and for upgrading the hospital's facilities and services. Dr Mao's problem was therefore much more serious than that of a management that 'wouldn't listen' to her, but a vicious circle with a negative impact not just on the financial health of health care but also on the quality of the hospital's service. The financial implica-tion of the vicious circle was serious. According to Dr Mao, expenditure on health care would very likely exceed Y8 million in 1995 and Y9 million in 1996.

Housing was the next big problem area. The plant had already built 160,000 sq. metres of housing for 3,700 families. But there was still a long queue of eligible applicants waiting for allocation. One-fifth of the plant's 5,225 employees were queuing and many others waiting to get on the queue.

Varying in sizes from around 25 sq. metres to around 60 sq. metres and rented at between Y0.2 and Y0.5 per sq. metre, *danwei* flats were heavily subsidized. From 1989, new flats were sold to workers. The first batch of such flats were sold at the much below market and below cost price of Y150 per sq. metre. At such a price, recovering costs was out of the question. Mr Dong explained how the plant's building programme had run into financial difficulty and upset its production plans:

> We are housing not just the employees but also their families. This is not a small thing. In 1991, we began a programme to build six multi-storey buildings for 480 families. The cost was originally estimated to be Y9.8 million. But it quickly shot past this figure. At the completion of the programme, it had reached Y20 million. The plant, to be honest with you, was not making much profit. We had to lay our hands on working capital. This was not right but there was no better way. You see, housing has got in the way of production.

In 1994, the plant had a budget of only Y1.2 million for housing. Lamented Mr Tang, the plant's accountant, 'This amount is not even enough for building a six-storey apartment building. You need at least Y3 million to build one.'

Retirement pensions, health care and housing took the lion's share of the plant's welfare budget. The rest of the budget was shared among various welfare services and facilities, including the school, nursery, canteens, recreation centre for retired workers and hardship subsidies. In 1994, these facilities and services together claimed one-fifth of the plant's Y23 million welfare budget.

The dilemma of efficiency and obligation

The plant was on the horns of a dilemma. The choice was between efficiency and obligation. Should the choice be obligation, it would have to deal with inefficiency. If the choice was efficiency, it would have to reduce its welfare responsibilities and cut welfare. There were, however, four main reasons against cutting welfare.

The first was a moral consideration. Plant management reckoned it had a moral obligation to its old workers and that they had a legitimate claim to what they deserved after many years of 'toil' and 'under-paid' service:

Old workers have gone through many ups and downs and much hardship: the Great Leap Forward, the difficulties in the 1960s, the Great Cultural Revolution and so on. Their toil, if not their contributions, should be recognized. (Mr Shi, Bureau Chief of Corporate Management)

Retired workers expect the plant to look after them in their old age because, for many years before retirement, they had been paid much less than they deserved. Their pay was not commensurate with their contributions. (Mr Dong, Deputy Party Secretary)

Old workers have been with us for many years. They have witnessed (the growth and development of the plant. The plant is like home to them and they feel they belong to it. In their view, the plant owes it to them to look after them and provide for their security in old age. Younger workers have a different view on this. In their view, it is up to workers to earn their own security through their own efforts and skills. (Mr Liao, Head of General Affairs Office)

But could it not leave the responsibility of looking after old workers to the family? While accepting that there was a role for the family, plant management believed the unit should not shirk its responsibility, as Mr Li, Deputy Head of Personnel, argued:

It is difficult for retired workers to live on a pension of merely 300–400 yuan. It's all right if their children are filial. Otherwise they will have a difficult time. But you cannot entirely depend on the children. The children themselves may be earning so little they themselves may have difficulty making ends meet. They may be filial children, but they may not have the means to support their parents. Retired workers have to depend on the *danwei*.

Compared to the average in the city, our pension is on the low side. But we have tried our very best and done all that we can. Retired workers appreciate what we have done for them. 'Money' and 'morals' are equally important and it is important to have both. We are just doing what is right in terms of traditional Chinese values.

Older workers had experienced not only 'toil' and 'hardship'. As living witness to the socialism of the pre-reform days, they had been through times when they enjoyed the prestige and status accorded 'proletarian' and 'state employees'. They believed they had a legitimate claim for the state's continuing obligation based on their *traditional* right as proletariat employees of the socialist state. To ignore such a claim was tantamount to denying the state's socialist past. Mr Chen, Director of Propaganda, and Ms Ma, a worker, explained why the plant had to honour its obligation to its older workers:

> The working class is after all the leading class. In the past, workers in large-scale state enterprises enjoyed not only prestigious status. They were also provided with benefits and welfare commensurate with their status. Old workers who have been with us for many years still see it this way. They believe they deserve what they should have. (Mr Chen)

> Older workers have all along been paid very low wages. How can we be convinced of the superiority of socialism if we can't even compensate old workers for what they have done for the plant? (Ms Ma)

There was also a political reason against cutting welfare. The plant could not simply give up its welfare role because the government was opposed to it. Cutting welfare could have wider social and political ramifications, as Mr Dong explained:

> We did consider cutting welfare. The government, however, stressed stability. What would happen if our workers take to the street or stage sit-ins at government offices? We would be in big trouble. Our problem could turn into a social problem. That's why we hesitate to cut welfare.

The plant, for example, could not simply lay off its surplus workers. According to Mr Xu, the general manager, about a third of the plant's labour force was redundant. However, it could not just lay off its surplus workers because of its traditional responsibilities and because there were no alternative institutions providing income maintenance, housing services, medical care and other basic social services to unemployed workers. Laid-off workers would be losing not just their income but all the benefits and essential services provided through the *danwei*. 'If too many workers lose their jobs,' Mr Han, Bureau Chief of the Office, said, 'they may become a cause of social instability.' Instead of laying off its surplus workers, the plant let them stay. Older workers were sent to its general service unit (*xingzheng chu*) where they took up such jobs as canteen assistants, cleaners, salesmen, shop assistants and so on. Those not assigned jobs at the '*xingzheng chu*' were given a '*daigan*' (waiting) wage of Y250 and sent home to 'rest and wait' for job offers. 'While on "*daigan*", they can look for jobs. If they want to quit, we let them go,' said Mr Han. Young workers were more fortunate. They were given the opportunity to go through a three-month course of retraining at the plant's vocational school. The school's principal, Mr Wang, explained:

> We just closed our iron-casting workshop because its '*xiaoyi*' was poor. Among those who lost their jobs some were young graduates from this vocational school. They would have wasted all these years of training if they could not get back to work. That we could not employ them for the time being did not mean that we would not be able to employ them forever. So we gave them retraining and prepared them for other jobs in the plant. Retraining should be good for them too. From retraining they acquired additional skills. During retraining, they were paid the same wage as '*daigan*' workers, Y250 a month.

A third major reason against cutting welfare was that welfare had become an indispensable means for motivating workers and inducing their commitment. Housing, in particular, had been instrumental in arresting the outflow of skilled labour and attracting new recruits (Dai 1995: 96). Cutting welfare would affect the plant's competitiveness in the labour market. Mr Chen, senior cadre in charge of propaganda, compared situations before and since reforms, and Mr Liao, Head of the General Affairs Office, explained the problem facing the plant:

> In the old days, a worker was very much dependent on his *danwei*: his fortune and the *danwei*'s fortune rose and fell together. He rarely if at all thought of changing his job. Not only was policy not for it, but there also was not much point going to a new job which paid more or less the same. For a second-grade worker, for example, no matter where he went, he was paid Y46.20. It is of course a very different story now. To win their loyalty, you must satisfy workers with welfare, not just wage. (Mr Chen)

> Because our performance is not as good as joint-venture companies, we cannot offer comparable terms. Hence we have difficulty recruit-

ing new employees. There is also a good deal of mobility. Many are prepared to go. Many professionals and skilled workers use their jobs here as springboards to other jobs. They leave us as soon as they secure '*hukou*' (residency status) and get better offers. (Mr Liao)

On average, workers in the country's state-owned enterprises earned 50 per cent less than workers in private and joint-venture enterprises. However, what they gained from welfare in both cash and in kind enabled them almost to bridge the gap. In other words, welfare was an important source of non-wage income. It helped to bring their incomes to a level almost on a par with the incomes earned by workers in private and joint-venture enterprises. Cutting welfare would in practice reduce what they earned. Mr Liao and Mr Dong, Deputy Party Secretary, explained the plant's instrumental use of welfare:

In general, workers in non-state enterprises are paid around 1,000–2,000 yuan a month. But that's all. They don't have allowances or subsidies for such things as housing and health care. Old enterprises like ours are different. Workers are paid only several hundred yuan, but they have housing, *laobao yiliao*, and so on. For old enterprises like us, welfare is an important means to retain workers, especially skilled workers and experienced administrative personnel. You see, the market price of a flat is easily between 100,000 and 200,000 yuan. We sell our *danwei* flats to workers at less than 50,000 yuan. The difference is very big. (Mr Liao)

Our workers earned on the average Y730 a month last year. This level of income was not bad among factory workers. It was, however, on the lower side if you compare it to the average level of wage in *Guangzhou*. We are in a difficult dilemma. If we can have our way, we will rid ourselves of the welfare burden as soon as we can. But in reality we can't. In fact, we have to rely on welfare to integrate and stablize the workforce. It would be nice, for example, for a young worker to share a two bedroom one sitting-room flat with another worker. But this is very ideal. In actual fact, he has to share a flat with three to seven others. So, recently, we have decided that we must do something about it. We decided to build a hostel for single workers. We hope that by providing better housing to young graduates, technicians and professionals, we can make them stay. You see, not everyone has a ready offer or a better place to go. There is a good chance that he may stay because of the welfare that he has from us. Let me give you another example. Two senior workers, a husband and wife couple, recently left us. The husband was 54. A township enterprise offered them a three bedroom apartment, a bank deposit of Y50,000, and a chauffeur-driven car. They wouldn't have left us had we been able to provide a comparable package. Enterprises like ours are facing this dilemma: we cannot afford welfare, but we cannot afford not to have it. (Mr Dong)

The fourth important reason why the plant could not give up welfare was that the government was not prepared to take over from the plant what it might want to give up. Mr Dong explained the plant's misgivings:

Welfare can be useful in integrating and motivating your staff. In turn this can bring about better '*xiaoyi*'. However, this shouldn't have been entirely our responsibility. The government should take over what should be its responsibility. If it cannot entirely take over, it should at least take over a major part of such responsibility. But this has not been the case. Instead the enterprise is entirely responsible. Education, for example, should not have been our responsibility. There are now more than 2,000 kids in our primary school, kindergarten and nursery. Less than half of them are local kids. Many kids from outside the neighbourhood have come to us because they couldn't get into government schools. It should have been the government's responsibility to provide enough school places. It is very unreasonable that we are doing the government's job instead.

Whether or not the plant should give up its school was an issue of great contention. The plant was eager to get rid of the school. The government, however, was reluctant to take over. Mr Wen, the school's principal, explained why the responsibility of education should be returned to the government:

The school building looks new, but it is in fact very old and dilapidated. Because the '*xiaoyi*' of the plant has not been good, we have not been given the money to do something about it. In 1992, we finally managed to paint the building. It cost us Y300,000. This at least gave the building a new look. Parents had been turned off by the shabby conditions of the building. So even though things were tight, the plant decided to put some money into face-lifting the building. The overall development of the school is, however, lagging behind. You see, in the past, education was not expensive. Running a school like this one cost you only one hundred to two hundred thousand yuan. The cost has now gone up to over 1 million yuan. This is a big burden to the plant. And because the '*xiaoyi*' of the plant is not good, it simply cannot put more money into the school to meet its many needs. There are so many things that we want to do to improve the school and we have got many good ideas. We cannot but shelve these plans and ideas. You see, since reform, the plant is supposed to be on its own. The government no longer comes to our help. The plant, on the other hand, is busy with its own problems. State enterprises like us feel very strongly that we should return to society what belongs to society. Why should we be responsible for compulsory education? Compulsory education should be the responsibility of the government.

Teachers were for the government taking over the school for a more practical reason. Should they become government-school teachers, they would benefit from a more favorable retirement pension package. Mr Wen explained:

In terms of wage, there is not really that much difference. Senior teachers in government primary schools are paid around Y800. Some may be paid more. Our senior teachers in the primary school are paid around Y700. There is, however, a big difference in their pensions. Government school teachers can have around 700 to 800 yuan a month for their pensions. Our retired teachers have much less, just around 300 to 400 yuan. Why? Because our pensions are largely calculated on the basis of basic wage. A major part of the Y700 earned by our senior teachers is made up of bonus and various types of subsidies. Their basic wage is just around Y200. There is therefore a big difference between their pensions and the pensions of government school teachers. My staff do worry a lot about retirement. However, it is not likely that in the recent future they will get a big increase in their wage. For, you see, education is not the plant's priority area. The plant's priority area is production.

There was general agreement that the plant should give up the school and return it to the government. This would be to the advantage of all parties: it would reduce the plant's welfare burden, give the school more resources for development and improve its teachers' retirement benefits. However, the government was not ready to take over. Mr. Wang, principal of the plant's vocational school, explained:

> It takes time. You see, there are more than 30 enterprise-run schools in Guangzhou. This is not a small number. The government cannot take over all of them all at once. Enterprises would, of course, want to pass their schools to the government. The government, however, has to think twice. The problem is that these schools do vary in standard. For good schools, there is no big problem. For schools which are not that good, the government may have to do many things about them and put in a lot of resources. Moreover, once it takes over these schools, it has to pay their teachers too. This will be a rather heavy burden for the government.

In 1994, the government held talks with the Guangzhou Ship-Builder (*Guangzhou Zaochuan Chang*) to return its school to the government through a pilot scheme. The ship-builder found the terms proposed by the government 'difficult to accept'. The talks broke down. Plans for returning enterprise-run schools to the public school system were also shelved.

Acting on the dilemma

The plant could neither give up its welfare responsibilities nor afford them were it to continue with its obligations. This section describes how the plant found a way out of its difficult situation and how in the end this ushered in a new welfare economy at the *danwei*.

The plant's primary strategy was to go quasi-market on welfare: to 'sell' to *danwei* members or external users or both parts of what used to be free or almost free benefits and services at prices calculated to either cover cost or make profit. The strategy, in other words, was partly to *commodify danwei* welfare: to be doing business and providing welfare at the same time. The strategy allowed the *danwei* to 'walk on two legs': to perform its welfare obligations on one hand, and to engage in profit-making activities on the other hand.

Commodified benefits and services were differentiated from non-commodified benefits and services in two main ways: (1) by way of *price differentiation*, i.e., there were 'price differences' between commodified and non-commodified benefits and services, and (2) by way of *product differentiation*, i.e., commodified and non-commodified benefits and services were different kinds of products. There was always a 'price difference' between commodified and non-commodified benefits and services. Users, in other words, paid more for commodified than for non-commodified benefits and services. Commodified housing was, for example, more expensive than rented housing. However, commodified benefits and services were not necessarily product-differentiated from non-commodified benefits and services. In other words, users could just be paying more for the same product. At the kindergarten, for example, pupils from outside the plant were paying a higher tuition fee than local pupils.

In addition to the quasi-market, the plant had also, in some areas, used the strategy of 'user contribution', which made users contribute to, hence share the cost of the welfare provided to them. In the area of health care, for example, patients had to be responsible for 20 per cent of their medical bills according to the hospital's cost-sharing formula.

Resulting from the changes introduced was a much more differentiated *danwei* welfare economy, one in which not just welfare but also commodities were distributed; not just the bureaucracy but also the market performed the distribution; users did not just receive benefits and services free but could also contribute to or pay for them; and they had an extended and more diversified range of products from which to make their choices. In the making was a *danwei* mixed economy of welfare.

There was, however, not just one model of quasi-market. The plant's various services had tried out different approaches to and applications of the quasi-market concept, and had varying extent of success. The case studies to follow take a closer look at and assess the application of the strategy in three areas: the hospital, the canteens, and the school.

The hospital

The strategy here was to market the service of the hospital to outside users.

DFMW provided Labour Insurance (*laobao yiliao*) to its employees through its in-house hospital and through reimbursing their referral visits to other hospitals in the city. It was a costly service because, in addition to reimbursing these visits, it was also maintaining a hospital staffed by more than 70 doctors, paramedical professionals and nurses. This was a medium-scale hospital among hospitals attached to work-units.

Could it not, to cut cost, give up the hospital, which was, after all, inefficient and very much underutilized? Dr Shan, deputy-director of the hospital, argued the case for a clinic of a much smaller scale:

> Myself being a medical professional, I will not be so extreme as to say that the hospital is totally useless. But if the enterprise could, instead of having the hospital, keep just a small clinic, it would solve many problems. Ring the ambulance if there are really serious cases. The money saved from radically downscaling the facility can be put to better uses. For example, it can be used to give every one a pay rise, or top up subsidies and allowances. Many township and joint-venture enterprises do it this way. Whether or not an old enterprise such as this one should continue to have a hospital very much depends on the attitude of management and the policy of the government. Nothing is impossible. You see, the primary function of the enterprise is production. It should concentrate on production. The hospital is a problem from the past. In the past, a large-scale enterprise was run just like a small society. It had its nurseries, hospitals, schools and canteens and so on. Whether or not this should continue is now very questionable.

But, according to Dr Mao, director of the hospital, it could cost the enterprise even more were it to give up the hospital. She explained why:

> The enterprise cannot be without its hospital. That you don't have one does not mean you won't have to pay for the health care of your employees. You'll still have to pay. The per capita cost of health care in the city last year was Y1270. Our per capita cost was just one-third as much, Y360. In other words, had all our patients been referred to outside hospitals, our medical bill would have been three times as expensive. We have saved a lot of money for the plant.

Though overstaffed and underutilized, the hospital had nevertheless rendered a service that was much cheaper than what was provided by other hospitals in the city. The plant could end up paying more for the health care of its employees if it did not have its in-house facility. Dr Mao explained how the hospital kept its cost down:

> Public hospitals are run like a business. The more patients they have, the more profits they can make, and the fatter is the pay for

their staff. We are in a different situation. All that we can do is to try to economize and spend our money carefully. Old drugs, for instance, though much cheaper than new drugs, are not always less effective. You could be spending many times more on new drugs than on old drugs for the same results. Treating leukaemia, for instance, costs around 700 to 800 yuan. Public hospitals can't do it even for 70,000 to 80,000 yuan. You do not have to spend more to cure. You can even spend less to achieve the same result. Because what has been given to us is a very lean budget, we need to be careful and reasonable with how we spend our money.

The hospital did not just spend less on drugs. Compared to public hospitals, it also paid its doctors less, the differences varying from around Y400 for junior to Y700 for senior doctors. Dr Mao, for example, earned around Y700, Y500 less than her public hospital counterparts.

But even if the plant was to give up the hospital, it was unlikely any public hospital would want to take it over. Dr Shan explained:

Would any big hospital want to have us? No. For, you see, our equipment is poor and the quality of our staff not that good. If no hospital is willing to give us a home, and if we are transferred out, we will have to stand on our own two feet, which means we will need to make a lot of adjustment. Beggers used to their way of life are reluctant to change. They don't jump at job offers.

The plant was therefore left with few options. Perforce it had to keep the hospital because, without one, it would have to pay even more for *laobao yiliao*. But even if it wanted to give up the hospital, the government was not likely to be welcoming. Its staff might also be against the change.

In September 1994, it was decided that the hospital should try also to market its service to outside users. The approach, as Dr Mao explained, was to 'save a fish by putting it back into the water', or, in other words, to allow the hospital to engage in profit-making business activities:

With our limited budget there is not much that we can do to either improve the service of the hospital or give our staff better pay. Plant management has now given us the green light to move over to new premises at Hostel 27. The new premises face the street and are much more accessible. Once we are there we can go in two directions. One, we'll carry on with our usual service. Two, we can also extend our service to the outside community. We will face competition from other hospitals, of course. But I think we can find our niche if we can keep our fees low and reasonable. Enterprises which cannot afford heavy '*laobao*' cost may come to us.

The hospital would share 20 per cent of its 'profit', if any, with the plant and divide the rest among its staff members as 'labour service fees' (*laowu fei*). While Dr Mao was confident that this new development would breathe life into the hospital, her deputy was sceptical. Dr Shan explained:

> This is a marvellous idea, but I don't think it is going to work. It is all right so long as the hospital remains an in-house operation. Once it opens up, it will be competing with hospitals at various levels of the city. These hospitals all have well-defined positions in the city's health care market. It will not be easy for us to get in. We will be competing with them for patients and they won't be happy about it. For, you see, this is a matter of economic interest. The Health Department has already made it very clear it does not welcome our move. It will set up many hurdles, require us to go through many procedures and make us pay heavily to obtain its approval.

There were all together 216 hospitals, nine sanatoria and 1,668 outpatient clinics in the city (*Guangzhou Shi Tongji Ju* 1995: 429). Were the hospital to enter the health market, it would be competing with a large number of competitors. The hospital did eventually get the required approval and in October 1995 its out-patient department was in operation at the new premises. Dr Mao updated its development during the researcher's return visit to the plant in December 1995:

> Business is not as good as expected. I would say only one-tenth of our patients are now from outside the *danwei*. Patients who are on '*laobao*' won't come to us. They'd rather see doctors at big hospitals. We are, after all, not that well equipped. Patients who are not on '*laobao*' but who are well-off, like *geti hu* (private entrepreneurs), also don't come to us. They can afford to go to big hospitals. We have managed to attract only a few local peasants and migrant workers. Do we charge them a different set of fees? No. We charge the same kind of fees. We just make them pay more by giving them more

check-ups and prescribing more drugs. But even our staff are not enthusiastic. You see, they do not find that many incentives.

The initial attempt of the hospital to go quasi-market appeared then to founder, for three reasons. First, its service was not competitive in a 'market' already dominated by major public hospitals. Secondly, it had failed to attract 'customers' on *laobao yiliao*. Because their medical expenses were covered by *laobao yiliao*, these 'customers' could afford the expensive service provided by major public hospitals. Thirdly, it did not have the support of its staff.

The strategy of 'user contribution' had also foundered. Beginning on 1 August 1994, users were required to contribute to, in the case of employees, 20 per cent and in the case of pensioners, 10 per cent, of their medical bills. The strategy foundered because of a 'protection point' (*baohu xian*) provision which limited the respective contributions by employees and retirees to Y500 and Y350 but at the same time committed the plant to all above-limit expenses. The 'protection point' provision had the unintended consequence of encouraging patients to spend beyond the 'point', their doctors to over-prescribe, and, as a result, the plant to over-spend its health-care budget. The plant soon recognized the overwhelming financial implications of the provision and decided that it be removed as from January 1995.

Towards the end of 1995, plans were also under way to 'contract out' *laobao yiliao* responsibility to the plant's subsidiary companies. The plan was to give to each subsidiary company a *laobao yiliao* grant, on head-count basis of Y500 for each employee, and make it responsible for the *laobao yiliao* expenses of its employees. This would mean that each subsidiary company would have to find its own method of meeting the health care expenses of its members. This would very likely lead to a proliferation of all kinds of cost-sharing formulae and arrangements between subsidiary companies and their employees. It would also mean that, because subsidiary companies did vary greatly in terms of '*xiaoyi*' and financial resources, those with unhealthy balance sheets would have difficulties providing the same degree of protection to their employees as the rest.

As subsidiary companies took over the financial side of *laobao yiliao* responsibilities, the hospital would be left with the specific responsibility of providing only direct service. According to these plans, the hospital would also be made party to a 'contract responsibility' (*chengbao*) arrangement with the plant. It would be given a much leaner budget than it used to receive and be expected to generate revenue from its own activities to finance any shortfalls. It would very much be standing on its own feet.

The canteens

The canteens were run on a somewhat different quasi-market model. While the hospital aimed its quasi-market at outside users, the canteens aimed its at internal users.

The canteens were managed by the Labour Services Company (*Laodong Fuwu Gongsi*), a subsidiary company incorporated in January 1994. The company was previously the plant's general service unit (*Xingzheng chu*). *Xingzheng chu* provided a wide range of 'domestic' (*houqin*) services to the plant community, including, besides canteens, nursery, kindergarten, pest control, sanitation and delivery of bottled gas. It had over 400 employees. *Houqin* units and services were regular features of state-owned enterprises. In 1995, *houqin* units in the country's state-owned enterprises employed as many as 20 million workers. Their total assets were worth Y1,000 million (Xiao 1996: 111).

Houqin services had always been provided free or heavily subsidized to *danwei* members. But, as Mr Qian, general manager of *laodong fuwu gongsi*, explained, this had to change:

> We could no longer provide these as welfare. *Houqin*, you see, was huge. It covered many areas and employed several hundred workers. We were talking about feeding 7,000–8,000 people, placing over 1,000 kids in kindergarten and nurseries, public sanitation, pest control and so on. It was a big financial burden for the plant. Also, you see, when it was the plant which paid for everything, we just didn't feel the need to improve and work hard. Welfare had made us all very lazy.

In 1991, the plant decided to give up 'pure welfare' (*chun fuli*) and instead operate *houqin* as a 'low profit-making' (*weili*) 'business' (*jingying*). Mr Qian explained the changes involved:

> It was *weili* because it was not operated entirely as a profit-making business. It was still very much welfare. But instead of providing all these services free or largely free, we were allowed to try to make some profit out of them and pay our own wage and bonus out of what we earned. At first, we were not sure if this was right. Could there be no welfare in a socialist enterprise? And if a socialist enter-

prise was to continue with welfare, could it be compatible with the socialist market economy? We had wondered about questions such as these.

What had obtained between the plant and *xingzheng chu* was a 'contract responsibility' (*chengbao*) arrangement. The responsibility of providing *houqin* services was 'contracted out' to *xingzheng chu*. *Xingzheng chu* could try to make profits out of its responsibility and keep whatever it earned. As a condition, however, it had to be responsible for the wage and bonus of its workers. *Xingzheng chu* applied the same *chengbao* arrangement to its sub-units: it further 'contracted out' its *houqin* responsibilities to units at the next lower level of administration. The canteens were one of these sub-units.

Mr Qian described how the canteens were operated as a subcontracted low profit-making business:

> We have four canteens. In the past, they were very heavily subsidized. Prices were more or less fixed and kept very low. At one time, you could have a hot meal with rice, vegetable and meat for just 8 cents! It was an impossible business. What we have done is this: we keep the canteens but turn part of each canteen into a more well decorated restaurant. The canteens continue to serve food at very low prices. The restaurants, however, provide better food and service, and charge accordingly. You see, we must make sure that, in the process of change, the welfare side of canteens is not affected. There should still be cheap food. At the canteens, for example, workers can have a meal for just 2 yuan. But if they can afford it, they can choose to spend more at the restaurants. There they can have a table and invite friends to a more decent lunch or dinner for one to two hundred yuan. The canteens more or less break even. The restaurants are making profits. The return is between 20 to 30 per cent.

The canteens had created a quasi-market by differentiating both its products and prices. The strategy enabled the canteens to combine welfare with business. The strategy was apparently successful, according to Mr Qian:

> We did worry at first. What would happen if we made losses? The livelihood of several hundred workers was at stake and we must not let things go wrong. We all felt a sense of urgency and crisis. All

worked doubly hard. Everybody worked more than eight hours and stayed until 10 p.m. No one complained about working overtime. And we did it. We were able to not only break even but also make profits. The pay of our workers has risen by 40 to 50 per cent in three years' time.

The *chengbao* contracts agreed between *xingzheng chu* and its sub-units provided neither 'profit ceilings' (*shang bu fengding*) nor 'subsidies for losses' (*xia bu budi*). Sub-units could keep whatever profits they made. But losses were also entirely theirs and *xingzheng chu* would not bail them out even if they suffered very bad losses. In other words, they had to stand on their own two feet and be responsible for all consequences. Removed was the security of the 'iron rice bowl' and workers could not but work hard to secure their livelihood.

The canteens had passed the 'first test of the market'. However, Mr Liang recognized that there were limits to what were essentially in-house operations:

There is not much room for development if we just stay where we are. There are, you see, plenty of opportunities beyond the *danwei* walls. We must reach out, find our position in the market, and be prepared to compete with other operations. We can, for example, sell boxed fast-food to workers in other units. Our competitors will do a better job than us if we don't prepare ourselves for the market beyond the *danwei*.

The quasi-market of the canteens was originally for *danwei* members. Over time it had evolved into one catering also to external users. By December 1995, two production lines for boxed food were in operation and the canteens were, as Mr Qian envisioned, beginning to sell beyond the *danwei* walls.

The canteens had successfully combined business with welfare. By going quasi-market, the canteens had ceased making a loss and begun making a profit. Their employees were earning more than before. The quality of food improved and users had more choices. And, by taking over from the plant what used to be its welfare responsibility, they had also relieved the plant of a part of its welfare burden.

The kindergarten, although also on *chengbao* contract with the *xingzheng chu*, had pursued a somewhat different quasi-market strategy. The kindergarten had more than 70 teachers and minor staff. What it had tried to do with an annual allocation of only Y60,000 from *xingzheng chu* was to open its doors to 'outside' students and charge them a much higher tuition fee. In 1994, of its more than 700 students nearly half were 'external' students paying tuition fees from Y92 to Y120 a month, treble that of Y36 paid by 'local' students. What the kindergarten had created was a quasi-market involving external users and using 'price differentiation' to distinguish between marketed service and welfare.

The school

The school was, by the city's standard, a big one: with 1,200 students in 14 primary and 12 junior secondary classes.

Unlike the kindergarten, the school was not on a contract responsibility, or *chengbao*, arrangement with the *danwei*. It was, as Mr Wen the principal put it, the 'last place in the *danwei* still not required to stand on its own feet'. In 1994, it had a budget of Y1.2 million to cover, among other expenses, the wage and bonus for its 98 teaching and supporting staff.

Importantly also, unlike the kindergarten, tuition fees were not a source of its income. Mr Wen explained:

> You see, because there are nine years' compulsory education in this country, students from the first year of the primary school to the third year of the secondary school do not have to pay tuition fees. This has important financial implications. Primary schools do not receive any revenue from tuition fees for six years and secondary schools for three years. Because ours is both a primary and a junior secondary school, this means we are not getting any revenue from tuition fees for nine years. Yes, we do have external students. Half of our secondary places are for external students. This is required by the government as a condition for allowing our students to progress to other public schools in the city after they have completed junior secondary school. Half of our secondary students are now from outside the *danwei*. But, just as local students, they do not have to pay tuition fees.

Hence the school could not use the same strategy as used by the kindergarten to generate income, i.e., charging external students higher tuition fees. What it had tried to do instead was to make use of its facilities and professional staff and to market educational facilities and services to users both inside and outside the school. The strategy, as Mr Wen described it, was one 'using the school to support the school' (*yi xue yang xue*). A variety of ways were used.

For example, it had rented its language laboratory on Sundays to schools without the facility for these schools to run English language enhancement classes for their students, charging Y60 to Y80 per student for each six-month course. The proceeds from the 'business' went into the school's staff welfare fund. It had also organized evening classes for students on a voluntary and fee-charging basis, each pupil paying Y5 to Y8 a month for 20 tutorial sessions. The revenue went to the teachers. More formally and with the permission of the government, the school had started a one-year pre-primary head-start programme for children who just completed kindergarten classes. There were 46 students in the head-start programme. Each student was paying a tuition fee of Y30 a month. But what had been most successful in terms of generating revenue and using the revenue generated to enhance the quality of education was its entrepreneurial experience in promoting computer education. Mr Wen described what had happened:

> Not many schools in the city are equipped with computer facilities. However, we believe we must give our kids a computer education and prepare them for the twenty-first century. The plant couldn't give us any help. So we had to find our own ways to raise funds. We knocked down one of the walls, the wall facing the street, and invited people to bid for the right to rent the seven stalls built on the space cleared from knocking down the wall. We made Y30,000. We topped this up to Y50,000, using savings from another line of business activity, bought ten PCs, set up a computer laboratory, and began running computer courses for our students. Each student paid Y10 a month to enrol in the course. We reinvested the revenue and bought more PCs. There are now all together 30 PCs. We intend to increase the number to 50 and upgrade the machines from 386 to 486. I think we have been right to work on computer education. Parents very much appreciate our initiatives and there is tremendous support for what we have done. All these would not have been possible if we were passive, just sitting and waiting for the *danwei* to give us what we wanted.

What the school had created was a quasi-market 'selling' a range of educational services to both external and internal users. In going quasi-market the school had achieved what would have been impossible were it to depend entirely on the enterprise: improving its equipment and facilities and providing a 'better' education for its students. Mr Wen was proud of the school's achievement:

> Our overall rating both among schools in the district and in the city as a whole has improved. Of the 140 students graduating from the junior secondary school this year, three have reached the city's best level and seven have been admitted into the city's top schools. These are very good news, and for our teachers this is very much the kind of incentives that they badly need, besides material incentives.

Conclusion

This chapter examined how one state-owned enterprise reorganized its *danwei* welfare economy in its attempts to reduce welfare burden without giving up welfare responsibilities.

Welfare had become a heavy financial burden. It was seriously affecting the enterprise's *xiaoyi*, diminishing its profit, draining capital funds and upsetting production. The burden was, moreover, becoming heavier and heavier as more and more workers retired and as it became increasingly costly to provide housing and health care to the *danwei's* members.

Though weighed down by the burden, the enterprise was hesitant about cutting welfare, for four main reasons. First, the plant reckoned it had a moral obligation to its older workers. Secondly, it was concerned that cutting welfare would cause hardship and precipitate unrest and disorder. Thirdly, welfare had become an important means for inducing incentives and commitment. Cutting welfare could make it even more difficult for the enterprise to stabilize its workforce and compete with non-state-sector enterprises for skilled workers. Fourthly, the government was not ready to take over from the enterprise what it wanted to give up; for example, its school.

To be or not to be? The answer was neither to give up welfare nor to do nothing about it. The enterprise's strategy was to 'go quasi-market': to commodify welfare in part; in other words, to combine welfare with business. The strategy allowed the enterprise to 'walk on two legs': to perform its welfare responsibilities at the same time as it tried to generate income from marketing its services.

The chapter has examined the application of the strategy in three case studies and found considerable variations. For example, while the strategy of the hospital was to 'market' its service to 'outsiders', that of the canteens was to 'sell' 'differentiated products' to 'local' buyers. The school provided a range of 'differentiated products' not only to 'local' but also to 'outside' users. It became involved in only not an 'internal', but also an 'external' market.

Users, in all cases, paid more for marketized services. But 'outsiders' did not always pay more than 'local' users for the same service. For example, 'external' students paid just as much as 'local' students for the school's computer classes.

Outcomes also varied. By bringing out 'differentiated products', the school and the canteens had extended the range of 'consumer choice' and improved the quality of their services. The hospital, unlike the school and the canteens, had not 'produced' any new 'product' or service. Its strategy was instead to extend its 'old' service to 'outsiders'. 'Local' users of its service had not benefited from a widened range of choice and an improved service.

Performance, in terms of generating income, also varied. The canteens were, compared to the hospital and the school, most 'successful'. 'Going quasi-market' enabled the canteens to generate enough income to stand on their own feet and substantially increase the income of their employees. The school was financially dependent on the enterprise. However, by 'going quasi-market', it had, without turning to the enterprise for help, built its computer laboratory and increased the income of its staff. The hospital was the least 'successful' of the three. 'Going quasi-market' had not made any significant impact on the income of its staff or the quality of its service.

There was not, therefore, a unified approach. Nor was there a formula or recipe for success.

But what seemed common in the experience of the canteens and the school was that they both began with 'internal markets': the canteens selling food to customers at the 'upper end' of the internal market and the school enrolling students in computer classes. In the case of the canteens, it was only after they had 'passed the test' of the internal market that they began eyeing the 'opportunities beyond the *danwei* walls'. The hospital never went through the test of the internal market. It got into the 'external market' at once and lost out in its competition with other hospitals in the city. The experience earned from the internal market appeared to have prepared the canteens for the much keener competition and greater risk in the external market. 'First the internal market, then the external market' (*Baogang* 1995: 129) seemed a safe strategy for 'going quasi-market'.

In 'going quasi-market', the three services had also become unequally dependent on the enterprise. The canteens had become, of the three, least dependent; they were becoming self-supporting. The school was still very dependent on the *danwei*. But, by being able to generate some income, it had also in its modest way reduced its dependence. The hospital remained highly dependent and a heavy financial burden to the enterprise.

In becoming less dependent, the canteens and the school had helped the enterprise reduce its welfare burden without giving up its welfare responsibilities.

But what the canteens, and to some extent the school, had gained was not only less dependence but also, importantly, more independence, the independence from a centrally planned budget and the managerial control of the *danwei* bureaucracy. This independence gave them a freer hand to do their jobs. It encouraged initiative and innovation. But at the same time as they exploited this newly gained independence, to good effect, the canteens were also exposed to risks of a new kind, business risks which they otherwise would not have were they entirely dependent on the enterprise.

The *danwei* economy of welfare emerging from these changes was more diversified and pluralistic than before. In the making was a *danwei* welfare economy in which not just welfare but also commodities were distributed; not only the bureaucracy but also the market performed the distribution; distribution was based not just on needs, but also on prices and the ability to pay; users could also be consumers; there were both internal and external markets; there were at once more products and services for distribution, giving users a wider range of choice; and there was not one singular and unified but different approaches to providing welfare. It was a mixed *danwei* economy of welfare.

7
Redistributing Risks and Responsibilities

Introduction

A key component of Chinese occupational welfare was a comprehensive 'Labour Insurance' (*laodong baoxian*) scheme which required, by law,[1] state enterprises to provide old age pensions and a wide range of benefits covering maternity and birth, illness, accidents and death to employees and their dependants (see Table 1.1, Chapter 1).

The scheme was non-contributory and insurance funds were borne in full by the employers. Enterprises participating in the scheme each made a contribution to a Labour Insurance Fund partly managed by the enterprises and partly managed by the trade unions, which would 'transfer about 30 per cent of the contributions to a higher level of trade union organization so that a certain degree of redistribution could be effected between enterprises of varying financial commitments' (Chow 1988: 40).

This arrangement was disrupted during the Cultural Revolution and formally ended in 1969, when the Ministry of Finance issued an order which in effect stopped the Labour Insurance Funds, ended the involvement of trade unions in the administration of the scheme and made enterprises responsible for administering and financing Labour Insurance.[2]

In other words, from then on the risk as well as the responsibility of providing Labour Insurance fell on the enterprises. Before reform, this was not a problem for the enterprises because it was the state which was ultimately responsible and because enterprises were not required to produce for profit. The occupational welfare of Labour Insurance was financed by the government.

Everything changed following economic reform: state enterprises had to produce for profit, be responsible for their own profits and losses, and they could no longer look to the state to bail them out of their difficulties. Labour Insurance entered into cost-efficiency considerations.

Since economic reforms, the problem rested with the fact that the scheme was both statutory and non-contributory. Because it was statutory, there was little that the enterprise could do to absolve itself of this responsibility. And because it was non-contributory, the enterprise had to bear full responsibility for it, as well as the entire risk.

In the new context of market transition, it had become increasingly clear that this was not a viable state of affairs. State enterprises held responsible for Labour Insurance could not compete as equals with non-state counterparts, which had few welfare responsibilities. In this chapter, we look at how the state took on and tackled the problem: how it tried to bring about a more viable scheme by redistributing the risks and the responsibilities involved between the state, the enterprises, and the individual workers. The result of what had been attempted so far was a system of Labour Insurance combining both statutory and non-statutory arrangements, giving the state, the enterprise and the individuals each a share of the risks and the responsibilities involved. Emerging from the change was a 'mixed' system of Labour Insurance.

Problems with the inherited system

There were three main problems with the system of Labour Insurance inherited from the pre-reform days. These were, first, its narrow coverage, or exclusivity; secondly, that it was not portable; and thirdly, that it made the enterprise bear all financial responsibility. In other words, risk and responsibility were highly 'localized' in separate enterprises. Let me take each in turn.

1. Exclusivity

The services available to state employees were largely denied rural workers and other occupational groups in the cities (Table 7.1). Such near-exclusive rights and benefits gave state workers a distinct 'status'[3] and divided them from other 'status groups' in the society.

Such a status division was meant to be strategic: its purpose was to induce discipline and co-operation from an elite sector of the labour force, which was expected to make strategic contributions to the goal of socialist industrialization.[4] However, what had been strategic and functional in the early years of the Republic had become anachronistic

Table 7.1 Labour Insurance and Benefits for Workers in Non-state Sectors

Item	Collectives by Municipal Bureau	Collectives by Urban District or Rural County	Collectives by Sub-district Government	Collectives by Township Government	Village Cooperative and Private Sectors
1. Health insurance					
Employees	Same as state coverage	Same as state coverage	Up to 75 per cent coverage	50–70 % per cent	None
Dependants	Up to 50 per cent coverage	Up to 50 per cent coverage	Limited amount	Limited amount	None
2. Pension as per cent of salary	60–90 per cent	60–90 per cent	60 per cent fixed	Vary, up to 60 per cent	None
3. Injury, disability and death benefits					
Injury	Same as state	Same as state	One-time limited payment	One-time limited payment	Ask help from government
Disability	Same as state	Same as state	One-time limited payment	One-time limited payment	Ask help from government
Death	Limited amount for funeral	Limited amount for funeral	Limited amount for funeral	Limited amount for funeral	None
4. Benefits for women workers					
3-month maternity leave	Same as state	Same as state	Same as state	50 per cent of salary	None
Longer maternity leave	Same as state	None	None	None	None
Infant nursery allowance	Limited amount	None	None	None	None
Day-care allowance	Limited amount	None	None	None	None
5. Holiday, sick leave and leave of absence benefits					
Holiday	Same as state	Same as state	Same as state	Same as state	None
Sick leave	Same as state	Same as state	50 per cent pay	Limited pay	None
Leave of absence	Same as state	Same as state	No pay	No pay	None
6. Other benefits	Limited	Limited	None	None	None

Source: Bian (1994: 184–5).

and dysfunctional in the new context of a socialist economy in a process of market transition.

From the point of view of equity such a status division is undesirable and difficult to justify, 'given that it is now accepted that the Chinese economy will retain diverse forms of ownership (state, collective, foreign and private), and that both state and collective ownership would undergo important changes' (Hussain 1993: 37). It was also difficult to justify given the declining importance and productivity of the state sector. In 1994, for instance, state-owned enterprises, employing two-thirds of the country's urban labour force, were producing just one-third of the country's total industrial output (see Table 1.4, Chapter 1). By limiting its coverage to state-sector employees, the scheme 'leaves out a significant section of the labour force which could be included' (Hussain 1993: 15): employees of town and village enterprises, private firms and joint ventures. This meant that, in 1991, it had left out around 96 million employees at town and village enterprises and 3 million employees with joint venture, foreign capital and private enterprises in the cities (State Statistical Bureau 1995: 84–5).

It was not fair from the point of view of equity to exclude these workers from benefits enjoyed by their state-sector counterparts simply because they were not state employees; such inequity flew in the face of citizenship rights enshrined in the Constitution.[5] Article 45 of the Constitution, for example, clearly states that 'citizens of the People's Republic of China have the right to material assistance from the state and society when they are old and disabled' and that 'the state develops social insurance, social relief and medical and health services that are required for citizens to enjoy the right'. Article 44 stipulates that 'the state applies the system of retirement for workers and staff of enterprises and institutions and for functionaries of organs of state according to law' and that 'the livelihood of retired personnel is ensured by the state and society'. Article 42 promises citizens 'the right as well as the duty to work' and pledges the state's commitment to creating conditions for employment and increasing 'remuneration for work and welfare benefits'. Clearly, according to the Constitution, non-state employees, as citizens, are as much entitled to the various rights and benefits provided by Labour Insurance as their state-sector counterparts.

The status division had also become increasingly dysfunctional because 'it hinders the mobility of labour across enterprises' (Hussain 1993: 37). It made non-state jobs less desirable and discouraged state workers from leaving their jobs. It slowed the flow of labour from state to non-state enterprises and thereby distorted the allocation of labour in what could have been a competitive labour market. Hence the 'best' persons might not have gone to the 'best' jobs. State enterprises 'kept' people who otherwise might have left and non-state enterprises did not get people who otherwise might have been recruited.

2.   Non-portability

What had also impeded labour mobility was that Labour Insurance was not portable: workers changing their jobs could not carry their insurance benefits with them to their new jobs. Quitting state-sector jobs meant, therefore, forfeiting the security and protection of Labour Insurance. It also meant that in the increasingly likely event of a worker losing his job, he and his dependants also lost the security and protection of Labour Insurance.

The non-portability of Labour Insurance had to do with four inter-related features of the scheme: (1) the absence of a specialized Labour Insurance administration (e.g. a governmental or professional agency); (2) the absence of some kind of pooling arrangements across enterprises; (3) the financing of Labour Insurance resting entirely with individual enterprises; and (4) the integration of Labour Insurance administration with enterprise management. In other words, because both the financing and the day-to-day administration of Labour Insurance rested with the enterprises, and because beyond individual enterprises there was no other administrative or financial arrangement for Labour Insurance, the scheme had become very much a 'localized' (within individual enterprises) scheme. In brief, the scheme had become characterized by 'extreme fragmentation' (Wong et al. 1995: 13).

This was not a problem before reform because there was more or less permanent employment in the same workplace for most workers and because there were few job transfers. It did not matter if each enterprise had its own administration of Labour Insurance and if there was no record of job changes and no across-enterprise administrative arrangements. But this degree of fragmentation was incompatible with an increasingly marketized economy with contractual employment, mobility of labour and increasing instances of unemployment arising from bankruptcies, mergers and enterprises reducing their surplus labour force. There clearly was the need for a less fragmented and more portable arrangement, one which could continue to give protection to workers when they either changed or lost their jobs.

Fragmentation was also undesirable from the point of view of equity. It meant that there could be great inter-unit variations in provision and coverage, hence not giving the same standard and quality of security and protection to workers in different enterprises. A less fragmented and more unified system would be less inequitable.

3. Localized financial responsibility

The financial responsibility for Labour Insurance was borne entirely by the enterprise. This was not a problem before reform because it was the government which carried the ultimate responsibility for maintaining Labour Insurance and, enterprises were not required to produce for profit and be responsible for their profits and losses. Nor was cost a big problem then because there were relatively few retired employees and because the cost of health care insurance was relatively low.

This state of affairs ceased to be viable when enterprises faced market competition and became responsible for their own profits and losses. Labour Insurance became a financial burden. Expenditures on Labour Insurance benefits raised production costs and reduced enterprise profits; they made state enterprises less competitive and aggravated the financial difficulties of many loss-making enterprises.

The size of this financial burden was reflected in the rapid growth of expenditures of state-owned enterprises on 'Labour Insurance and Welfare Funds', which increased from 14.3 per cent of their total wage bill in 1978 to 31.5 per cent in 1994. The total number of retired workers in state-owned enterprises increased nearly ten-fold, from 2.84 million in 1978 to 22.49 million in 1994. Expenditures on retirement benefits increased more than 60 times during the same period. The cost of medical care increased almost six-fold between 1984 and 1994 and was expected to rise at an annual rate of 30 per cent (see Tables 1.1 and 1.2, Chapter 1).

The aim of the enterprise reforms was to invigorate state enterprises and turn them into profit- and market-oriented actors. But unless they were shorn of their welfare responsibilities or had these reduced, state enterprises could never compete on equal terms with enterprises which had fewer or none of these responsibilities. Labour Insurance had become such a financial burden for state enterprises that change was inevitable. An important aim of this change had to be a reduction in their financial responsibilities. In short, the system of Labour Insurance inherited from the pre-reform days was unsuitable for a socialist economy in market transition.

The system had to change in three vital respects. First, it needed to extend its coverage to include new urban occupational groups – employees of private, joint ventures and foreign capital enterprises – as well as employees of fast growing town and village enterprises in the precincts of cities. Secondly, the system had to be made more portable. This would necessitate the separation of Labour Insurance administration from enterprise management, the setting up of some specialized Labour Insurance administration, and the development of some kind of financial arrangement for labour insurance across enterprises. Thirdly, the system needed to find ways of reducing the financial responsibility of the enterprises. This could be done by implementing one or more of the following changes: a new formula for employees' contribution, the introduction of a more equitable risk-sharing arrangement between enterprises, persuading the government to share part of the financial responsibility, and providing a new scheme of supplementary non-statutory benefits and protection. It is difficult to say in retrospect which combination of these policy options would have worked out in the 1980s. All of these were under consideration.

Reforms along these lines would not be easy, for five main reasons.

1. Wages were still very low.[6] This made it difficult to make workers contribute to Labour Insurance. Contributions which were of only a very low level would be insignificant both in terms of providing for their old age and security and in terms of reducing the financial burden of the enterprise. Contributions set at a level high enough to have significance could be difficult for workers to afford.
2. The 'old' system had been in existence for over three decades and workers had become accustomed to their benefits and entitlements. 'Anything less favourable or even slight changes would immediately arouse their resistance as the benefits provided are directly affecting their present and future standard of living' (Chow 1988: 71–2).
3. The entire scheme was immensely complex, covering many kinds of benefits, ranging from health insurance to injury, disability and death benefits, to pension, to holiday, sick leave and leave of absence benefits. It was inevitable that as these reforms were implemented they would develop in different directions and at different speeds with regard to different groups of workers. Such a complex pattern of change was certain to result in a major problem of 'reintegrating' a diversity of schemes in the future.
4. It would be difficult to bring enterprises of very diverse profiles and backgrounds together within some common administrative and financial framework. Serious conflicts of interest between them would become unavoidable. For example, a pooling arrangement for pension funds helped share risk among enterprises. However, in the

short run, such an arrangement would be likely to benefit enterprises with many older and retired workers and disadvantage those with many young workers and few old workers and retirees. It would not be in the interest of the enterprises with few older workers to participate in a scheme that produced benefits only in the long run.

5. Given the significant regional variations in levels of economic development as, for example, between coastal and inland cities,[7] it would be unrealistic to have a single and unified nation-wide system. As Chow (1983: 73) observes, 'as incomes in most parts of China are still very low, it implies that contributory insurance schemes can only be applied in the more affluent regions'. This problem of inter-regional and inter-city diversity continues to pose a major problem with regard to the future reintegration of the Chinese social security system.

Reforming labour insurance

By the mid-1980s, it was widely acknowledged among professionals and government officials that there were serious flaws with the 'old' system of Labour Insurance.[8] Various reform proposals,[9] including some from the Ministry of Civil Affairs and the Ministry of Labour and Personnel, were also drafting new blueprints for future reforms.[10] Four salient concepts or principles underpinned the proposals drafted by the two Ministries. The first of these was the idea that the sources of funding should be diversified and that they should come from the state, the enterprises and individuals. The second was the idea that there should not be just one fund for many purposes but different funds for different purposes. For example, there could be a fund specifically for old age insurance and another fund for health care insurance. There could be, in other words, a functionally differentiated Labour Insurance system. The third idea was that enterprises could pool their resources to share and reduce risks. The fourth principle embodied in these proposals was that users should contribute to or pay fees for benefits or services received. It was, for example, suggested that part of the medical expenses which were currently provided free of charge to employees in state enterprises should henceforth be recovered by charging fees.

Reforms were heralded by the introduction of a contributory old age pension scheme for workers on 'contract employment' and the establishment of a special fund to provide protection to unemployed workers.

In 1986, the government promulgated four regulations to further reforms in contract employment (*Guowuyuan* [State Council] 1986). Two of these regulations announced the setting up of a dual programme consisting of a contributory pension fund for workers on 'employment contracts' and an unemployment insurance fund for state-sector employees who had been laid off for one reason or another (see Chapter 4).

The 'Temporary Regulations on the Implementation of Labour Contracts in State-owned Enterprises' required enterprises to contribute a sum equivalent to 15 per cent of the basic wage of contract workers towards an old age pension fund managed by a social insurance organ set up under the supervision of the appropriate labour bureau. Workers were also required to contribute a sum not exceeding 3 per cent of their basic wage.

The 'Temporary Regulations on Unemployment Insurance for Workers in State-owned Enterprises', on the other hand, required enterprises to set up an insurance fund by contributing to it a sum equivalent to 1 per cent of the basic wages of all workers employed. The fund would be managed by designated banks and given subsidies by local government if it fell short of the amount required to meet its obligations. The regulation specified the level of benefits which unemployed workers were to receive from the insurance fund up to a maximum of two years. During the first 12 months of their unemployment, they were to receive 60–75 per cent of their sbasic wage. Thereafter, for the next 12 months they were to receive 50 per cent of their basic wage. The insurance fund also provided assistance for their dependants while they were awaiting employment and covered against future medical and burial expenses.

These reforms, while still modest, were important breakthroughs and 'will go down in history as a milestone in the development of the social security system in China' (Chow 1988: 80). They embodied some of the most important concepts and principles which were to guide subsequent reforms, namely, the concept of pooling, the idea of workers making contributions to their old age pensions, the principle of an independent insurance administration which was separate from enterprise management, and the provision of functionally demarcated insurance funds designed to cover different contingencies and different groups of employees.

Reforming old age pensions

The State Council's decision in 1991 to introduce on a nationwide scale a new system of old age pensions for state-sector employees was the next milestone in Labour Insurance reforms (*Guowuyuan* [State

Council] 1991). The 'Decisions' (as they were described in Chinese nomenclature) required all state-owned enterprises to set up contributory pension funds for their employees. In addition to this 'basic pension fund' (*jiben yanglao baoxian jijin*), it also required enterprises to provide, from their own funds, 'enterprise supplementary pensions' (*qiye buchong yanglao baoxian*) for their employees when they reached a specified level of productivity. In addition, it encouraged employees, on a voluntary basis, to put aside savings for 'individual pensions plans' (*geren chuxuxing yanglao baoxian*).

There were a number of noteworthy features in this three-tiered insurance system which consisted of three levels of income provision – basic, supplementary and individual.

1. It combined both statutory and non-statutory components. While the basic and the supplementary plans were statutory, the individual plans were non-statutory and optional. In this respect, this added a pluralist dimension to the scheme.
2. It required all three parties – the state, the enterprise and the employees – to contribute to basic pensions. The contributions of the enterprise and the employees were respectively 24.5 per cent of the total wage bill of an enterprise and up to 3 per cent of a worker's basic wage. The state contributed indirectly by allowing the enterprise to include its own contribution as a cost item. As such it was not taxed. In other words, the state made its contribution by not taxing what could have been part of an enterprise's pre-tax profit.
3. Basic pension costs were pooled (*tongyi chouji*, or *shehui tongchou*). The costs of 'enterprise supplementary pensions' were borne entirely by the enterprises. In the case of 'individual pension plans', all the cost fell on individual employees. The 'three-tiered system' combined, therefore, both a risk-sharing and a non-risk-sharing component.
4. The 'three-tiered system' provided both 'basic' and 'supplementary' forms of protection. 'Basic' protection was provided at a more or less uniform level. 'Supplementary' protection depended on the enterprise and the individuals concerned. With regard to enterprises, the system took into account their performances, and in the case of individuals, their income levels. Thus we can see that it was a complex and diverse system which was designed both to guarantee basic levels of subsistence provision and to make allowance for performance-related criteria of provision. It was these criteria that added to the system's diversity and complexity.

5. The pension plans were portable. All participating workers had a 'worker old age insurance handbook' (*jigong yanglao baoxian shouce*) listing their basic pension entitlements. The handbook included both the employer's and the worker's record of contributions. When they changed jobs, workers could take their 'handbooks' to their new employers. The social insurance agency then completed the necessary paperwork and recorded the transfer. All workers who were members of the 'enterprise supplementary pensions' also had their individual 'handbooks' (*jigong buchongyanglao baoxian chubeijin shouce*). Once again, when workers left their jobs, they took their 'handbooks' with them to their new employers. In summary, both the 'basic' and 'supplementary' pension schemes were part of a personalized pension account system designed to encourage portability.

6. Pension funds were deposited in designated banks, administered by a social insurance agency and supervised by a government pension committee. The administration and supervision of Labour Insurance had become, in other words, dissociated from enterprise management and made the responsibility of specialized professional and administrative bodies.

What was emerging from these reforms was a system of old age insurance that combined both contributory and non-contributory, statutory and non-statutory, compulsory and optional, basic and supplementary, and pooling and non-pooling features. It was also a system that provided portability and made sure there was separation of insurance administration from enterprise management.

In 1993, 'basic pension funds' covered 83 million state-sector employees and 17.7 million pensioners, or, in terms of percentage, 71.8 per cent and 81.2 per cent respectively, of all state-sector employees and retired workers (Liu 1995: 32). In Guangzhou, in 1994, 'basic pensions' covered 376,000 state-sector and 134,000 collective-sector workers (*Guangzhou Shi Tigaiwei* [Guangzhou City Economic Restructuring Commission] 1994: 29).

In 1995 the State Council formally announced the extension of the system (with some modifications) to cover non-state as well as state sector employees (*Guowuyuan* [State Council] 1995). The 'basic' part of the system was now officially designated as one 'combining the pooling of costs for basic old age insurance with personalized accounts for the individual workers' (*qiye jigong jiben yanglao baoxian shehui tongchou yu geren zhanghu xiang jiehe*). Instead of a 'handbook', all workers would have a 'personalized basic old age insurance fund account' (*jiben yanglao baoxian geren zhanghu*), which they would keep for the rest of their life. Members would be identified either by a newly established social security number or by their resident identity card numbers. The account would keep a record of their employers' contributions as well as their own contributions. Each individual contribution began with no more than 3 per cent of the member's average wage in the previous year which was scheduled to increase by 1 percentage point every two years thereafter. On retirement, members would be paid a monthly pension equal to the accumulated amounts in their accounts, divided by 120. Depending on whether there were 'enterprise supplementary pensions' and on whether they had saved for an 'individual pensions plan', the amount could be topped up by additional pension contributions and benefits.

Reforming health insurance

Reforms in old age insurance had pointed the way forward for reforms in health insurance, which did not really begin until 1994. Under Labour Insurance, health insurance covered a comprehensive range of benefits, including primary health care and hospital treatment, surgery, maternity benefits and drugs. There was, in effect, almost a free medical service. Other benefits included pay during sickness and maternity leave. Medical benefits could also be extended to cover the immediate dependents of employees.

As in the case of old age insurance before 1995, health care costs were not pooled and each enterprise was responsible for the cost of its employees and retirees. With the rise in health insurance cost in the 1980s (Hussain 1993: 26), this had become a serious problem. Enterprises had responded by shifting part of the cost to users. There were various ways of cost-sharing. One common formula for cost-sharing was that each year the enterprise paid the full cost up to a fixed amount, and thereafter the user paid the full cost or a percentage of the amount. Another common formula was for the user to pay up to a fixed amount; the enterprise then paid whatever exceeded the fixed amount.[11] To keep medical cost under control, some enterprises also entered into contracts with hospitals for the medical care of their employees (Hussain 1993: 27). Employees were only reimbursed for visits to hospitals designated under the contracts.

Cost-sharing was at best, however, a stop-gap measure. Enterprises varied greatly in their financial resources and there were also wide variations in the formula for cost-sharing. These differences produced inequities in levels of provisions and coverage, sometimes resulting in under-provision and inadequate coverage. There were no incentives to control cost because the scheme did not impose limits on what the medical care providers could charge for individual services. Consequently, costs continued to escalate. These problems pointed to the need for further reforms in the new scheme of things, such as requirements to pool cost, to create a centralized system of health insurance management, to standardize payments for particular services and to specify which services and needs could be covered.

With these objectives in mind, a new set of health insurance reforms were introduced in 1994 (*Guojia Jinji Tizhi Gaige Weiyuanhui* [State Economic Restructuring Commission] 1995: 156–69). This took the form of two pilot programmes jointly initiated by four government departments: the State Economic Restructuring Commission, the Ministry of Finance, the Ministry of Labour and Personnel and the Ministry of Health. These pilot programmes were started in the cities of Zhen Jiang in the province of Jiang Su and Jiu Jiang in the province of Jiang Xi. They were designed to establish 'a social insurance system combining the pooling of medical funds with a personalized medical care account' (*jianli shehui tong zhou yiliao jijin yu geren yiliao zhanghu xian jiehe ti shehui baoxian zhidu*). The concept, simply, was to have two types of fund: a pooled 'basic' fund and funds for individual medical care accounts. As in the 'basic pensions' model, all three parties – the state, the enterprise, and the employees – made contributions to both funds. The enterprise contributed an amount equal to 10 per cent of the sum of its total annual wage bill and its total expenditure on retirement benefits. One part of this fund was put into the pool; the other was put into the individual medical insurance accounts of employees and retired employees. Each employee made a contribution equal to 1 per cent of his annual wage income. As in the case of 'basic pensions funds', the state contributed only indirectly, by not taxing the enterprise's contributions.

As in the case of 'basic pensions', each insured worker had a portable 'personalized account'. The account recorded their shares in the enterprise's contributions and their own contributions. They could use their accounts to pay expenses incurred as a result of visits to designated hospitals. If in any given year their expenditures exceeded what they had in their accounts by more than 5 per cent of their annual wage, they would make a contribution towards meeting the excess costs. The more a member 'overspent', the more he or she had to reimburse the overspent amount.

Both the pooled and the non-pooled parts of the funds were deposited in a designated bank, managed by a specialized insurance agency and supervised by a special government body. In order to control costs, coverage and payment terms were laid down and standardized.

In neither Zhen Jiang nor Jiu Jiang did the pilot programmes provide universal coverage, i.e., coverage of all kinds of workers in all kinds of enterprises. The Zhen Jiang programme excluded employees of private enterprises and village and town enterprises. Except for these, all others, including workers on contract employment and temporary workers, were covered. The Jiu Jiang programme excluded employees of private enterprises, village and town enterprises and individual entrepreneurs but did not rule out the possibility of including them in the future.

But what was particularly noteworthy was that both programmes covered not just workers who used to be covered by Labour Insurance, but also employees in government departments who used to be covered by another health care insurance scheme, the 'government-funded health care insurance' programme (*gongfei yiliao*). In other words, these initiatives cut through sectoral-administrative boundaries, unified two different schemes and brought them both under a common administrative and financial framework.

The pilot programmes were hailed as a success. Their achievements were described as having 'set up new fund-raising mechanisms; raised the standards of security and protection in health care; curbed rising costs; induced changes within hospitals; and gained much experience useful for deepening reforms of the health care insurance system' (*Guojia Tigai Wei* [State Economic Restructuring Commission] et al. 1996). In 1996, the State Council decided that the pilot programmes should be tried out in more cities. Though still on an experimental basis, it was already clear that the government sees these as a model with great potential for the future.

Reforms in other areas of Labour Insurance have not moved as fast and covered as much ground as have the reforms in health, old age and unemployment insurance. In 1994, a non-contributory maternity insurance scheme covering maternity leave and hospitalization expenses was introduced on a trial basis (Liu 1995). Funds for maternity insurance were pooled; each enterprise contributed up to 1 per cent of its total wage to the pool. In 1993, a non-contributory accident insurance scheme was also launched. It appeared at the time of writing, however, that this scheme had not been implemented on a nation-wide basis. As late as May 1995, an official spokesman for the Ministry of Labour wrote a significant article in a collection of essays published by the State Economic Restructuring Commission. In the article (Zheng 1995) the official outlined a plan for the future reforms of accident insurance. He proposed the setting up of a non-contributory insurance programme with each participating enterprise contributing not more than 1 per cent of its total wage to a pool of funds.

Such uneven development notwithstanding, there has been, on the whole, very significant progress. As a result of the reforms, particularly with regard to the three core programmes – old age, health and un-employment insurance – Labour Insurance has moved away from what it was before the economic reforms, when it was an entirely non-contributory and enterprise-based system of benefits. From a unified and undifferentiated package of benefits it has been transformed into a system of functionally differentiated insurance programmes each with its own set of policy, rules, administration and financial arrangements. From being a programme exclusively concerned with state-sector employees it has been extended to include many employees who were previously excluded from Labour Insurance. This extension of membership has been greater in some programmes than in others. Furthermore, the enterprise-based system of social insurance has been dissociated from enterprise management and its control and supervision has been taken over by specialized professional and administrative bodies. It has become at one and the same time both much less localized and much more portable.

Four themes in these changes are particularly noteworthy. The first has been the redistribution of risks and responsibilities. All three parties – the state, the enterprise and the individual employees – now carry a share of the risks and the responsibilities involved. The second change is the trend towards 'universalization' – the extension of benefits and rights to other occupational groups who were previously excluded. The third trend is the process of increasing functional differentiation. Schemes that were once combined in one unified framework have become independent and separate, with each assuming a distinct set of purposes and functions. The fourth trend of significance has been the growth of professionalization. Services hitherto undifferentiated from enterprise management have now been taken over by specialized professional and governmental agencies.

The new system of Labour Insurance is not without its problems, however. The biggest problem has to do with the fact that individual contributions are very modest. For old age pensions, they account for no more than 3 per cent of a worker's standard wage; for health insurance, for only 1 per cent of his annual wage; and, for other insurance programmes, workers make no contribution at all. The modest levels of workers' contributions have to be compared with the very substantial contributions of the enterprise. In the case of the three core programmes alone – old age, health and unemployment insurance – the enterprise's contributions amounted to 35.5 per cent of their total wage bill. The relative contributions of the enterprise and the individual members can, therefore, be seen to be very unequal.

From the point of view of individual welfare this was not desirable because it does not do much to help the individual to appreciate the value and importance of his own role and responsibility.

This division of responsibility is equally undesirable in its effect on the efficiency of the enterprises. They are still carrying a very heavy responsibility for the welfare and security of their employees. It has become quite common for enterprises and particularly loss-making enterprises to default on their contributions – despite the introduction of penalties for overdue payment. In Guangzhou in 1994, for example, the overdue payments to the city's pension pool amounted to Y50 million. Pool revenues and expenditures are supposed to balance on an annual basis. Overdue payments increase the risk of insolvency.

Clearly, the balance of responsibilities between the enterprises and the individuals will have to be further adjusted and fine-tuned in order to give the individuals more and the enterprises less responsibilities.

Conclusion

The pre-reform system of Labour Insurance was unsuitable for a socialist economy in market transition. It was too exclusive; it was non-portable; and most importantly, it made the enterprise carry all the risks and responsibilities. These arrangements were not appropriate for an economy that was becoming increasingly characterized by contractual employment arrangements, higher rates of labour mobility, more market competition and more production for profit.

In this chapter, we have examined what has been done since 1986 to reform Labour Insurance. Reforms began in 1986 with the introduction of old age pensions for workers on contractual employment and an unemployment insurance programme for state employees. These were followed in 1991, and subsequently in 1995, by the introduction of a system of old age insurance combining both statutory and non-statutory features and combining both the concept of pooling and the concept of a personalized account. Reforms in health insurance began in 1994 with two pilot programmes, which were also based upon these concepts. Though still on a trial basis, these new initiatives and pilot schemes are pointing the way for further reforms.

The reform process has been incremental in character. The separate reforms of the various programmes making up Labour Insurance have not all moved in the same direction all at the same pace. Some general themes, however, can be identified: (1) there has been some redistribution of risks and responsibilities between the state, the enterprise and the individual; (2) what had hitherto been the exclusive rights and benefits of state-sector employees have been increasingly universalized; (3) the old system of Labour Insurance has become more functionally differentiated; and (4) the management and administration of the various insurance programmes has become notably more professionalized.

Emerging from the reforms is a 'mixed' system of social security, one combining both contributory and non-contributory, statutory and non-statutory, compulsory and optional, basic and supplementary, and pooling and non-pooling features.

8
Conclusion: Towards a Chinese Model of Welfare Pluralism

Introduction

China has since the 1950s developed a system of occupational welfare which provides 'cradle to grave' benefits and services to urban state-sector employees. This study sets out to explain the origins of such a system and to describe the processes of radical change which are transforming it into a more pluralistic system. Using the empirical evidence and field data collected in a large-scale state-owned enterprise in Guangzhou, it attempts to explain how and why these changes took place and to reappraise the relevance of a number of key Western concepts and theories to Chinese models of welfare.

In seeking to explain the origins of Chinese occupational welfare, we have taken the 'new institutional' position which regards state socialism as a distinct social formation with its own institutional logic and dynamics of development. It follows from this position that Chinese occupational welfare should best be studied in its national and historical contexts and as part of an institutional configuration characteristic of state socialism.

In this perspective, we have found it useful to explain the origins of Chinese occupational welfare in terms of the unique state formation experiences of the Chinese socialist state. Specifically, these were the experience of guerrilla warfare, the experience of rehabilitating a war-devastated urban economy, and the experience of socialist industrialization.

We then used the concept of 'dependence' to help anchor and organize our analysis of Chinese occupational welfare. We argued that Chinese occupational welfare is a rare and extreme case of 'near-complete dependence', a situation in which the employer assumes a comprehensive range of responsibilities for meeting the needs of the employees and the employees have few alternatives for satisfying these needs. This situation is in marked contrast with the more common situation of 'limited dependence' in which the employer assumes only a limited range of responsibilities and the employees have access to other alternative sources for satisfying their needs.

We posited that, in the Chinese case, 'near-complete dependence' on occupational welfare explains a range of significant outcomes: the *Gemeinschaftlich* character of the *danwei* community, the control of the *danwei* over many aspects of the life of its members, the paternalism and egalitarianism in *danwei* life, inefficiency and waste, and the consent and acceptance of communist rule, or, in other words, the legitimating function of occupational welfare.

We hypothesized that, in the course of market transition, Chinese occupational welfare has undergone very significant changes: it has moved away from 'near-complete dependence' towards a model of 'limited dependence' that combines in a unique way strategic uses of the mixed economy. This results in a mixed economy of welfare with distinct institutional and cultural characteristics.

These concepts and hypothesis have been sustained by the study. Empirical evidence and field data have, furthermore, borne out the relevance and validity of several other key concepts, and added specificity and details to the hypothesis proposed, as follows.

First, besides the concepts of 'near-complete dependence' and 'limited dependence', empirical evidence and field data have also drawn our attention to 'entitlements and obligations', 'equity and inequity', 'alternatives and choices', 'efficiency and inefficiency', 'distribution of risks and responsibilities' and 'legitimacy and growth' as significant and useful perspectives and themes for describing the nature of Chinese occupational welfare and for understanding this system of occupational welfare undergoing a process of change. The meanings and implications of these concepts will be discussed under 'The Nature of Chinese Occupational Welfare' later in this chapter.

Secondly, while confirming the hypothesis that in market transition Chinese occupational welfare is moving away from 'near-complete dependence' towards a distinctive pattern of 'limited dependence', empirical data has also shown that this change has come about through three separate yet interrelated processes at the individual, the work-unit and the government level: the process reshaping dependence, the process reshaping the *danwei* welfare economy and the process reforming Labour Insurance. These processes of change have jointly transformed Chinese occupational welfare and put a mixed economy of welfare in its place. Emerging from the change is a model of welfare pluralism with unique cultural and institutional characteristics.

The origins of Chinese occupational welfare

As we studied the origins of Chinese occupational welfare we were impressed by three striking features. First, the *danwei* was more than a workplace. It assumed many functions and was in fact an all-important channel for making available a wide range of goods and services to its members. Secondly, the system was highly exclusive. It mainly covered urban workers in employment in the state sector, excluding rural workers and other non-state sector workers in the cities. Thirdly, the Chinese socialist state was involved in a wide range of functions and responsibilities. These included determining wages, allocating people to jobs and the distribution of goods and services.

We argued in this study that these distinct features had arisen from the unique historical experience of the Chinese socialist state. More specifically, we showed that the institutional and policy features characteristic of Chinese occupational welfare had evolved from three sets of state-formation experiences of the Chinese socialist state: the experience of guerrilla warfare, the experience of rehabilitating the postwar economy and the experience of socialist industrialization.

1. Guerrilla warfare

The communist ascendancy to power in 1949 was preceded by nearly a decade of guerrilla warfare fought in the border region of Shansi-Kansu-Ninghsia against the armies of Japanese and Guomindang governments. For most of the time the border region was besieged and blockaded. There was severe shortage of supplies and great economic hardship. To overcome its difficulties the guerrilla government had developed a number of key policies and measures. The most important of these included the involvement of troops and public-sector organizations in self-supporting production activities, the practice of a supply system (*gongji zhi*) among 'institutional households', the adoption of the 'mass line' which required the party and the government to care for the people and consider their problems and needs, and, towards the later phase of war, militarizing and mobilizing peasants for war and production.

These wartime experiences had important bearing on the development of subsequent policies and institutions. The 'institutional households' of armies, government organs and schools were the organizational prototype of the *danwei*, the socialist work-unit, which performed many functions for its members. The supply system foreshadowed the system of rationing and bureaucratized distribution of goods in the cities since the 1950s. The spirit of egalitarianism and the welfare value implied in the 'mass line' had become a persistent part of the ideology of the socialist state.

2. Rehabilitation of the postwar economy

After they gained control of the cities, the communists proceeded to tackle two difficult economic problems: curbing chronic hyperinflation and providing jobs to several million unemployed urban residents.

A number of drastic measures were introduced to bring inflation under control. These included taking over the entire banking system to gain control of credit, paying public employees in subsistence goods with a small cash supplement and setting up nation-wide trading associations in each major commodity to gain control of goods. As a result of these and related counter-inflationary measures, the state had, in a very significant way, gained control over the economy. This then paved the way for even more drastic measures introduced in less than ten years to nationalize the economy.

The government used a combination of radical measures to reduce unemployment. These included the policies of re-engaging *en bloc* Guomindang officials, requiring private enterprises to apply for permission to hire or discharge workers, job introductions through government labour bureaux and centralized allocation of jobs.

As a result of these measures, the state assumed an all-important role and responsibility in urban employment. Urban residents looked to and depended on the state, instead of the market, for jobs and, once allocated, jobs were more or less for life.

3. Socialist industrialization

The overriding concern of the Chinese Communist Party in the early years of the Republic was to achieve industrialization – to develop industrial production and realize economic growth.

We argued in this study that in pursuance of this goal the Chinese Communist Party followed a distinct socialist industrialization strategy, characterized by the importance attached to the strategic role of the urban-industrial labour force, by its emphasis on heavy industry, its neglect of services and consumption, and by the enforcement of a system of strict rural–urban migration controls.

In this study, we showed that these policy features explained the privileged status of urban workers in employment in the state sector, the introduction of a system of rationing and distribution through the workplaces, and the provision by the workplaces of a wide range of facilities and services.

In short, we have shown that Chinese occupational welfare originated from important policies and institutions shaped in China's state formation experiences.

The nature of Chinese occupational welfare

In the course of this study, we found seven sets of concepts valid and relevant for describing the nature of Chinese occupational welfare and the system undergoing a process of change. Let me recapitulate these.

1. Near-complete and limited dependence

In the pre-reform days, Chinese workers were almost completely dependent on occupational welfare. We found this very much the case with workers in Dongfang Heavy Machinery Works. In the pre-reform days, they depended on the *danwei* for a wide range of facilities and services typical of a 'large and comprehensive' (*da erh chuan*) state-owned enterprise. They had access to its many facilities and services, including its hospital, nursery, day-care centre, school and canteens. Many of them lived in *danwei*-provided housing, for which they paid only nominal rentals. They enjoyed retirement, health care and various benefits provided through *laobao yiliao* (Labour Insurance). They were regularly given various kinds of allowances and subsidies (*butei*) which considerably topped up their money wage income. During the 1960s and most of the 1970s, it was also through the *danwei* that they obtained ration coupons for various commodities and basic necessities. Because employment was more or less permanent during these years and wages were low; and also because there were few alternative sources providing these benefits and services, they were very heavily dependent on the *danwei*. It was a situation of near-complete dependence.

When this study was undertaken, very important changes had taken place to social and economic life in the country and to the enterprise. As described in Chapter 4, economic reforms and market transition had ushered in a mixed economy and induced many changes at various levels of the economy. There were now many more alternatives to what used to be distributed through the *danwei*. Workers were earning many times more than in the past. There were now also many opportunities for moonlighting, or *chaogang*, in the non-state sector. Workers could even change jobs or set themselves up as 'private entrepreneurs' (*gete hu*). 'Exit' from the *danwei* had become a real option.

In other words, since reform, workers were moving away from the situation of near-complete dependence towards one of limited dependence on occupational welfare.

How limited was such dependence? Field data showed that this varied both between workers and between different types of benefits and services.

Findings described in Chapter 5 showed that workers' dependence on occupational welfare varied importantly between male and female workers, between workers in different age-groups, and between workers who had and workers who did not have the advantage of a supportive family strategy. There were, in other words, gender, generational, as well as family differences in welfare dependence.

Workers' dependence also varied with different benefits and services. They were still very dependent on *danwei* housing, but were less dependent on such other collective facilities as the school and the hospital. They were still very dependent on Labour Insurance (*laobao yiliao*), but would become less dependent on it when it assumed more contributory and non-statutory features. They were now much less dependent on rations and 'in-kind distributions', but still depended on various allowances and subsidies to top up their wage income.

In other words, moving away from near-complete dependence, workers' dependence on occupational workers was at once also more varied and differentiated both among workers and with regard to different benefits and services.

2. Entitlements and obligations

The situation of 'near-complete dependence' is one in which the employer assumes many obligations and the employees have many welfare entitlements. In the pre-reform days, what was obtained in the *danwei* was also 'paternalistic dependence', a situation in which it was taken for granted that the *danwei* had an obligation to take care of and provide for nearly every aspect of the life of its members and its members had the right to its unlimited care and benevolence. As observed in Chapter 1, 'paternalistic dependence' had become very much a *danwei* culture. The culture made the *danwei's* and its members' role as respectively 'carer' and 'cared for' obligatory. While workers were expected to be co-operative and obedient, the *danwei* was expected to do whatever it could to take 'good' care of its workers. The culture of paternalistic dependence stabilized their reciprocal expectations and set moral standards for their behaviour.

Field data showed that this pre-existing pattern of dependence had been upset by the process of change. The *danwei* had been suffering from poor *xiaoyi* (profitability and performance) and it was clear that, to help itself out of its difficult situation, it had to try to reduce its welfare burden. This implied redefining, and perhaps also reducing, welfare obligations and entitlements.

This was not easy. It would be difficult, for example, to change obligations and entitlements in ways that would affect old workers. In part this was because plant management still believed it had a moral obligation to its older workers, to take care of them in their old age after they had given their best years to the enterprise. In part this was also because older workers reckoned they had a legitimate claim. They 'expect[ed] the plant to look after them in their old age because, for many years before retirement, they had been paid less than what they deserved' (Mr Dong). And, in their view, 'the plant owes it to them to look after them and provide for their security in old age' (Mr Liao). There were, in other words, commonly shared moral values and expectations about the *danwei*'s and the workers' respective obligations and entitlements.

Changes side-stepping these shared values and expectations had nevertheless been introduced and, as could be expected, evoked strong reactions. Older workers, for example, were upset when the plant decided on a policy which advantaged high-fliers in the allocation of *danwei* housing. They were also upset by a policy which required users to pay 20 per cent of their medical bills.

The process was fraught, therefore, with difficulties because it upset paternalistic values and expectations about the *danwei*'s welfare obligations and its members' welfare entitlements. The pre-existing pattern of welfare dependence became an obstacle to change.

3. Equity and inequity

Chinese occupational welfare was characterized by a paradoxical combination of equitable and inequitable features.

Its inequitable features can be seen when the *danwei* is considered in its total social context. Chinese occupational welfare was the near-exclusive right of urban workers employed in state productive units. The *danwei* made state employees a distinct 'status group' enjoying benefits and services largely denied to rural workers and other occupational groups in the cities. In other words, Chinese occupational welfare 'stratified' China's working population in ways which significantly and differentially shaped their welfare and life chances. It engendered inequality, and this was not fair because, according to the Chinese Constitution, rural workers and non-state employees were as much entitled to their citizenship rights as state employees. This was also difficult to justify, given the declining importance and productivity of the state sector and the rising importance and productivity of the non-state sector.

Nevertheless within the relatively privileged world of state employees the distribution of occupational welfare was generally equitable. Most benefits and services were distributed or made available on an egalitarian basis to all members of the same unit and, with regard to statutory benefits, across all units.

What had happened since reforms had upset these pre-existing patterns, in two important ways. First, as described in Chapter 7, important changes had been brought about through reforms of the Labour Insurance system to make it a less exclusive scheme and gradually to extend its rights and benefits to other occupational groups which were previously excluded. For example, beginning in 1995, 'basic pensions' were to cover non-state as well as state-sector employees. The exclusive rights and benefits of state-sector employees became increasingly universalized.

Secondly, as described in Chapter 6, within the *danwei*, reforms were underway reshaping the *danwei* welfare economy. Emerging from the changes introduced was a mixed economy of welfare, one combining welfare and business and using both the bureaucracy and the market in the distribution of goods and services. Housing, for example, was becoming commodified. Increasingly its distribution was on a basis reflecting differences in the ability to pay. The implication, from the point of view of equity, was very clear: workers unable to pay would be disadvantaged. As observed in Chapter 5, the inequitable implication of commodified housing had been a cause of much frustration and anger among ordinary workers.

The transformation of Chinese occupational welfare involved, in other words, both the redistribution of interests between different social and economic groups in the society and the redistribution of interests between different groups of workers in the *danwei*. On the one hand, this was giving rise to more equitable consequences and on the other hand, inequitable consequences. The exact impact of these consequences has yet to be observed and studied.

4. Alternatives and choices

There were few alternatives and choices over what to have and what not to have when workers were almost completely dependent on occupational welfare. They had to take whatever was provided through the *danwei* however poor its quality might be. They had no choice; because there were no options. Before the reforms, there was no private trade and service sector which might have provided alternative sources for the satisfaction of many needs. Even if such a sector had existed, most workers would not have been able to afford its services because their wages were very low.

Danwei workers had so little choice also because Chinese occupational welfare was not organized to meet the needs of 'consumers'. It was neither market- nor profit-oriented in its approach to service delivery. Consumers' preferences and choices were deemed to be irrelevant in the *danwei* scheme of things.

Field data showed that, as workers moved away from near-complete dependence, they were also having more choices than before. Chapter 5 found evidence of workers exercising preferences and using occupational welfare more selectively and calculatively. No longer just passive recipients, they were making choices of, and from, *danwei* benefits and services. With more alternatives and with a better income, they could afford to choose between making greater or lesser use of, or even not using, a *danwei* service altogether. They were also more quality conscious and more demanding. For example, they could choose not to send their children to the *danwei* school. They could choose to have better food in the canteens. They could choose not to see doctors at the *danwei* hospital. They could even choose not to move into *danwei* flats.

In other words, as they moved away from near-complete dependence, workers were also becoming less recipients and more consumers of services, exercising their preferences and more ready to articulate their demands.

5. Efficiency and inefficiency

Chinese occupational welfare was meant to be an efficient system. The bureaucracy distributed benefits and services to their recipients without reference to any kind of market criteria. It minimized market transaction costs. It was also efficient from the welfare point of view because it provided a range of basic services 'cheaply' – at cost or even below cost – and equitably, to their recipients.

This system turned out, however, to be very inefficient. Field data described in Chapter 6 showed that it was poorly run; there was considerable waste; the quality of its goods and services was poor; and consumers were given few choices. The *danwei* hospital, for example, was over-staffed. Its 'doctors and nurses outnumbered their patients' and were consulted only for 'minor illnesses and cuts and wounds'. It was, as one informant put it, 'a sub-standard and filthy facility where patients hated to go'. Patients turned away from the hospital; they preferred to see outside doctors. Doctors at the *danwei* hospital were ready to give referrals. As Dr Mao the director of the hospital explained, 'Doctors, you see, don't care. After all, it is not their money. It is public money, the state's money. And why not, when they can use the power to sign referral letters to exchange favours with *guanxi*.' Patients were reimbursed for their consultations with outside doctors. Because these consultations were expensive, heavy use of such referrals consumed the *danwei*'s health care budget, leaving very little to upgrade the hospital's facilities and services. Because facilities and services were poor, patients turned to outside doctors. The vicious cycle came full circle.

The system was inefficient primarily because expenditures were passed directly to the state budget and did not represent a cost to enterprise management: hence there were few incentives to control cost. Secondly, it was inefficient because there was no competition from within or outside the *danwei*. It was a closed system and there was no pressure on the system to improve. Thirdly, it was inefficient because its staff and workers could afford to be inefficient. Just like their colleagues in production units, their jobs were 'iron rice bowl' jobs. Even if they performed poorly, it was unlikely that they would lose their jobs. The situation in the hospital, the school and other units providing welfare services mirrored exactly that of the *danwei* of which they were sub-units.

Reforms reshaping the *danwei* welfare economy had brought about very important changes. These were not uniform across all units providing welfare. Some units had moved faster and had introduced more radical changes than others. The general direction of the changes were, however, very clear. These changes opened up the previously closed system, brought the market in, introduced competition, increased the managerial autonomy of these units, and made them responsible for their own profits and losses. The overall effects of these changes, as had happened to the canteens, were to make these units more efficient service-providers. As described by Qian, general manager of the Labour Service Company, what had happened was most remarkable: 'We all felt a sense of urgency and crisis. All worked doubly hard. Everybody

worked more than eight hours and stayed until 10 p.m. No one complained about working overtime. And we did it. We were able to not
only break even but also make profits. The pay of our workers has risen
by 40 to 50 per cent in three years.'

Field data showed that the *danwei* welfare economy emerging from
the changes that had happened had become on the whole more
efficient. As a result it had also become less a burden and liability to
the *danwei*.

6. Distribution of risks and responsibilities

The Chinese system of occupational welfare made state-sector units
bear all risks and responsibilities. This was both unsound and unfair:
unsound because it gave rise to substantial costs which in the long run
could not be met; unfair because it exempted employees from all
reasonable risks and responsibilities.

The changes that had occurred through reforms of the Labour
Insurance system involved an important move in the direction of
redistributing these risks and responsibilities. Instead of the state enterprises bearing all risks and responsibilities, individual workers and their
families were to assume an increasing share of risks and responsibilities. Old age pensions, for example, were no longer the sole responsibility of employers. Workers were required to contribute to 'basic
pensions', beginning with a modest 3 per cent of a worker's wage in
the previous year, but scheduled to increase by 1 percentage point
every two years thereafter. They were also encouraged to set aside
savings for 'individual pensions plans'.

Besides the shifting of parts of the risks and responsibilities to the
workers and their families, there was also the significant move to pool
risks between enterprises. The three key insurance programmes,
'unemployment insurance', 'basic pensions' and 'health insurance', all
contained important pooling features.

As described in Chapter 7, these developments significantly reduced
the risks and responsibilities concentrating on individual enterprises
and redistributed these both across enterprises and between enterprises
and their workers.

7. Legitimacy and growth

Chinese occupational welfare was an important source of regime legitimation. As Walder (1986: 249) points out, 'The extraordinary job security and benefits, the goods and services distributed by the state
enterprise in a situation of scarcity that affects other sectors of the

workforce more severely, is an important source of acceptance of the system.'

More specifically, Chinese occupational welfare secured the loyalty and support of urban workers in employment in the state sector. This was very important in the early years of the Republic because the socialist state was then embarking on a course of socialist industrialization which placed strategic emphases on heavy industry and on the accumulation of capital through forced saving and low wages. As we explained in Chapter 3, the success of this industrialization strategy depended to no small extent on the co-operation and support of a hard-working industrial labour force. Chinese occupational welfare performed the important function of inducing productivity and discipline from this strategic sector of the working population. In other words, the legitimating function of Chinese occupational welfare was crucial for 'growth' – for creating wealth and prosperity and economic development.

However, by the late 1970s, it was clear that the socialist economy had failed in its task. After three decades of socialism, China remained a very poor country. Its per capita GNP was among the lowest of centrally planned economies. The economy had almost ground to a standstill. Stagnation in agricultural production had posed serious problems for urban food supplies. In industry, there were serious problems of inefficiency and poor co-ordination. Stagnant wage rates and a breakdown in workplace discipline produced extremely low worker morale and high absenteeism. As described in Chapter 4, these problems pointed to the need for some type of economic reforms.

The response of the reform leaders was to liberalize the economy – to reduce the role and presence of the bureaucracy and to bring the market back in. More importance was attached to market forces, to competition and to profit and wage incentives in the allocation of resources and the distribution of goods. Alternative forms of ownership were allowed to coexist with state ownership. State enterprises were to assume a greater degree of independence. They were to produce for the market and be responsible for their own profits and losses.

The pre-reform system of occupational welfare was incompatible with these new developments. It was too exclusive; it failed to cover new occupational groups; it impeded mobility; it was inefficient and it undermined productive efficiency; and, most importantly, it had become a heavy financial burden for state enterprises. From a political asset – an important means for obtaining the loyalty and support of state industrial workers – it had become an economic liability – an obstacle to growth.

These then called for change – revamping the old system and putting in its place a new system of welfare compatible with the growth strategy of a socialist economy in market transition.

The emergence of a pluralistic system of Chinese occupational welfare

In short, the pre-reform system of Chinese occupational welfare engendered and perpetuated dependence. It provided few alternatives and choices. It was inefficient and was inequitable because it gave unjustifiable privileges to a particular group of workers. The way in which it distributed risks and responsibilities was both unsound and unfair. From an asset providing a source of legitimation it had turned into a liability, an obstacle to growth.

This study has explored the process by which the pre-reform Chinese system of occupational welfare has been superseded by a new system in which 'near-complete' dependence has given way to a model of 'limited' dependence. The new arrangements allow more autonomy and more choice to workers. It is more efficient, more flexible, more equitable and characterized by a more viable division of risks and responsibilities. It also compels the bureaucracy to take more account of market forces and encourages closer interaction between the public and private sectors and the formal and informal aspects of social and economic life. Chinese occupational welfare is, in brief, evolving from a unitary into a pluralistic system – a mixed economy of welfare.

Empirical evidence and field data showed that three separate yet interrelated sets of processes have been responsible for bringing about these changes. At the individual, the enterprise and the government level, these processes have reshaped patterns of dependence and the manner in which the *danwei* operates its welfare services. They have also led to a major reform of Labour Insurance involving significant changes in the redistribution of risks and responsibilities.

1. Reshaping dependence

The rise of the mixed economy had opened up new opportunities and options for *danwei* members. It was now possible to have second jobs, to retire early and, while on pensions, collect a second pay-cheque from a new job in the private sector, or simply give up and quit work altogether. Workers were no longer as near-completely dependent on and tied to the same *danwei* as in the past.

Workers had devised various strategies to enable them to make the most of these new options and opportunities. The exemplary case of Ms Feng, an unskilled worker, illustrated some of the most commonly followed strategies. Ms Feng planned to retire in three years' time when she reached the retirement age of 45. Upon retirement, she intended to take up a job in the non-state sector. As a pensioner, she would be entitled to not just her monthly pensions but also *danwei* housing and most *danwei* benefits. The strategy would allow her to hold on to what she was enjoying at the *danwei* at the same time as it enabled her to collect a second pay-cheque from a non-state job.

But, even more strategically, Ms. Feng's husband, a co-worker, would also be quitting his job in one or two years' time to take up a job in the non-state sector. The strategy, in other words, was to combine the concept of 'one family, two systems' with the concept of 'husbands go, wives stay'. Positioning key members of the family in both the state and the non-state sectors, the strategy enabled the family to maximize what it could gain from both sectors and minimize the risks of the couple either both staying in the same *danwei* or both quitting their jobs. What was being worked out was an arrangement straddling two systems of advantages and opportunities, enabling the family to have the best of both worlds – the security and welfare of the public sector and the profits and challenge of the private sector.

The 'one family, two systems' and 'husbands go, wives stay' strategy did not always work out. It depended on whether one was young or old, whether one was married or not married, whether both husband and wife were working, whether they were both working in the same *danwei*, whether both were approaching retirement age, and so on. Gender, generational and familial differences such as these opened up, just as they also closed off, different options and opportunities for workers in different stages of life and family situations. Because there were these differences, there were also many variations in the strategies actually worked out. These then led to differential outcomes: some workers were more able than other workers to gain from arrangements straddling two systems of advantages and opportunities. As a result they became also better able than other workers to move away from their near-complete dependence on the *danwei*.

What was happening was, in short, a process reshaping dependence. Emerging from this process was increasingly a pattern of limited instead of near-complete, and differentiated instead of uniform dependence on occupational welfare.

2. Reshaping the *danwei* welfare economy

The *danwei* had to reshape its welfare economy because it was inefficient and not cost-effective. The quality of its service and what it distributed to its members was poor. Choice by users was limited. Most importantly, welfare was becoming a financial burden to the enterprise.

However, the *danwei* had but few options. Giving up welfare altogether was out of the question because (a) it had a responsibility to its workers, (b) the government was not always willing and ready to take over what the *danwei* gave up, (c) the government was against the *danwei* giving up their welfare responsibilities altogether because this might have wider social and political ramifications, and (d) welfare was a valuable work incentive, instrumental for motivating workers and inducing them to stay within their enterprises.

The *danwei* was given the 'impossible' task of reducing its financial welfare burden without giving up its welfare responsibilities. The main strategy to accomplish this, as exemplified in our case study, has been to combine welfare with business and to link the bureaucracy to the market, or, in other words, to 'go quasi-market'.

Specifically, this involves pricing and selling for profit part of what used to be free or almost free benefits and services to users either within or outside the *danwei*, or both. Such policy changes, however, require some kind of product or price differentiation between 'commodified' and 'non-commodified' goods and services. It also requires the creation of markets – either internal or external or both internal and external, in which to sell 'commodified' goods and services.

The strategy of 'going quasi-market' has resulted in a differentiated *danwei* welfare economy, one which uses the bureauracy to distribute benefits and services at the same time as it employs the service of the market to sell for profit price- and product-differentiated goods and services. In these respects the *danwei* system is becoming a mixed economy of welfare.

This mixed *danwei* economy of welfare extends the range of goods and services made available to its members. It offers more choices. By bringing in the market, it generates competition and gives more priority to consumer preferences and consumer needs. It encourages the *danwei* to be more productive.

What is also important is that it enables *danwei* sub-units like canteens and nurseries to generate income from their business activities which goes towards improving their services or increasing what they pay their workers. The mixed economy of welfare helps reduce, therefore, their dependence on the *danwei* and to some extent enables them to stand on their own feet. By helping these sub-units to stand on their feet, welfare becomes less a financial burden for the *danwei*.

As a result of 'going quasi-market', *danwei* sub-units providing welfare become differentiated both in terms of their performance and their financial dependence.

The *danwei* economy of welfare emerging from the changes that have occurred is at once more efficient, more open, more flexible and more responsive. It is also more pluralistic and more differentiated. The monolithic, rigid, closed and inefficient system of the past has given way to a mixed *danwei* economy of welfare.

3.   Reforming Labour Insurance

The hallmark of Chinese occupational welfare was a comprehensive Labour Insurance scheme covering old age pensions, maternity and birth, health insurance, and accidents and death for state-sector employees and their dependants.

The scheme was non-contributory, non-portable and it excluded rural workers and other urban occupational groups. Starting in 1969, the scheme also made the state enterprises bear all the financial responsibility. While it had worked in the past, by the 1980s it had become unfit for an economy increasingly characterized by contractual employment and mobility of labour, by the rise of new occupational groups outside the state sector, by market competition, and by increasing instances of bankruptcies, mergers and workers becoming unemployed. It had also become, for the state enterprises, a big financial burden, as insurance costs increased and as more and more workers joined the growing army of retired workers.

The Labour Insurance reforms were based on six key concepts and ideas – of risk pooling, of a personalized insurance account to which the employer and the employee both made contributions, the sharing of responsibilities between the state, the enterprise, the individual, the idea that 'basic' statutory insurance should be supplemented by additional non-statutory, optional insurance programmes to provide for more flexibility and protection, the idea that the financing and administration of insurance should be separate from enterprise management, and the idea that there could be different insurance programmes for different groups of workers and for different purposes.

These reforms started in 1986 with the introduction of old age pensions for workers on contractual employment and unemployment insurance for state workers displaced from their jobs. They were followed, in 1991, by the introduction of a new nation-wide system of old age pensions combining the concept of pooling and individual contributions for state-sector employees. Further changes took place in 1995 with the extension of this system to non-statutory employees. In 1994, two pilot programmes in health insurance were launched in two cities and subsequently extended to more cities in 1996. At the same time a non-contributory maternity insurance scheme was implemented on a trial basis in 1994. Finally, a non-contributory accident insurance scheme was launched, again on a trial basis, in a few selected cities in 1993.

Although the pace of development has been uneven, much significant progress has been made. As a result of these reforms, Labour Insurance has ceased to be the kind of enterprise-based, non-contributory and non-portable system which it was before the reforms. It has been transformed into a system of insurance programmes embodying the concepts of pooling of risks, of employee contribution, of portability, and the separation of insurance administration and enterprise management. From being the exclusive rights of state employees the new system has been extended to cover also other occupational groups in the cities. Most importantly, the new system has also achieved the redistribution of risks and responsibilities away from the enterprise to the state and to individual workers.

Towards a Chinese model of welfare pluralism

In short, the three processes of reshaping dependence, reshaping the *danwei* economy of welfare and reforming Labour Insurance have jointly transformed Chinese occupational welfare. The system emerging from the change is no longer a unitary system worked entirely through the *danwei* bureaucracy and is no longer the exclusive rights and privileges of a special group of workers. The new system has broken with the near-complete and paternalistic dependencies of the past and it no longer exempts individuals from their shares of risks and responsibilities.

The system emerging from the change combines the state with the non-state sector and the bureaucracy with the market. It depends both on formal structures and on the informal organizations of the family and social networks. Its formal plans and policies leave plenty of scope for individual values and initiatives. The emerging system of occupational welfare is at once more diversified, more differentiated and more pluralistic. It is also, therefore, becoming more like the welfare systems of Western capitalism, suggesting, perhaps, that there is a tendency in the change towards 'convergence', a theme alluded to by Mishra (1977:

149) in his earlier reflections on the nature of social policy in the former Soviet-type societies:

> Moreover, recent economic reforms in Soviet and East European societies point toward a greater use of market mechanism in the economy and wide income differentials. These economic policies cannot help affecting social policy. The situation remains somewhat unclear but in the long run their general effect may be to limit movement toward the increasing 'social' distribution decreed in Marxist ideology. This no doubt suggests a tendency toward 'convergence', namely that both Western and socialist societies may have to work with some kind of institutional welfare – a mixture of social and economic (market) distribution of goods and services.

Indeed there are striking parallels and similarities between the Western and the Chinese models of development. In the British case, for example, the development during the 1980s, under successive Conservative administration, had been one of 'reducing the role of the state and encouraging the growth of welfare pluralism' (Pinker 1992: 277). This development has led to the proliferation of a great variety of models of and approaches to funding and providing social services (Le Grand et al. 1993; Wistow et al. 1994). The trend is unlikely to reverse under a Labour administration, however. 'Stakeholder welfare' (Field 1996), a key Labour concept, for example, recognizes that there are limits to what the state can do to satisfy the needs of the people and that they will have to resume greater responsibility for their own welfare. Labour has advocated, for instance, the 'compulsory universalization of second pension provision to run alongside the state retirement pension' (Field 1996: 35).

In both China and Britain, therefore, there have been developments converging on a model of welfare pluralism characterized by the diversity of welfare institutions. Both recognize the limitations of a model of welfare giving the state an all-important position. Both seek a bigger and more active role for non-state institutions, particularly the market and the individuals and their families.

That, notwithstanding their very different political systems and cultural traditions, there are nevertheless converging developments in these two countries suggests, perhaps, that, as Isaiah Berlin observes, 'the world that we encounter is one in which we are faced with choices between ends equally ultimate, and claims equally absolute, the realization of some of which must inevitably involve the sacrifice of others' (Berlin 1969: 168). In other words, there cannot be 'a total acceptance of any single end' and governments in these societies, be they politically pluralist, as in Britain, or authoritarian, as in China, should accept that there is a plurality of means to reach these ends. These include not just 'a policy mix of the invisible hand of the market and the visible hands of public institutions' (Keegan 1993: 104, cited in Pinker 1994) but also, filling the gaps between and negotiating with both the market and the public institutions, 'familial and community-based forms of mutual aid' (Pinker 1994).

The social and political implications of the transformation of Chinese occupational welfare

The transformation of a system of occupational welfare which is as important to the life of the people as is the Chinese system will no doubt have very significant social and political implications. Let me, therefore, conclude this study by pointing out and speculating on some of the most significant implications which are likely to follow from the changes.

First, the end of near-complete dependence on the *danwei* and the redistribution of risks and responsibilities away from the enterprise implies inevitably a shifting of more responsibilities and risks back to the family. How might these changes affect the family? Both 'positive' and 'negative' outcomes are possible. On the one hand, 'given new incentives for individuals to develop family- and kin-based strategies of cooperation, one would … expect a resurgence of … risk-sharing institutions' (Davis and Harrell 1993: 18) and the emergence of new forms of family solidarity. On the other, the 'greater competition at the workplace and more approval of individualistic striving undermined the willingness of some family members to sacrifice for another' (ibid.: 19). The assumption by the family of more welfare functions and responsibilities could accentuate the tension between two core traditional values of urban Chinese families: the desire to sacrifice for dependents, and the commitment to 'judicious investment of family resources … [for the advancement] of the social status of the family' (Phillips 1993: 298). In other words, it could also generate new tensions and undermine family solidarity.

Secondly, the *danwei* is becoming less and less the *Gemeinschaft* model that it once was. It is ceasing to be the kind of 'total community' (Shirk 1993: 31) which embraced and controlled so many aspects of the life of its members. The availability of alternatives and exit options, the rise of a *danwei* mixed economy of welfare, the shifting of risks and responsibilities to the individual workers and the end of near-complete dependence are all contributing to its decline. The demise of the *danwei* as a total community implies a decline in the control of individuals by a society that has been labelled 'intrusive, supervised, molded, centrally planned, totalistic'. As pointed out by Litwak (1965: 310), 'Where the giver is never in a position to provide the entire service, then he is not in a position to ask for complete subservience.' The decline of the *danwei* community implies the decline of control over the individuals and their families by the socialist state and, for the individuals and their families, increasing independence, autonomy and individuality.

Thirdly, the extension to other occupational groups in society of rights previously enjoyed only by state-sector employees has two important implications. First, it means the decline of state employees as a 'status group' and of the function of occupational welfare in status stratification. Secondly, as the importance of 'status' declines and as other groups in society come to share the rights previously enjoyed by one privileged sector, the concept of citizenship begins to assume a more universalist character.

Citizenship begins where status ends. The transformation of Chinese occupational welfare heralds the beginning of the end of status and status privileges. The next big status division to be crossed in the long march to universal and uniform citizenship rights will be the division between rural and urban workers. This was a system of unequal rights which has been legitimated since 1958 with the introduction of household registration requirements.

It is perhaps appropriate, therefore, that this study should end on a Marshallian note. In his classic formulation, Marshall describes social rights as embracing 'the whole range from the right to a modicum of economic welfare and security to the right to share to the full in the social heritage and to live the life of a civilized being according to the standards prevailing in society' (Marshall 1963: 74). Chinese occupational welfare should be seen as part of a broader progressive history of expanding citizenship and citizenship rights in China.

Qualifications regarding relevance

China is a big country. The province of Guangdong alone is geographically as big as the United Kingdom. Within China, there are great inter-regional economic as well as cultural differences. These are most pronounced between the cities and the countryside and between coastal and inland cities. It is appropriate, therefore, that we should end this study by pointing out its limitations. This is, after all, a case study carried out in one industrial enterprise in one coastal city in a large country. It is important that it should refrain from over-claiming what it could generalize about situations in the country as a whole.

At the present time, much interesting empirical research is being undertaken in different parts of China.[1] Large parts of this huge country are still unresearched. It may very well be that as the process of marketization proceeds, a number of different models or sub-models will emerge in the Chinese context. In brief, future comparisons may show not only that the Chinese system is markedly different from the Western model in some key respects, but also that there are some very significant differences within China.

The natural interest in developing broad comparative models as quickly as possible should nevertheless be resisted. In our view, the best way forward is by careful case studies over a period of time undertaken in key localities which will reveal differences as well as similarities. With regard to the quality of life enjoyed by ordinary people and the notion of justice which they entertain, it may well be that the differences will prove to be politically more important than their similarities.

Notes

Chapter 1

1 In 1991, for instance, the country spent Y109.4 billion on Labour Insurance, a key component of occupational welfare, but only Y7.1 billion on direct services and poor relief, and Y14 billion on poor families in the rural areas (Zhu 1993: 46, 47, 53). Poor families in rural villages have access to a 'Five Guarantee Scheme' (see, for example, Chow 1988: 51), which 'guarantees' food, housing, clothes, medical care and burial expenses. In 1991, while only 2.66 million rural poor people benefited from the 'scheme', 60 times as many (162.7 million) urban workers and retired workers were enjoying welfare and protection provided through their work-units (Zhu 1993: 47, 49). In 1991, there were 343 million urban and 2.5 times as many (855 million) rural residents (State Statistical Bureau 1995: 59).

2 'Danwei, "work-unit", is an administrative term referring to the organization of almost all urban workplaces under the authority of the central government' (Henderson and Cohen 1984: 139).

3 Dagang Petroleum, for example, had 189 canteens, 37 nurseries, 9 hospitals, 37 clinics, 30 primary schools, 21 secondary schools, and numerous shops, grocery stores, bathrooms and other facilities. It was a typical example of a 'da erh chuan' work-unit, i.e. it was large and all-embracing (Dagang Shiyou Guanli Ju, 1996: 70–1). Smaller work-units may not have as many facilities and services. Nevertheless, they tend to be 'xiao erh chuan', i.e. small but also all-embracing.

4 See, for example, Moonman (1973: xi) and Titmuss (1958).

5 This position is not shared by 'modern conservatives' who are critical of a social policy based on rights, citizenship and entitlement because it neglects the importance of obligation, responsibility, and duty (Meade 1986).

6 The index to Esping-Andersen's widely cited The Three Worlds of Welfare Capitalism (1990), for example, does not have any entry on 'occupational welfare'.

7 '[P]ermanent workers in state industrial enterprises are the only segment of the industrial labour force to participate fully in the welfare state' (Walder 1986: 40). Temporary workers are largely denied these benefits. Benefits for workers in the collective sector are unstable and never approach the same level of the state sector.

8 It appears that this is not unique to China. Simpura (1994: 165), for instance, also remarks that in Russia and the Baltic States there was a system very similar to what was found in China: 'Production and consumption were, in a way, organized in the same units. Production units, and all other workplaces as well, were not only a source of monetary income but also distributive channels for various commodities and services to the workers ... The workplaces were responsible for the satisfaction of a large part of the

material and social needs of the employees. Commodities and services were distributed through the workplace. The technical management ran the production, trade unions were in charge of the distribution of goods and services, and party organs dealt with control and coordination. All these three functions were intertwined, both on the level of workplaces and of the municipalities. In western terms, the need for services outside the workplaces was relatively limited.' Manning (1992: 42) also notes that 'soviet welfare was, in Titmuss's terms, largely reminiscent of occupational welfare'. What distinguishes the Chinese system from its Soviet counterparts was that Chinese workers were dependent on occupational welfare to a much greater extent, as explained by Walder (1986: 74–5): 'The Chinese pattern differs from the Soviet in two important respects. First, the Soviet Union has not had a system of job allocation through labour bureaux since the early 1930s, relying instead on local advertisements, word of mouth, and, in recent decades, employment agencies. Second, the rates of labor turnover there are considerably higher in the state sector than interviewed and document suggest is the case in China.' Granick (1991) concludes that China is the norm rather than the exception among centrally planned socialist economies in providing some form of an iron rice bowl for state employees.

  9 Two-thirds (65.2 per cent) of the workers interviewed in a 1988 survey of urban residents had never worked for another work-unit. Around one quarter (24.0 per cent) had changed their jobs only once (Li and Wang 1992: 278).

10 On the concept of 'gatekeeper', see also Pahl (1975: 206) who defines 'gatekeepers' as 'those crucial urban types ... who control or manipulate scarce resources and facilities'.

11 The concepts 'rent' and 'rent-seeking behaviour' also throw light on the strategic position of the 'gatekeepers'. In the light of these concepts, rent can be 'administratively generated' (Krueger 1974), as when, within the *danwei*, power to mediate the distribution of welfare is given to certain 'gate-keeping' positions. Occupants of these positions appropriate the value of the rent in the form of bribes (financial corruption) or political loyalty.

12 The cultivation of personal connections (*guanxi*) is not, however, new. It is a prominent feature of Chinese society (Fried 1954).

13 The crucial notion here is that unequal exchange between two parties, in which one depends on the other for services or resources, results in a power relationship between them. See Emerson (1962) and Blau (9164) for some classic statements on this perspective.

14 See Yu (1991) for an insightful discussion of this culture.

15 The proportion of the population aged 60 and above increased from 7.6 per cent in 1982 to 8.9 per cent in 1989 (Zhou 1995: 158).

16 The number of state-sector employees receiving medical care insurance provided through the workplace increased by 90 per cent from 72 million in 1980 to 137 million in 1991 (Zhou 1995: 158).

17 A survey of 28 state-owned enterprises in Guangzhou found 15 of them spending all their Labour Insurance and Welfare Funds on health care (Bo and Dong 1993: 196).

18 Kornai visited China in 1985 and found that the phenomenon of 'soft-budget constraint' was prevailing there too: 'In the course of our talks with Chinese economists they used this expression, which they had learnt from Hungarian literature, repeatedly' (Kornai 1990: 192).

19 The State Council introduced the Bankruptcy Law in November 1988, but few enterprises took that course in the beginning. In the first six months of 1992, 'fifteen state-operated and forty-one other enterprises declared bankruptcy. These figures are minuscule ... However, this small number of bankruptcy is a great improvement over the previous five years during which only two state-operated and ninety-eight other enterprises went bankrupt' (Field 1993: 251).

20 In 1994, the ratio of employees to retirees was 5.1 in state-owned enterprises and 12.5 in the non-state sector. Expenses on retirement benefits were respectively Y102.20 billion and Y2.73 billion (State Statistical Bureau 1995).

21 The taxation of enterprises depends on their ownership. State-owned enterprises, urban collectives, rural collectives, private enterprises, individual household enterprises, foreign enterprises and joint ventures are all taxed differently. Joint ventures and foreign enterprises are taxed more lightly than domestic enterprises, except village and township enterprises. Large and medium-sized state-owned enterprises pay 55 per cent of their profits in tax, while small enterprises are subject to a progressive tax scale rising from 10 to 55 per cent. Urban collectives pay taxes on the same progressive rate structure as small state-owned enterprises. Township and village enterprises pay only a 20 per cent tax. 'The application of different rates of tax to different bases for different types of enterprises distorts the economy by preventing equal competition' (Wong et al. 1995: 59).

22 The 'triangular debt' problem indicates a debt chain in which firm A is indebted to firm B, firm B to firm C, and firm C to firm A (see, for example, Lee 1996: 274–7). As a result, all have found excuses not to repay their debt. Triangular debts are bad debts.

23 The accumulated losses among state banks during the first six months of 1995 amounted to 2.9 billion yuan (Li 1996: 63).

24 There were reports of an alarming increase of incidents of 'fights, strikes, petitions and demonstrations'. Many of these had to do with social security and welfare issues, for instance, workers frustrated by their displacement from jobs in loss-making enterprises without adequate compensation and assistance (Feng 1996: 11, 284).

25 Castells so describes the 'crisis in the provision of collective consumption': the more the state assumes responsibility for the provision of social resources, the more the whole area of collective consumption becomes politicized; the fiscal crisis of the state forces it to react by cutting its level of expenditures and redirecting resources from the support of labour-power to the direct support of capital; a reduction in the level of such provision carries with it the possibility of a strong and politically organized lower-class reaction against the state itself (Castells 1977). O'Connor argues that the capitalist state must try to fulfil two basic and often mutually contradictory functions – accumulation and legitimization. 'This means that the state must try to maintain or create the conditions in which capital accumulation

is possible. However the state also must try to maintain or create the conditions for social harmony. A capitalist state that openly uses its coercive forces to help one class accumulate capital at the expenses of other classes loses its legitimacy and hence undermines the basis of its loyalty and support. But a state that ignores the necessity of assisting the process of capital accumulation risks drying up the source of its own power, the economy's surplus production capacity and the taxes drawn from this surplus (and other forms of capital)' (O'Connor 1973: 6). The contradictory nature of these two basic functions gets the capitalist state into successive fiscal and legitimacy crises.

26 The consumer price index in cities (preceding year = 100) was 114.7 in 1993 and 124.1 in 1994 (State Statistical Bureau 1995: 233).

27 According to one official source, in 1990, private sector entrepreneurs were earning 2.2 times more than the average state sector workers (State Statistical Bureau 1991: 18–20).

Chapter 2

1 I visited the enterprise again in December 1995.
2 Pseudonyms are given to protect the identity of the informants.
3 Pseudonym.
4 Chinese industrial firms are categorized as 'small', 'medium' or 'large' according to sector-specific productive capacities rather than by the numbers of workers. However, as a rule, large and medium-sized firms have more than 1,000 employees, and small firms have fewer than 1,000 employees (Shirk 1993: 30). DFMW was, by this standard, a large industrial firm.
5 In terms of population size, Guangzhou is China's 20th largest city. In terms of gross output value of industry, it ranks fourth, after Shanghai, Beijing, and Tianjin (State Statistical Bureau 1995: 312).

Chapter 3

1 These questions have also intrigued Susan Shirk (1993), who could not understand why China had created 'unitism', the system in which work-units assumed wide-ranging responsibilities towards their members: 'Why unitism was created in China in the early 1960s remains something of a mystery because it was economically irrational in the context of China's abundant supply of labour. In fact, it would have been more economically logical for Soviet industry, facing a labour shortage, to extend generous welfare and security privileges to its permanent workers than it was for Chinese industry, with its plentiful supply of labour' (Shirk 1993: 31).
2 On this see the authoritative study of Wright (1957).
3 This will be discussed in the next section.
4 Skocpol defines in the Weberian tradition a state as 'any set of relatively differentiated organs that claims sovereignty and coercive control over a territory and its population, defending and perhaps extending that claim in competition with other states' (Skocpol 1992: 43). In the Weberian perspective, states are compulsory associations claiming control over territories and

the people within them. For Max Weber's principal writings on states, see Roth and Wittich (1968).

5 Skocpol and Weir suggested that, in the case of capitalist-industrializing countries, '"state formation" includes constitution-making, involvements in wars, electoral democratization, and bureaucratization – macropolitical processes, in short, whose forms and timing have varied significantly in capitalist-industrializing countries' (Weir et al. 1988: 17).

6 In 1941, the Border Region consisted of 29 counties, 266 districts and 1,549 townships, with a population of around 1,500,000. *Yan'an* was the administrative and political centre of the Border Region (Watson 1980: 13).

7 Though promulgated in 1951, its history went back to the early days of the Chinese Communist Party, which at various times during its struggle for power with the Nationalist Government advocated labour welfare and the provision of labour insurance. In 1948, when the CCP gained control over the Manchurian provinces, then China's most important industrial provinces, it introduced some form of labour insurance on a trial basis in state enterprises in railways, mining, arsenal, military supplies, post office and telecommunications, electricity and textiles' (Kallgren 1969: 544). But it was not until 1951 that a labour insurance scheme in its present form was introduced. For a brief description of this part of the history of labour insurance, see Chow (1988). An English translation of the full text of the Regulations can be found in an appendix to Hoffmann (1974).

8 Perceived inequalities in the treatment received by the industrial workers and the peasants had understandably evoked the latter's dissatisfaction, as expressed in a letter to the editors of *Nanfang Jihbao* (*Southern Daily*), which wrote: 'The industrial workers don't do much work and get a lot to eat, while the peasants do a lot of work and don't get much to eat. The Party takes care of the industrial workers and doesn't take care of the peasants' (*Nanfang Jihbao*, 25 October 1957).

9 'Welfare funds' were equivalent to 2.5 per cent of an enterprise's total payroll. In 1969, this percentage was increased to 11 per cent.

10 Schurmann (1968) drew attention to the meanings of heavy and light industry in the Chinese context. In contrast to the Russians, the Chinese have defined heavy industry as a 'general term for all industrial production which has a decisive function for realizing industrialization and modernization and which supplies all branches the national economy with modernized material and technical equipment'. Light industry is defined as a 'general term for all industrial production that, in the process of industrialization and modernization, only supplies all branches of the national economy with general producer and consumer goods'. According to Schurmann, the distinction is not economic but political. 'What the Chinese call heavy industry consists of industries strategically important for the developmental goals of the regime; whatever remains falls into the category of light industry' (Schurmann 1968: 80).

Chapter 4

1 'Individual firms' had fewer than eight employees and 'private firms' had eight or more employees.

2 The Joint Venture Law and the creation of Special Economic Zones were formally approved in 1979. For one insightful account of China's open policy, see (Vogel 1989).

3 Bian's (1994: 184–5) study in *Tianjin* found that the private sector firms there had none of the following benefits: health insurance for employees and their dependants, pension, injury, disability and death benefits, benefits for women workers, holiday, sick leave and leave of absence benefits, and other benefits.

4 It was not uncommon for loss-making enterprises to be doing what their profit-making counterparts were doing. In so doing they even borrowed from the bank (Liu 1993: 61).

5 In 1978, the average bonus and cost-of-living allowance comprised 10 per cent of an individual's total wage; this share increased to 40 per cent in 1988 (Hu and Li 1993: 165). In 1984, non-wage income comprised 17.4 per cent of a state worker's pay; in 1990, this share increased to 23 per cent (Di and Sun 1993: 184).

6 These were: 'Temporary Regulations on the Implementation of Labour Contracts in State-owned Enterprises', 'Temporary Regulations on the Recruitment of Workers in State-owned Enterprises', 'Temporary Regulations on the Dismissal of Workers in State-owned Enterprises Who Violate Discipline' and 'Temporary Regulations on Unemployment Insurance for Workers in state-owned Enterprises'.

7 The consumer price index in cities (preceding year = 100) was 120.7 in 1988, 116.3 in 1989, 116.1 in 1993, and 125.0 in 1994 (State Statistical Bureau 1995: 233; Zhu 1995: 195).

8 Among others, the contract committed the enterprise to: (1) produce an aggregate total of Y350 million of industrial output in the next four years and increase industrial output at an annual growth rate of 10.4 per cent; and (2) make Y40 million of profit in the next four years (Feng 1990: 29).

9 There were all together 50 bidders. Of these 29 were middle-ranking cadres, 19 were ordinary cadres and two were workers. Of the 15 successful bidders, there were 12 middle-ranking cadres, two ordinary cadres and one worker (Feng 1990: 31).

10 According to 'contract', they would be paid twice the average wage if they fulfilled targets; be given additional increases in their wages if their performance exceeded targets; be paid only subsistence wages if their performance fell short of targets by 10 to 15 per cent; and their suitability for their jobs be reconsidered if their performance fell short of targets by more than 15 per cent (Feng 1990: 33).

11 Workers displaced from their jobs as a result of this '*youhua*' process were transferred to new jobs within a newly created unit called *Laodong Fuwu Gongsi* (Labour Services Company), which looked after various 'domestic' services like nursery, canteens, cleaning, and delivery of bottled gas (Feng 1990: 32).

Chapter 5

1 In 1995, the average wage of workers in the non-state sector was 33 per cent more than that of their counterparts in the state-sector (Huang 1996: 11).

2   Even more serious than this was *daogong*, or 'robbing the public'. An instance of *daogong* occurred in 1995 when the unemployed workers of a state-owned enterprise in the province of Hunan raided their work-unit and seized whatever was valuable. They did so because they had not been paid their unemployment insurance six months after it was due (Feng 1996: 286).

3   At DFMW, skilled jobs were dominated by male workers. Female workers mostly occupied jobs requiring low level skills, unskilled jobs and menial jobs. About 80 per cent of the plant's female workers were in these jobs. Male dominance in the sexual division of labour at the workplace was common among Chinese industrial enterprises.

4   For example, Article 13 of 'The Marriage Law of the People's Republic of China' promulgated on 1 May 1950 stipulates that 'Parents have the duty to rear and to educate their children; the children have the duty to look after and to assist their parents. Neither the parents nor the children shall maltreat or desert one another' (Yang 1965: 221–6).

5   There are occasional reports of abusive children who have been reprimanded and forced to provide support (Davis-Friedmann 1983: 126).

6   A large-scale survey of 10,959 elderly persons aged 60 and above in three provinces (Hubei, Jilin, Liaoling) and two cities (Beijing, Shanghai) found 20.8 per cent of them living with their spouses, 48.9 per cent with married children, 18.3 per cent with unmarried children, 6.7 per cent alone and 5.3 per cent in institutions and homes for elderly people (Zhang 1990: 185). In the majority of the cases, elderly persons lived with their children.

7   One important way was to pass the father's job to a son or a daughter through 'replacement' (*ting-ti*).

8   The same three-province–two-city survey found 31.2 per cent of the interviewed elderly respondents receiving their principal sources of income from children; 35.2 per cent relying mainly on their pensions; and 19.2 per cent earning their own incomes from employment. Pertaining mainly to principal sources of income, these figures do not reflect supplementary or in-addition kinds of income. Had these latter kinds of incomes been taken into account, the actual extent of children financially supporting their parents could be of a level much higher than 31.2 per cent (Zhang 1990: 189).

9   Myron L. Cohen cogently described this as follows: 'The arrangement of familial economic roles such as redistributor, manager or worker and the pooling and redistribution of resources are characteristics of [Chinese] family life adaptable to a great variety of economic activities' (Cohen 1976).

10 During 1983 there were many local efforts to crack down on private business. Again, in 1986, there was a crackdown on private business (Gold 1990: 164–5).

11 Per-worker welfare cost of female workers was 1.34 times as much as that of male workers (Sha 1995: 27).

12 Importantly, female workers were entitled to maternity leave on very favourable terms. On the whole, female workers did take more leave and for longer leave period than male workers. According to one study, the leave taken by female workers in state-owned enterprises was 7.29 times as long as the leave taken by male workers. Leave taken by female workers aged between 26 and 35 was 9.6 times as long (Sha 1995: 14).

13 A survey conducted by the All-China Federation of Trade Unions in 1997 found less than 30 per cent of its respondents still believed in communism. This result was 40 per cent down from the result of a similar survey conducted in 1982. (*Apple Daily* 6 May 1997).

Chapter 6

1 'It was characterized by its *"fuli xing"* (free or heavily subsidized benefits and services), its *"fengbi xing"* (its being a closed system), and its *"ziwo fuwu xing"* (self-serving)' (Gu 1996: 41).
2 The Tai Yuan Steels Works, a huge state-owned enterprise established in the 1930s, had 30 schools, 7 hospitals, 12 nurseries and a large number of other services and facilities for workers. It successfully 'dissociated' itself from its schools and hospitals through 'returning' these to the Tai Yuan City Government (Zhang 1996: 2).
3 Usually, the contract would specify the minimum amount of profits the sub-unit must remit to the enterprise. The contract could also lay down other terms. For a brief introduction to the evolution of the Contract Responsibility System, see Koo et al. (1993: 33–80).
4 For example, *Baogang* Steel Works, a huge steel manufacturing plant in Shanghai, tried this approach in recent years (Zhang 1996: 3).
5 In the case of retirees, the formula required them to contribute to only 10 per cent of their medical bills. Their '*baohu xian*' was fixed at Y350.

Chapter 7

1 The 'Labour Insurance Regulations of the People's Republic of China' promulgated in 1951. See Chapter 3 on its origins.
2 See Chapter 3 on the origins of Labour Insurance.
3 T. H. Marshall defined 'status' in a manner applicable here as 'a position to which is attached a bundle of rights and duties, privileges and obligations, legal capacities and incapacities, which are publicly recognized and which can be defined and enforced by public authority' (quoted in Poggi 1978: 43).
4 See Chapter 3, above, on the nature of China's socialist industrialization strategy and its commitment to labour welfare.
5 Constitution of the People's Republic of China adopted at the Fifth Session of the Fifth National People's Congress and Promulgated for Implementation by the Proclamation of the National People's Congress on 4 December 1982. Foreign Language Press, Beijing, 1987.
6 In 1985, for example, the average annual wage of employees in state-owned units was only Y1213, or just slightly more than Y100 a month (State Statistical Bureau 1995: 113).
7 The gross output value of industry in 1994, for example, was, for Eastern Cities, Y5168.96 billion, for Central Cities, Y1544.53 billion, and, for Western Cities, Y734.83 billion (State Statistical Bureau 1995: 298–9).
8 On this see a good discussion in (Chow 1988: 59–74).

9   Among these was a proposal from the World Bank. The World Bank sent an economic mission to China in 1984 and completed a report in 1985 on the key developmental issues that China might face in the next two decades. The report, entitled *China: Long-Term Development Issues and Options*, included a discussion on the Chinese social security system. For an outline on relevant issues in this report, see (Chow 1988: 70–2).
10 Chow (1988: 66–70) outlines main points presented in these proposals.
11 For an example of this formula of cost-sharing, please refer to the case of the *danwei* hospital discussed in Chapter 6.

Chapter 8

1   These include, among others, Henderson and Cohen (1984), Nee (1989), Oi (1989), Wong (1992), Bian (1994) and Yang (1994).

Appendices

I Fieldwork Checklist

The Dongfang Heavy Machinery Works

1. The evolution and development of the plant up to the present

When was it established?

What did/does it produce?

How and when did it become a state enterprise?

How has the size and composition of its workforce changed over time?

Its supervisory structure (from which government departments did/does it receive orders)

Its management structure – has it changed over time?

Its labour, wage and bonus systems

'Workers' Congress': its position and role in the plant

The Party: its position and role in the plant

How had it fared (e.g. during the Great Leap Forward, 1958–60, and during the Cultural Revolution 1967–76)? What happened?

Its economic performance: output, productivity, profits and losses.

2. The plant's evolution into a 'mini-welfare state':

Past and present: the range and nature of welfare and benefits (subsidies, Labour Insurance, pension, hardship allowances, single-child allowance, health care, housing, canteen, nursery, housing, etc.) provided through the *danwei*.

Past and present: who were/are entitled to what; how were/are benefits actually distributed; through what policies, rules, norms, procedures and mechanisms were/are these distributed; who were/are involved in making decisions which have bearing on the distribution of welfare and benefits? Which departments/ sections/bureaus were/are involved? How equally and equitably were/are these benefits distributed?

Past and present: How did/do *danwei* members regard and use welfare benefits? the meanings of welfare and benefits to them.

Why had the *danwei* taken on more and more welfare responsibilities? How and when did these changes occur? Had there been 'cutbacks' in the welfare and benefits distributed through the *danwei*? What had changed? What had not changed during all these years?

What explained these changes and developments?

- historical contexts (e.g. state formation, First Five Year Plan, Great Leap Forward, Cultural Revolution);

- urban political economy (e.g. planned economy, employment problems, strict control over rural-urban migration, retarded development of the tertiary sector);

- ideas (how were these changes and developments explained?);

- state policies (e.g. policies favouring urban and industrial development);

- values and ideology (e.g. PRC's Constitution, socialist ideology, traditional cultural values);

- macro-politics (e.g. state's quest for legitimacy and control, inter-departmental competition);

- micro-politics (interaction between Party, plant management, workers, *guanxi* and local bureaucrats, party cadres, and community elites).

3.   The challenge of the market

How did economic reforms since 1979 – emergence of a dual-track economy, financial reforms which give more autonomy to the enterprises, director responsibility system, contract labour and bankruptcy law, and so on – impact on the plant?

What has happened to its economic performance, operations and management, size and composition of its staff, labour and wage policies?

In what ways have these affected the *danwei*'s policies and provisions of welfare and benefits?

Do these have different kinds of impacts on *danwei* members?

How do *danwei* members regard these changes?

Have these caused changes in their values, orientations and relations? Have they become more individualistic and instrumental in their relations with one another and with the danwei collectivity?

Have these affected management-worker relations? How?

Are new policies being considered and debated? Who have espoused which positions?

II Interviewing Schedule

Name:
Sex:
Age:
Marital Status:
Job/Position:
Party Member: yes/no
Cadre: yes/no
Household Information:

Name	Age	Relation with	Occupation
(same danwei?)		Interviewee	(Yes/No)

1. When did you join the plant?
2. What was your job and position then?
3. Do you remember the wage that you earned then?
4. Besides wage, what other non-wage income and benefits did you receive from the *danwei*, on a regular basis and then on special occasions? Could you itemize them for us?
5. (a) Were you and/or your family entitled to *danwei* housing?
   (b) Did you live there?
   (c) Could you describe its size?
   (d) How much rent did you pay for it?
6. Did you and/or your family make much use of other facilities and services provided by the *danwei*?
7. Much of what you have just told us must have changed between then and now. Could you describe to us how things have changed? What are some of the more recent changes? (Check: wage, non-wage income and benefits, housing, other facilities and services.)
8. Let us concentrate on changes since 1979.
   (a) Were these changes related to changed policies in the plant?
   (b) What were these? (Probe: wage reform, employment reform, housing reform, pension reform ...)
9. In your view, what were the reasons behind such policy changes?
10. (a) Were the changes related also to wider social, political and economic changes?
    (b) What were/are these?
11. (a) In what ways have the changes which you have just told us affected you and your family?
    (b) How have you and your family adjusted to these changes? (Probe: for example, moonlighting.)
12. Are the experiences of you and your family quite typical or exceptional? (If typical) Do you know of workers and their families whose experiences are atypical? Could you tell us about their experiences? (for example: contract and young workers).

(If exceptional) Do you know of workers and their families whose experiences are very common in the *danwei*? Could you tell us about their experiences?

13. In your view, are the changes for the better, or for the worse:
    (a) for yourself and your family?,
    (b) for workers like yourself, and their families?,
    (c) for other categories of *danwei* members (check where applicable: cadres, managerial staff, professional staff, technical staff, ordinary workers, service workers)?, and
    (d) for the plant as a whole?

14. We have talked about *danwei* welfare and benefits. Let us now look at the people. Workmates can be good friends.
    (a) In your experience, has it been easy to make friends in the plant? With whom?
    (b) What do friends do? Please give us some examples of what good friends do for each other.

15. In your own experience, are friends becoming more or less easy to make? Are they as 'good' as in the past?

16. (a) Besides friends, would you say that there are *guanxi* (personal connections) which would be important and/or useful for people to have?
    (b) In what ways are these *guanxi* important and/or useful?

17. (a) Has the nature of *guanxi* in the *danwei* changed much during your time here? In what ways?
    (b) How would you explain such changes?
    (c) Do you like or dislike such changes?

18. (a) Could you describe to us the guanxi that are important to *you personally*?
    (b) In what ways are they important?
    (c) Who are your important *guanxi*?
    (d) How do you nurture your *guanxi*?

19. (a) Has your own *guanxi* changed much during your time here? In what ways has it changed?
    (b) Could you explain the changes?
    (c) Do you like or dislike such changes?

20. (a) *Danwei lingdao* (leaders) are important people in the plant. Could you tell us why in your view they are important?
    (b) Are they becoming more important or less important? Why?

21. What about the Party? Do you find any difference in its position and role in the plant?

22. (a) Let's come to the trade union. Has it been able to do much for workers? What has it done?
    (b) Has the trade union changed much during your time here?

23. We all try to improve our lot, and some have done it better than the others. In your view, what are the sorts of things that one should try to *do* or *have*, the *right* kind of behaviour and attitudes, so to speak, in order to keep up with, let alone to be better than, the others in the *danwei*?

24. It is common for workers to feel a sense of belongingness to their *danwei*. Some feel it stronger than the others.

(a) In your view, do workers in your plant generally feel a sense of belongingness to the *danwei*? Why would you say so?

(b) Now during your time here, would you say that workers' sense of belongingness has grown stronger, or weaker? Why's that?

25. Now, on the whole, would you say that your *danwei* has become a better place or a worse place to work in?

26. (a) Given the chance, would you quit and look for better opportunities elsewhere?

(b) If you were to quit and go elsewhere, where would you go?

27. If you could do it all over again, would you still have preferred this *danwei*? (If yes) Tell us why.
(If no) Tell us what could have been a better *danwei* for you and why you think it could be better?

28. There is now much discussion and debate about reforming *danwei* benefits and welfare. One viewpoint has it that *danwei* should no longer be as heavily committed to welfare and that workers should pay, at least partially, for what they are getting. What is your own view on this?

29. Now, talking about the future, do you have particular changes or contingencies in mind?

III   List of Informants Interviewed

Informants interviewed. Pseudonyms given, age when interviewed, jobs held.

1. Ms Cao, 43, semi-skilled worker
2. Mr Chen, 50's, head of propaganda department
3. Ms Chen, 50's, teacher at vocational school
4. Mr Deng, 50, director of a subsidiary company
5. Mr Dong, 50's, deputy party secretary
6. Ms Feng, 42, unskilled worker
7. Mr Han, 30's, chief of secretariat of the general affairs office
8. Miss He, 20's, computer programmer
9. Mr Li, 40's, deputy head of personnel department
10. Mr Liao, 50's, head of the plant's general affairs office
11. Ms Ma, 43, skilled worker
12. Dr Mao, 40's, director of hospital
13. Mr Peng, 40, skilled worker
14. Mr Qian, 40's, general manager of the plant's labour services company
15. Mr Qiao, chief of secretariat of the general affairs office
16. Dr Shan, 40's, deputy director of hospital
17. Mr Shi, 40's, deputy head of corporate management department
18. Mr Tai, 50's, chairman of labour union
19. Ms Tan, 40's, headmistress of nursery
20. Mr Tang, 30's, senior accountant
21. Mr Tao, 24, driver
22. Mr Wang, 50's, principal of vocational school
23. Mr Wei, 40's, deputy general manager of the plant
24. Mr Wen, 30's, principal of the plant's school
25. Mr Wu, 40's, deputy head of propaganda department
26. Mr Xu, 40's, general manager of the plant
27. Ms Zhou, 41, semi-skilled worker
28. Mr Zhu, 37, skilled worker

Glossary of Terms

Anlau fenpei	按勞分配	Distribution to each according to his/her work
Baohu xian	保護線	Protection point
Bao xia lai	包下來	Take on all and be responsible for all
Butei	補貼	Subsidies
Changzhang fuzezhi	廠長負責制	Factory director responsibility system
Changping cang	常平倉	Ever-normal granary
Chaogang	炒更	Moonlighting
Chejian	車間	Workshops
Cheng bao	承包	Contract responsibility
Chengshi hukou	城市戶口	Urban residence
Chun fuli	純福利	Pure welfare
Da erh chuan	大而全	large and comprehensive
Da qingnian	大青年	'Old' young people
Daigan	待崗	Rest and wait for a job; wait for a posting
Danwei	單位	Work-unit
Daogong	盜公	Robbing the public
Digongzi, gao jiuyie, gao fuli	低工資，高就業高福利	Low wage, high employment, high welfare
Dongfang Qiye Jituan Gongsi	東方企業集團公司	Dongfang Group Holding Company
Duan qui wankuai chi nou, fang xia kuaizi ma liang	端起碗筷吃肉，放下筷子罵娘	Cursing between mouthfuls

Fang shui yang yu	放水養魚	Save a fish by putting it back into the water
Fei shengchanxing jianshe touji	非生產性建設投資	Non-production-related construction and investment
Fenchang	分廠	Branches
Fengbi xing	封閉性	Its being a closed system
Fenli qiyie ban shehui zhineng	分離企業辦社會職能	disassociating the enterprise from its welfare functions
Fuli jijin	福利基金	Welfare fund
Fuli xing	福利性	Free or heavily subsidized benefits and services
Fuyu jigong	富余職工	Surplus workers
Gangau tongbao	港澳同胞	Chinese people in Hong Kong and Macau
Geren chuxuxiang yanglao baoxiang	個人儲蓄性養老保險	Individual pension plans
Geti hu	個体戶	Private entrepreneurs; individual firms
Gongfei yiliao	公費醫療	Government-funded health care
Gongji zhi	供給制	Supply system
Gongling	工齡	Seniority
Guanxi	關係	Connections
Guanli fei	管理費	Management expenditure
Hei hu	黑戶	Black household
Huiguan	會館	Guilds
Hukou	戶口	Residency status
Hukou bu	戶口簿	Residence booklet
Houqin	後勤	Domestic services
Jianli jijin	獎勵基金	Bonus fund
Jianli shehui tongzhou yiliao jijin yu geren yiliao	建立社會統籌醫療基金與個人醫療帳戶相結合的	Establish a social insurance system combining the pooling of medical funds with personalized

zhanghu xian jiehe ti shehui baoxian zhidu	社會保險制度	medical care account
Jiben yanglao baoxian geren zhanghu	基本養老保險個人帳戶	Personalized basic old age insurance account
Jiben yanglao baoxian jijin	基本養老保險基金	Basic pension funds
Juan ban	捐辦	financing and implementing
Laobao yiliao	勞保醫療	Labour Insurance
Laodong fuwu gongsi	勞動服務公司	Labour service company
Laodong hetung zhi	勞動合同制	Contract employment system
Laodong jieshao suo	勞動介紹所	Job introduction offices
Laowu fei	勞務費	Labour service fees
Lingdao	領導	Cadres and managers
Nancho nu liu	男走女留	Husbands go, wives stay
Nongcun hukou	農村戶口	Rural residence
Pingjun zhuyi	平均主義	Egalitarianism
Puji tang	普濟堂	Poor houses
Qiaojuan	僑眷	Dependants of overseas Chinese
Qing	清	Manchurian dynasty
Qinshu wang	親屬網	Networks of kin
Qiye buchong yanglao baoxian	企業補充養老保險	Enterprise supplementary old age insurance
Qiye zhigong jiben yanglao baoxian shehui tongchou yu geren zhanghu xiang jiehe	企業職工基本養老保險社會統籌與個人帳戶相結合	Combining the pooling of costs for basic old age insurance with personalized accounts for the individual workers
Qiyie ban shehui	企業辦社會	Enterprises run the society
Quan yu	勸諭	Prompt and endorse
Quane jijian	全額計件	Fully floating piece rate
San ge ren di fan wu geren chi	三個人的飯五個人吃	Share the rice for three among five persons

Shangpin hua	商品化	Commodifying
Shantang	善堂	Benevolent halls
Shang bu fengding	上不封頂	No profit ceilings
She cang	社倉	Community granaries
Shehui hua	社會化	Socializing
Shehui tongchou	社會統籌	Pooling of funds
Shuangxian xuanze	雙向選擇	Bilateral choices
Siying qiye	私營企業	Private business
Tingchan ban tingchan	停產半停產	Stopping or half-stopping production
Tingti	頂替	Replacement of parents' jobs by their children
Tongyi chouji	統一籌集	Pooling of funds
Tou gai dai	投改貸	Converting fund allocation to bank loans
Weili jingying	微利經營	Low profit-making business
Wu fang	五反	The 'five-antis'
Xia bu budi	下不補底	No subsidies for losses
Xia gang	下崗	Leave their posts
Xiang qian kan	向錢看	Money-oriented
Xiao shehei	小社會	Small society
Xiao erh chuan	小而全	Small but comprehensive
Xiaoyi	效益	Profitability
Xingzheng chu	行政處	General service unit
Xin ren xin banfa, jui ren jui banfa	新人新辦法，舊人舊辦法	New workers new method, old workers old method
Yi cang	義倉	Public granaries
Yi jia liang zhi	一家兩制	One family, two systems
Yi xue yang xue	以學養學	Using the school to support the school

Yuying tang	育嬰堂	Orphanages
Youhua laodong zuhe	优化勞動組合	Prioritizing workforce composition
Zhigong buchong yanglao baoxian chubejian shouce	職工補充養老保險儲備金手冊	worker's supplementary pensions handbook
Zhigong fuli	職工福利	Employee welfare
Zhigong yanglao baoxian shouce	職業養老手冊	Worker's old age insurance handbook
Zi gongsi	子公司	Subsidiary companies
Zifu yingkui	自負盈虧	Self-responsible for profits and losses
Ziwo fazhan	自我發展	Self-developing
Ziwo fuwu xing	自我服務性	Self-serving
Ziwo jingying	自我經營	Self-managing
Ziwo yaoshu	自我約束	Self-regulating

Bibliography

Abel-Smith, B. and R. Titmuss, 1974. *Social Policy: An Introduction*. London: Allen & Unwin.

Apple Daily. Hong Kong. Various issues.

Baird, I.S., M.A. Lyles, S. Ji and R. Wharton, 1990. 'Joint Venture Success: A Sino–U.S. Perspective', in *International Studies of Management and Organization*. Vol. 20, Nos. 1 and 2, pp. 125–34.

Beijing Shi Fu Lian (Beijing Federation of Women Associations) et al., eds. 1993. *Jing. Sui. Gang Zaizhi Nuxing Jiuye Diaocha Baogao (Reports on Three Studies of the Employment Situations of Female Workers in Beijing, Guangzhou, and Hong Kong)*.

Bennett, John W., and Iwaoshino, 1963. *Paternalism in the Japanese Economy: Anthropological Studies of Oyabun-Kobun Patterns*. Westview, Con.: Greenwood Press.

Berger, Suzanne, 1981. 'Introduction', in *Organizing Interests in Western Europe*. Ed. by Suzanne Berger, pp. 1–23. Cambridge: Cambridge University Press.

Berlin, Isaiah, 1969. *Four Essays on Liberty*. Oxford: Oxford University Press.

Bian, Yanjie, 1994. *Work and Inequality in Urban China*. Albany: SUNY Press.

Blau, Peter, 1964. *Exchange and Power in Social Life*. New York: John Wiley.

Bo, Xian-feng and Dong Jian-zhen, 1993. 'Zhong-guo yiliao weisheng gaige di xianzhuang fenshi yu yuce' ('Analysis and Forecast of Medical System Reform (1992–1993)', in *1992–1993 Nian Zhongguo: Shehui Xingshi fenshi yu yuce (China in 1992–1993: Analysis and Forecast of the Social Situations)*. Ed. by Jiang Liu et al., pp. 191–211. Beijing: Zhongguo Shehui Ke Xue ChuBan She (Social Science Press).

Bo, Yi-bo, 1991. *Ruogan Zhongda Juece yu Shijian di Huigu (Looking Back on Several Important Decisions and Issues)*. Beijing: Zhonggong Zhongyang Dangxiao Chuban She (Chinese Communist Party Central Party School Press). Vol. 1.

Boisot, M. and John Child, 1988. 'The Iron Law of Fiefs: Bureaucratic Failure and the Problem of Governance in the Chinese Economic Reforms', *Administrative Science Quarterly*. Vol. 33, pp. 507–27.

Bryson, Lois, 1992. *Welfare and the State: Who Benefits?* London: Macmillan.

Burawoy, Michael, 1991. 'The Extended Case Method', in *Ethnography Unbound*. Ed. by M. Burawoy et al., pp. 271–90. Berkeley: University of California Press.

Burawoy, Michael, and Janos Lukacs, 1985. 'Mythodologies of Work: A Comparison of Firms in State Socialism and Advanced Capitalism', *American Sociological Review*, Vol. 50, pp. 723–37.

Castells, M., *The Urban Questions*. London: Edward Arnold.

Chandler, Alfred D, 1977. *The Visible Hand*. Cambridge, Mass.: MIT Press.

Chang, Kai, 1995. 'Gong you zhi giye zhong nu zhigong di shi ye ji zai jiu ye wenti di diao cha yu yanjiao' ('An Investigation and Study of the Problems of Unemployment and Re-employment of Female Workers in Public Ownership Enterprises'), in *Shehuixue Yanjiao (Sociological Studies)*, Vol. 3, pp. 83–93.

Chen, Li-wu et al., 1990. 'Guangzhou Zhong Xing Jiqi Chang Lishi Jianjie' ('A Brief History of the Guangzhou Heavy Machinery Works'), in *Guangzhong Ren*

(The Guangzhong Workers). Ed. by Liu Zhao-ding, pp. 1–12. Guangzhou: Guangzhou Zhong Xing Jiqi Chang (Guangzhou Heavy Machinery Works).

Cheng, J., 1986. *A Chronology of the People's Republic of China 1949–1984*. Beijing: Foreign Languages Press.

Chevrier, Yves, 1990. 'Metropolis and the Factory Director Responsibility System, 1984–1987', in *Chinese Society on the Eve of Tiananmen: The Impact of Reform*. Ed. by Deborah Davis and Ezra F. Vogel. pp. 109–134. Cambridge, Mass.: Harvard University Press.

Chow, Nelson, 1988. *The Administration and Financing of Social Security in China*. Hong Kong: Centre of Asian Studies, University of Hong Kong.

Ch'u, T'ung-Tsu, 1962. *Local Government Under the Ch'ing*. Stanford, CA: Stanford University Press.

Cohen, Myron L., 1976. *House United, House Divided*. New York and London: Columbia University Press.

Dagang Shiyou Guanli Ju (Dagang Petroleum Management Bureau), 1996. 'Cong woju shenghuo houqin gaige kan jiejue wenti di tujing' ('A Discussion of Our Experience in Reforming Domestic Services and Ways to Solve Our Problems'), in *Zhongguo Houqin Gaige Zhonglun (An Overview of Reforms in Domestic Services in China)*. Ed. by Quanguo Houqin Guanli Yanjiuhui (National Association for Research on the Management of Domestic Services). pp. 70–75. Beijing: Zhongguo Qingongye Chuban She (Light Industry Press).

Dai, Yuan-chen, Li Han-ming, 1991. 'Shuangchong tizhi xia di laodongli liudong yu gongzi fenpei' ('Labour Mobility and Wage Distribution in the Dual Economy'), in *Zhongguo Shehui Kexue (Chinese Social Science)*. Vol. 5, pp. 93–108.

Dandai Zhongguo Congshu Pianji Bu (Contemporary China Series Editorial Office), 1987. *Dandai Zhongguo Di Zhigong Gongzi Fuli He Sshehui Baoxian (Employee Wage, Welfare and Social Insurance in Contemporary China)*. Beijing: Zhongguo Shehui Keshe Chuban She (Social Science Press).

Davis, Deborah, 1988. 'Unequal Chances, Unequal Outcomes', *China Quarterly*, Vol. 114, pp. 223–41.

—— 1990. 'Urban Job Mobility', in *Chinese Society on the Eve of Tiananmen*. Ed. by Deborah Davis and Ezra F. Vogel. pp. 85–108. Cambridge: The Council of East Asian Studies, Harvard University.

Davis-Friedmann, Deborah, 1983. *Long Lives: Chinese Elderly and the Communist Revolution*. Cambridge, Mass. and London: Harvard University Press.

Deacon, Bob, 1992. 'East European Welfare: Past, Present and Future in Comparative Context', in *The New Eastern Europe: Social Policy Past, Present and Future*. Ed. by Bob Deacon et al., pp. 1–30. London, Newbury Park, New Delhi: Sage.

Dernberger, Robert F., 1989. 'Reform in China: Implications for U.S. Policy', in *American Economic Review*. Vol. 79, No. 2.

Di, Huang, Sun Qun-yi, 1993. 'Guan yu quo you qiyie fenpei geju zhong zhigong shouru fenpei zhuangkuang di fenxi' ('An Analysis of the Current Situation of the Distribution of Income among Employees of State-owned Enterprises'), in *Guomin Shouru Fenpei Geju Di Pinjia Yu Juece (Evaluation and Policies Regarding the Pattern of Distribution of Income Among the Chinese People)*. Ed. by Weng Tian-zhen, et al., pp. 181–97. Beijing: Zhongguo Laodong Chuban She (Chinese Labour Press).

Doeringer, Peter B., 1984. 'Internal Labor Markets and Paternalism in Rural Areas', in *Internal Labour Markets*. Ed. by P. Osterman. pp. 271–90. Cambridge, Mass.: MIT Press.

Doeringer, Peter, and Michael J. Piore, 1971. *Internal Labor Markets and Manpower Analysis*. Lexington, Mass.: D.C. Heath.

Dore, Ronald, 1973. *Origins of the Japanese Employment System*. London: Allen & Unwin.

Elbaum, Bernard, 1984. 'The Making and Shaping of Job and Pay Structures in the Iron and Steel Industry', in *Internal Labour Markets*. Ed. by P. Osterman, pp. 71–108. Cambridge, Mass.: MIT Press.

Edwards, Richard, 1979. *Contested Terrain: The Transformation of the Workplace in the Twentieth Century*. London: Heinemann.

Edwards, Richard, M. Reich and D. M. Gordon, eds, 1973. *Labor Market Segmentation*. London: D.C. Heath.

Emerson, R. M., 1962. 'Power-dependence Relations', *American Sociological Review*, Vol. 27, pp. 31–41.

Esping-Andersen, G., 1990. *The Three Worlds of Welfare Capitalism*. Cambridge: Polity.

Fairbank, John King, 1992. *China: A New History*. Cambridge, Mass.: The Belknap Press of Harvard University Press.

Fang, Sheng, 1982. 'The Revival of Individual Economy in Urban Areas', in *China's Economic Reforms*, Ed. by Lin Wei and Arnold Chao. Philadelphia: University of Pennsylvania Press.

Fehér, Ferenc, 1982. 'Paternalism as a Mode of Legitimation in Soviet-type Societies', in *Political Legitimation in Communist States*. Ed. by T. H. Rigby and Ferenc Fehér. pp. 64–81. London: Macmillan.

Feng, Tong-ji, 1990. 'Shi nian cangsang hua zhaangrong' (Achievements in the Last Ten Years'), in *Guangzhong Ren (The Guangzhong People)*. Ed. by Liu Zhaoding. pp. 29–38. Guangzhou: Guangzhou Zhong Xing Jiqi Chang (Guangzhou Heavy Machinery Works).

Feng, Tong-qin, 1995. '1994–1995 nian: Zhongguo zhigong zhuangkuang ji qi dongxian' ('Chinese Workers and Employees in 1994–1995'), in *1994–1995 Nian Zhongguo: Shehui Xingshi Fenxi Yu Yuce (China in 1994–1995: Analysis and Forecast of Social Situations)*. Ed. by Jiang Liu et al., pp. 294–308. Beijing: Zhongguo Shehui Kexue Chuban She (Chinese Social Science Press).

—— 1996. '1995–1996 nian Zhongguo zhigong zhuangkuang di fenshi yu yuce' ('Workers and Employees in 1995–1996'), in *1995–1996 Nian Zhongguo: Shehui Xingshi Fenxi Yu Yuce (China in 1995–1996: Analysis and Forecast of Social Situations)*. Ed. by Jiang Liu et al., pp. 270–86. Beijing: Zhongguo Shehui Kexue Chubana She (Chinese Social Science Press).

—— Xu Xiao-jun, 1992. 'Guoyou qiye zhigong neibujieceng fenhua di xianzhuang' ('The Current Situation of Stratification and Differentiation among Employees in State-owned Enterprises'), *Shehuixue Yanjiao (Sociological Studies)*, No. 6, pp. 21–7.

—— Xu Xiao-jun, 1993. 'Zou xiang shichang jingji di Zhongquo qiyie zhigong neibu quanxi he jiegou' ('The Relations and Structure among Workers in Chinese Enterprises Moving Towards the Market Economy'), *Zhongguo Shehui Kexue (Chinese Social Science)*. Vol. 3, pp. 101–19.

Field, Frank, 1981. *Inequality in Britain*. London: Fontana.

—— 1996. *Stakeholder Welfare*. London: IEA Health and Welfare Unit.

Field, Robert Michael, 1993. 'Macroeconomy: Fluctuation and Change', in *China's Economic Reform*. Ed. by Walter Galenson, pp. 231–61. South San Francisco: The 1990 Institute.

Fried, Morton, 1954. *The Fabric of Chinese Society*. New York: Athlone.

Gans, Herbert, 1982. *The Urban Villagers*. New York: The Free Press.

Gaulton, Richard, 1981. 'Political Mobilization in Shanghai, 1949-1951', in *Shanghai: Revolution and Development in An Asian Metropolis*. Ed. by Christopher Howe, pp. 35–65. New York: Cambridge University Press.

George, Vic and Robert Page, 1995. *Modern Thinkers on Welfare*. London: Prentice Hall/Harvester Wheatsheaf.

Geertz, Clifford, 1973. *The Interpretation of Cultures*. New York: Basic Books.

Giddens, Anthony, 1973. *The Class Structure of the Advanced Societies*. London: Hutchinson.

Golas, Peter J., 1977. 'Early Ch'ing Guilds', in *The City in Late Imperial China*. Ed. by G. William Skinner. pp. 555–580. Stanford, CA: Stanford University Press.

Gold, Thomas B, 1990. 'Urban Private Business and Social Change', in *Chinese Society on the Eve of Tiananmen*. Ed. by Deborah Davis and Ezra F. Vogel, pp. 157–80. Cambridge, Mass.: The Council of East Asian Studies, Harvard University.

Granick, David, 1991. 'Multiple Labour Markets in the Industrial State Enterprise Sector', *China Quarterly*, No. 126, pp. 269–89.

Green, F., G. Hadjimatheou and R. Small, 1984. *Unequal Fringes: Fringe Benefits in the United Kingdom*. London: Low Pay Report.

Gu, Shui-gen, 1996. 'Houqin gaige yao fangzhi jinru sige wu gu' ('Reforms in Domestic Services Should Try to Avoid Getting into Four Wrong Areas'), in *Zhongguo Houqin Gaige Zonglun (An Overview of Reforms in Domestic Services in China)*. Ed. by Quanguo Houqin Guanli Yanjiuhui (National Association for Research on the Management of Domestic Services), pp. 41–8. Beijing: Zhongguo Qingongye Chuban She (Light Industry Press).

Guangzhou Shi Tigaiwei (Guangzhou City Economic Restructuring Commission), 1994. 'Guangzhou Shi shehui baoxian, baozhang zhidu gige di jiben qingkuang, cunzai wenti ji weilai fazhang' ('The Current Situations of Social Security Reforms, the Problems, and the Future Development of Social Insurance and Social Security in Guangzhou City'), in *Gaige Yu Fazhang: Guangzhou Shi Jianli He Wanshan Shehui Baozhang Tixi Guo Yantao Hui (An International Conference on the Establishment and Improvement of Social Security System in Guangzhou)*. Ed. by Gaifang Shidai Zazhi She (Open Times Journal), pp. 29–32. Guangzhou: Gaifang Shiddai Zazhi She (Open Times Journal).

Guangzhou Shi Tongji Ju (Guangzhou City Statistical Bureau), 1995. *Guangzhou Tongji Nianjian (Annual Report on Guangzhou Statistics)*. Beijing: Zhongguo Tongji Chuban She (Chinese Statistical Press).

Guo, Shu-qing, et al., 1990. 'Wo guo di zhigong fuli ji qi dui guomin shouru fenpei di yingxian' ('China's Employee Welfare and its Implications for Income Distribution'), in *Cankao Ziliao (Reference Materials)*. Vol. 8. Beijing: Jiwei Jingji Yanjiao Zhongxin (Research Centre of the State Economic Planning Commission).

Guojia Jinji Tizhi Gaige Weiyuanhui (State Economic Restructuring Commission), ed., 1995. *Shehui Baozhang Tizhi Gaige (Reforms of the Social Security System)*. Beijing: Gaige Chuban She (Reform Press).

Guojia Ti Gai Wei (State Economic Restructuring Commission) et al., 1996. 'Guanyu zhigong yiliao baozhang zhidu gaige kuoda shidian i yijian' ('On Increasing the Number of Pilot Projects on Reforming Employee Health Care Insurance System').

Guowuyuan (State Council), 1986. 'Guowuyuan guan yu fabu gaige laodong zhidu si ge guiding di tongzhi' ('The State Council's Announcement Regarding the Promulgation of Four Regulations on the System of Employment').

——— 1991. 'Guowuyuan guan yu qiye zhigong yanglao baoxian zhidu gaige di juiding' ('Decisions of the State Council Regarding Reforms of Old Age Insurance System for Enterprise Employees').

——— 1995. 'Jiujiang Shi zhigong yiliaoshehui baoxian zanxing guiding' ('Provisional Rules and Regulations for Employee Health Care Insurance in Jiujiang City'), in *Shehui Baohang Tizhi Gaige (Reforms of the Social Security System)*. Ed. by Guojia Jingji Tizhi Gaige Weiyuanhui (State Economic Restructuring Commission), pp. 163–9. Beijing: Gaige Chuban She (Reform Press).

——— 1995. 'Zhenjian Shi zhigong yiliao zhidu gaige shishi fangan' ('Plans for the Implementation of Reforms in Employee Health Care in Zhenjiang City'), in *Shehui Baozhang Tizhi Gaige (Reforms of the Social Security System)*. Ed. by Guojia Jingji Tizhi Gaige Weiyuanhui (State Economic Restructuring Commission), pp. 156–62. Beijing: Gaige Chuban She (Reform Press).

Hall, Peter, 1986. *Governing the Economy: The Politics of State Intervention in Britain and France*. New York: Oxford University Press.

Han, Guojian, 1990. 'China's Moonlighting Craze', *World Press Review*. March, p. 64.

He, Guang et al., eds, 1990. *The Labor Force Management in Contemporary China (Xiandai Zhongguo Laodongli Guanli)*. Beijing: Zhongguo Shehui Kexue Chuban She (Chinese Social Sciences Press).

Henderson, Gail E. and Myron S. Cohen, 1984. *The Chinese Hospital: A Socialist Work Unit*. New Haven, Conn. and London: Yale University Press.

Hirschman, Albert O., 1970. *Exit, Voice, and Loyalty*. Cambridge, Mass. and London: Harvard University Press.

Hoffmann, Charles, 1974. *The Chinese Worker*. Albany: SUNY Press.

Hoven, Finn Holmer, 1982. 'Regressive Welfare: Distributive Effects of Occupational Welfare Benefits', *Acta Sociological*, Vol. 25, pp. 65–73.

Howe, Christopher, 1981. 'Industrialization under Conditions of Long-Run Population Stability: Shanghai's Achievement and Prospect', in *Shanghai: Revolution and Development in An Asian Metropolis*. Ed. by Christopher Howe, pp. 153–87. New York: Cambridge University Press.

Hu, Teh-Wei and Elizabeth Hon-Ming Li, 1993. 'The Labor Market', in *China's Economic Reform*. Ed. by Walter Galenson, pp. 147–76. South San Francisco: The 1990 Institute.

Hu, Wei-lue, 1996. '1995–1996 nian xiang shicang jingji zhuanbian zhong di laodong jiuye wenti' ('Labour and Employment in 1995–1996'), in *1995–1996 Nian Zhongguo Shehui Xingshi Fenshi Yu Yuce (China in 1995–1996: Analysis and Forecast of Social Situations)*, Ed. by Jiang Liu et al., pp. 125–37, Beijing: Zhongguo Shehui Kexue Chuban She (Chinese Social Science Press).

Huang, Ping, 1996. '1995–1996 nian Zhongguo shehui xingshi fenxi yuce zhong baogao' ('China in 1995–1996: Analysis and Forecast of the Social

Situation'), in *1995–1996 Nian Zhongguo Shehui Xingshi Fenxi Yu Yuce (China in 1995–1996: Analysis and Forecast of Social Situations)*. Ed. by Jiang Liu et al., pp. 3–15. Beijing: Gaige Chuban She (Reform Press).

Hussain, Athar, 1993. 'Reform of the Chinese Social Security System'. The Development Economics Research Programme CP No. 27. London: London School of Economics Suntory-Toyota International Centre for Economics and Related Disciplines.

Jacoby, Sanford M., 1984. 'The Development of Internal Labour Markets in American Manufacturing Firms', in *Internal Labour Markets*. Ed. by P. Osterman, pp. 23–70. Cambridge, Mass.: MIT Press.

Johnson, Graham E., 1993. 'Family Strategies and Economic Transformation in Rural China: Some Evidence from the Pearly River Delta', in *Chinese Families in the Post-Mao Era*. Ed. by D. Davis and S. Harrell, pp. 103–38. Berkeley, Los Angeles, London: University of California Press.

Kalleberg, Arne L., Michael Wallace and Robert Althauser, 1981. 'Economic Segmentation, Worker Power, and Income Inequality', *American Journal of Sociology*, Vol. 87. pp. 651–83.

Kallgren, Joyce, 1969. 'Social Welfare and China's Industrial Workers', in *Chinese Communist Politics in Action*. Ed. A. Doak Barnett, pp. 540–73. Seattle: University of Washington Press.

Keegan, William, 1993. *The Spectre of Capitalism*. London: Vintage.

Kendall, J., 1984. 'Why Japanese Workers Work', *Management Today*. January, pp. 72–5.

Kirkby, R.J.R., 1985. *Urbanisation in China: Town and Country in a Developing Economy*. London & Sydney: Croom Helm.

Koo, Anthony Y. C., Elizabeth Hon-Ming Li and Zhaoping Peng, 1993. 'State-Owned Enterprises in Transition', in *China's Economic Reform*. Ed. Walter Galenson, pp. 33–80. South San Francisco: The 1990 Institute.

Kornai, Janos, 1984. 'Bureaucratic and Market Co-ordination', *Osteuropa Wirtschaft*, Vol. 29, pp. 306–19.

—— 1986. *Contradictions and Dilemmas: Studies on the Socialist Economy and Society*. Cambridge, Mass.: MIT Press.

—— 1989. 'The Hungarian Reform Process: Visions, Hopes, and Reality', in *Remaking the Economic Institutions of Socialism: China and Eastern Europe*, pp. 32–94. Stanford, CA: Stanford University Press.

—— 1990. *Vision and Reality, Market and State: Contradictions and Dilemmas Revisited*. London: Harvester Wheatsheaf.

Krueger, Anne, 1974. 'The Political Economy of the Rent-Seeking Society', *American Economic Review*, Vol. 64, pp. 291–302.

Lee, Chi-Wen Jevons, 1996. 'The Reform of the State-owned Enterprises', in *China Review 1996*. Ed. by Maurice Brosseau, Suzanne Pepper and Tsang Shu-ki, pp. 263–80. Hong Kong: The Chinese University Press.

Lee, Ming-Kwan, 1994. 'Zhongguo zhi shehui fenceng: Weibo xueshuo zhi zaitan' ('Social Stratification in China: the Weberian Thesis Revisited'), in *Fazhan Yu Bupingdeng: Dalu yu Taiwan Zhi Shehui Jieceng Yu Liudong (Inequalities and Development: Stratification and Mobility in Mainland China and Taiwan)*. Ed. by Lau Siu-kai, Wan Po-San, Lee Ming-Kwan and Wong Siu-Lun, pp. 1–26. Hong Kong: Hong Kong Institute of Asia-Pacific Studies, The Chinese University of Hong Kong.

—— 1995. 'The Family Way', in *Indicators of Social Development: Hong Kong 1993*. Ed. by Lau Siu-kai, Lee Ming-kwan, Wan Po-san and Wong Siu-lun, pp. 1–20. Hong Kong: Hong Kong Institute of Asia-Pacific Studies, The Chinese University of Hong Kong.

Le Grand, Julian and Will Bartlett, 1993. *Quasi-Markets and Social Policy*. Basingstoke: Macmillan.

Leung, Joe C.B., 1992. 'The Transformation of Occupational Welfare in the People's Republic of China: from a Political Asset to an Economic Burden', Monograph Series, Social Welfare in China No. 3, Hong Kong: Department of Social Work and Social Administration, The University of Hong Kong.

—— 1994. 'Dismantling the "Iron Rice Bowl": Welfare Reform in the People's Republic of China', *Journal of Social Policy*, Vol. 23, No. 3, pp. 341–61.

Li, Jiang-Tao, 1994. 'Danwei zai shehui fen ceng zhong di yiyi' ('The Implications of Danwei for Social Stratification', in *Fazhan Yu Bupingdeng: Dalu Yu Taiwan Zhi Shehui Jieceng Yu Liudong (Inequalities and Development: Stratification and Mobility in Mainland China and Taiwan)*. Ed. by Lau Siu-kai, Wan Po-San, Lee Ming-Kwan and Wong Siu-lun, pp. 43–64. Hong Kong: Hong Kong Institute of Asia-Pacific Studies, The Chinese University of Hong Kong.

Li, Lu-lu and Wang Fen-yu, 1992. *Dandai Zhongguo Xiandaihua Guocheng Zhong Di Shehui Jiegou Ji Qi Bian Ge (Structure and Change in China's Modernization)*. Chejiang: Chejiang Renmin Chuban She (Chejiang's People's Press).

Li, Pei-lin, 1996. '1995–1996 nian guoyou qiye gaige di jincheng he zouxian' ('The Reform of State-owned Enterprises in 1995–1996'), in *1995–1996 Nian Zhongguo Shehui Xingshi Fenxi Yu Yuce (China in 1995–1996: Analysis and Forecast of Social Situations)*. Ed. by Jiang Liu et al., pp. 57–68. Beijing: Zhongguo Shehui Kexue Chubanshe (Chinese Social Science Press).

Lin, Cyril, 1989. 'Open-ended Economic Reform in China', in *Remaking the Economic Institutions of Socialism: China and Eastern Europe*. Ed. by Victor Nee and David Stark, pp. 95–136. Stanford, CA: Stanford University Press.

Litwak, Eugene, 1965. 'Extended Kin Relations in a Democratic Industrial Society', in *Social Structure and the Family: Generational Relations*. Ed. by Ethel Shanas and Gordon F. Streib, pp. 290–323. Englewood Cliffs, NJ: Prentice Hall.

Liu, Bo-xiong, 1995. 'Zhongguo nuxing jiuye zhuang kuang' ('The Conditions of Female Employment in China'), *Shehuixue Yanjiao (Sociological Studies)*, Vol. 2, pp. 39–48.

Liu, Mei, 1995. 'Shengyu baoxian zhidu gaige' ('Reforms of the Maternity Insurance System'), in *Shehui Baozhang Tizhi Gaige (Reforms of the Social Security System)*. Ed. by Guojia Jinji Gaige Weiyuanhui (State Economic Restructuring Commission), pp. 181–4. Beijing: Gaige Chuban She (Reform Press).

Liu, Zhi-feng, 1995. 'Shenhua shehui baozhang tizhi gaige cujin xiandai qiye zhidu jianli' ('Deepen Reform in the Social Security System and Foster the Establishment of a Modern System of Enterprises'), in *Shehui Baozhang Tizhi Gaige (Reforms of the Social Security System)*. Ed. by Guojia Jingji Tizhi Gaige Weiyuanhui (State Economic Reform Commission), pp. 28–53. Beijing: Gaige Chuban She (Reform Press).

Lu, Feng, 1989. 'Danwei: yi zhong teshu di shehui zuzhi xingshi' ('Danwei: a special form of social organization'), in *Zhongguo Shehui Kexue (Chinese Social Science)*, No. 1 pp. 71–88.

Manning, Nick, 1992. 'Social Policy in the Soviet Union and its Successors', in *The New Eastern Europe: Social Policy, Past, Present and Future*. Ed. by Bob Deacon, pp. 31–66. London: Sage.

Mao, Zedong (Mao Tsetung), 1953. *Mao Zedong Xuanji (Selected Works of Mao Zedong)*. Vol. I. Beijing: Beijing People's Press.

—— 1967. *Selected Works, Vols. I-IV*. Peking: Foreign Languages Press.

—— 1976. 'Jingji wenti yu caizheng wenti' ('Economic and Financial Problems'), in *Mao Zedong Ji*, Vol. 8, pp. 183–354. Hong Kong: Yi Shan Tu Shu (One Hill Press).

Marshall, T.H., 1963. 'Citizenship and Social Class', in *Sociology at the Crossroads and Other Essay*, pp. 67–127. London: Heinemann.

Minami, Ryoshin, 1994. *The Economic Development of China: A Comparison with the Japanese Experience*. New York: St. Martin's Press.

Ming Pao Daily. Hong Kong. Various issues.

Mishra, Ramesh, 1977. *Society and Social Policy: Theoretical Perspectives on Welfare*. London: Macmillan.

—— 1984. *The Welfare State in Crisis*. Brighton: Wheatsheaf.

Moonman, Jane, 1973. *Fringe Benefits in Industry*. London: Gower Press.

Naughton, Barry, 1995. 'Cities in the Chinese Economic System: Changing Roles and Conditions for Autonomy', in *Urban Spaces in Contemporary China*. Ed. by Deborah Davis, Richard Kraus, Barry Naughton and Elizabeth Perry, pp. 61–75. New York: Woodrow Wilson Center Press and Cambridge University Press.

Nee, Victor, 1989. 'A Theory of Market Transition: From Redistribution to Markets in State Socialism', *American Sociological Review*, Vol. 54, pp. 663–81.

—— 1991. 'Social Inequalities in Reforming State Socialism: Between Redistribution and Markets in China', *American Sociological Review*, Vol. 56, pp. 267–82.

—— 1992. 'Organizational Dynamics of Market Transition: Hybrid Forms, Property Rights, and Mixed Economy in China', *Administrative Science Quarterly*, Vol. 37, pp. 1–27.

—— 1994. 'Institutional Change and Regional Growth', in *The Economic Transformation of South China*. Ed. by Thomas P. Lyons and Victor Nee, pp. 1–16. Ithaca, NY: Cornell East Asia Program.

Nee, Victor and David Stark, eds, 1989. *Remaking the Economic Institutions of Socialism: China and Eastern Europe*. Stanford, CA: Stanford University Press.

O'Connor, James, 1973. *The Fiscal Crisis of the State*. New York: St. Martin's Press.

Oi, Jean Chun, 1989. *State and Peasant in Contemporary China: The Political Economy of Village Government*. Berkeley: University of California Press.

Oliver, N. and B. Wilkinson, 1988. *The Japanization of British Industry*. London: Blackwell.

Ouyang Jun, 1994. *Gaige Yu Gonghui (Reform and Unions)*. Beijing: Zhongguo Gongren Chuban She (Chinese Workers' Press).

Pahl, R., 1975. *Whose City?* (2nd edition). London: Penguin.

Pan, Yun-kang and Lin Nan, 1992. 'Zhongguo di zhong xiang jiating guanxi ji tui shehui di yingxiang' ('China's vertical family relations and their social implications'), in *Shehui She Yanjiao (Sociological Studies)*, Vol. 6, pp. 73–80.

Papadakis, Elim and Peter Taylor-Gooby, 1987. *The Private Provision of Public Welfare: State, Market and Community*. Brighton: Wheatsheaf Books.

Parish, William L. Jr, 1981. 'Egalitarianism in Chinese Society', *Problems of Communism*, Vol. 29, pp. 37–53.

Perkin, H., 1969. *Origins of Modern English Society, 1780–1880*. London: Routledge & Kegan Paul.

Perkins, Dwight H., 1966. *Market Control and Planning in Communist China*. Cambridge, Mass.: Harvard University Press.

Phillips, Michael R., 1993. 'Strategies Used by Chinese Families Coping with Schizophrenia', in *Chinese Families in the Post-Mao Era*. Ed. by D. Davis and S. Harrell, pp. 277–306. Berkeley: University of California Press.

Pinker, Robert, 1986. 'Social Welfare in Japan and Britain: A Comparative View. Formal and Informal Aspects of Welfare', in *Comparing Welfare States and Their Futures*. Ed. by Else Oyen, pp. 114–128. London: Gower.

—— 1991. 'On Rediscovering the Middle Way in Social Welfare', in *The State and Social Welfare*. Ed. by Thomas and Dorothy Wilson. pp. 280–300. London and New York: Longman.

—— 1992. 'Making Sense of the Mixed Economy of Welfare', in *Social Policy and Administration*. Vol. 26, No. 4, pp. 273–84.

—— 1994. *Golden Ages and Welfare Alchemists*. Revised version of Maxwell Cummings Lecture delivered at McGill University on 21 March 1994.

—— 1995. 'T.H. Marshall,' in *Modern Thinkers on Welfare*. Ed. by Vic George and Robert Page. London: Prentice Hall/Harvester Wheatsheaf.

Poggi, Gianfranco, 1978. *The Development of the Modern State*. Stanford, CA: Stanford University Press.

Polanyi, Karl, 1977. *The Livelihood of Man*. New York: Academic Press.

Rankin, Mary Backus, 1986. *Elite Activism and Political Transformation in China: Zhejiang Province, 1965–1911*. Stanford, CA: Stanford University Press.

Reddin, M., 1982. 'Occupation, Welfare and Social Division', in *The Year Book of Social Policy in Britain 1980–1981*. Ed. by C. Jones and J. Stenenson. London: Routledge and Kegan Paul.

Rein, Martin, 1982. 'The Social Policy of the Firm', *Policy Sciences*, Vol. 14, pp. 117–35.

Rein, Martin and Lee Rainwater, 1986. *Public/Private Interplay in Social Protection – A Comparative Study*. Almonk, NY: M. E. Sharpe, Inc.

Renmin Ribao (People's Daily). Beijing. Various issues.

Rimlinger, Gastron, 1971. *Welfare Policy and Industrialization in Europe, America and Russia*. New York: John Wiley.

Riskin, Carl, 1987. *China's Political Economy: The Quest for Development Since 1949*. Oxford: Oxford University Press.

Roth, Guenther and Claus Wittich, eds, 1968. *Max Weber: Economy and Society*. New York: Bedminster Press.

Rowe, William T., 1989. *Hankow: Conflict and Community in a Chinese City, 1796–1895*. Stanford, CA: Stanford University Press.

Russell, Alice, 1991. *The Growth of Occupational Welfare in Britain*. Aldershot: Avebury.

Saich, T., 1984. 'Workers in the Workers' State: Urban Workers in the PRC', in *Groups and Politics in the PRC*. Ed. by D. Goodman, pp. 152–75. Cardiff: University College of Cardiff Press.

Schran, Peter, 1976. *Guerrila Economy: The Development of the Shensi-Kansu-Ningsia Border Region, 1937–1945*. Albany: SUNY Press.

210   *Bibliography*

Schurmann, Franz, 1968. *Ideology and Organization in Communist China*. Berkeley, Los Angeles, London: University of California Press.

Seith, S., N. Namiki and C. Swanson, 1984. *The False Promise of the Japanese Miracle*. London: Pitman.

Selden, Mark, 1971. *The Yenan Way in Revolutionary China*. Cambridge, Mass.: Harvard University Press.

Sha, Ji-cai, ed., 1995. *Dang dai Zhongguo Funu Jiating Diwei Yanjiao (Study on the Status of Women in the Family in Contemporary China)*. Tianjin: Tianjin Renmin Chuban She (Tianjin People's Press).

Shirk, Susan L., 1981. 'Recent Chinese Labor Policies and the Transformation of Industrial Organization in China', in *China Quarterly* 88 (December), pp. 575–93.

—— 1993. *The Political Logic of Economic Reform in China*. Berkeley: University of California Press.

Simpura, Jussi, 1994. 'Social Problems and Social Policy in Russia and the Baltic Countries', in *Change and Continuity in Eastern Europe*. Ed. by Timo Piirainen, pp. 148–72. Aldershot: Dartmouth.

Sinfield, A., 1978. 'Analyses in the Social Division of Welfare', *Journal of Social Policy*, Vol. 7, No. 2.

Skinner, G. William, 1977. 'Introduction: Urban Development in Imperial China', in *The City in Late Imperial China*. Ed. by G. William Skinner, pp. 3–32. Stanford, CA: Stanford University Press.

Skocpol, Theda, 1985. 'Bringing the State Back In: Strategies of Analysis in Current Research', in *Bringing The State Back In*. Ed. by Peter B. Evans, Dietrich Rueschemeyer and Theda Skocpol, pp. 3–43. Cambridge: Cambridge University Press.

—— 1992. *Protecting Soldiers and Mothers: The Political Origins of Social Policy in the United States*. Cambridge, Mass.: The Belknap Press of Harvard University Press.

Solinger, Dorothy J., 1984. *Chinese Business Under Socialism*. Berkeley: University of California Press.

Stacey, Judith, 1983. *Patriarchy and Socialist Revolution in China*. Berkeley and Los Angeles: University of California Press.

Stark, David, 1986. 'Rethinking Internal Labor Markets: New Insights from a Comparative Perspective', *American Sociological Review*, Vol. 51, pp. 492–504.

Stark, David and Victor Nee, 1989. 'Toward an Institutional Analysis of State Socialism', in *Remaking the Economic Institutions of Socialism: China and Eastern Europe*. Ed. by Victor Nee and David Stark, pp. 1–31. Stanford, CA: Stanford University Press.

State Statistical Bureau, 1960. *Ten Great Years*. Peking: Foreign Languages Press.

—— 1988. *Zhongguo Laodong Gongzi Tongji Zilio, 1978–1987 (Statistical Information on Labour Wage in China)*. Beijing: Zhongguo Tongji Chuban She (Statistical Press of China).

—— 1989. *Zhongguo Tongji Nianjian (China Statistical Yearbook)*. Beijing: Zhongguo Tongji Chuban She (Statistical Press of China).

—— 1989. *Zhongguo Laodong Gongzi Tongji Nianjian (China Statistical Yearbook on Labour Wage)*. Beijing: Zhongguo Laodong Chuban She (Statistical Press of China).

—— 1995. *Zhongguo Tongji Nianjian (China Statistical Yearbook)*. Beijing: China Statistical Publishing House.

Steiner, H. Arthur, 1950. 'Chinese Communist Urban Policy', *American Political Science Review*, Vol. 44, No. 62.

Steinmo, Sven, K. Thelen and F. Longstreth, eds, 1992. *Structuring Politics: Historical Institutionalism in Comparative Analysis*. Cambridge: Cambridge University Press.

Su, Si-jin., 1994. 'Hybrid Organizational Forms in South China: "One Firm, Two Systems"', in *The Economic Transformation of South China*. Ed. by Thomas P. Lyons and Victor Nee, pp. 199–214. Ithaca, NY: Cornell East Asia Program.

Szalai, Julia, and Eva Orosz, 1992. 'Social Policy in Hungary', in *The New Eastern Europe: Social Policy Past, Present And Future*, Ed. by B. Deacon, pp. 144–44. London: Sage Publications.

Szelenyi, Ivan, 1978. 'Social Inequalities in State Socialist Redistributive Economies', *International Journal of Comparative Sociology*, Vol. 19, pp. 63–87.

—— 1983. *Urban Inequalities Under State Socialism*. New York: Oxford University Press.

Takahara, Akio, 1992. *The Politics of Wage Policy in Post-Revolutionary China*. London: The Macmillan Press.

Tan, Shen, 1994. 'Dandai Zhongguo zhiye funu: you zhengfu anzhi gongzuo huo jinru laodongli shicang' ('Working Women in Contemporary China': to be Allocated Jobs by the Government or to Move into the Labour Market'), in *Xingbie Yu Zhongguo (Gender and China)*. Ed. by Li Xiao-jiang et al., pp. 78–92. Beijing: Shenghuo. Dushu. Xinzhi Sanlian Shudian (Joint Bookstore).

Taylor-Gooby, P. and J. Dale, 1981. *Social Theory and Social Welfare*. London: Edward Arnold.

Titmuss, Richard M., 1958. *Essays on 'The Welfare State'*. London: George Allen & Unwin.

Tsou, Tang, 1991. 'The Tiananmen tragedy: the state-society relationship, choices, and mechanisms in historical perspective', in *Contemporary Chinese Politics in Historical Perspective*. Ed. by Brantly Womack, pp. 265–328. Cambridge: Cambridge University Press.

Van Velsen, Jaap, 1961. 'The Extended Case Method and Situational Analysis', in *The Craft of Social Anthropology*. Ed. by A.L. Epstein, pp. 129–49. London: Tavistock.

Vogel, Ezra, 1979. *Japan as Number One: Lessons for America*. Cambridge, Mass.: Harvard University Press.

—— 1989. *One Step Ahead in China: Guangdong Under Reform*. Cambridge, Mass.: Harvard University Press.

Walder, Andrew G., 1986. *Communist Neo-Traditionalism: Work and Authority in Chinese Industry*. Berkeley: University of California Press.

—— 1989. 'Factory and Manager in an Era of Reform', *China Quarterly*, Vol. 118, pp. 242–64.

—— 1992. 'Property Rights and Stratification in Socialist Redistributive Economies', *American Sociological Review*, Vol. 57, pp. 524–39.

Walker, Alan, 1984. 'The Political Economy of Privatization', in *Privatization and the Welfare State*. Ed. by J. Le Grand and R. Robinson, pp. 19–44. London: Unwin Hyman.

Wang, Xue-li, 1993. 'Guan yu guomin shouru fenpei geju bianhua wenti di yanjiao' ('A Study on the Changing Pattern of Income Distribution in China'), in *Guomin Shouru Fenpei Geju Di Pinjia Yu Juece (Evalutaion and Policies*

Regarding the Pattern of Income Distribution Among the Chinese People). Ed. by
Weng Tian-zhen, et al., pp. 166–180. Beijing: Zhongguo Laodong Chuban She
(Chinese Labour Press).

Ward, Colin, 1982. *Anarchy in Action.* London: Freedom Press.

Watson, Andrew. 1980. *Mao Zedong and The Political Economy of the Border
Region: A Translation of Mao's Economics and Financial Problems.* Cambridge:
Cambridge University Press.

Weir, Margaret, Ann Shola Orloff and Theda Skocpol, 1988. 'Introduction:
Understanding American Social Politics', in *The Politics of Social Policy in the
United States.* Ed. by Margaret Weir, Ann Shola Orloff and Theda Skocpol,
pp. 37–80. Princeton, NJ: Princeton University Press.

Wen Hui Bao (Wen Wei Po Daily). Hong Kong. Various issues.

Weng, Tian-zhen, et al., eds., 1993. *Guomin Shouru Fenpei Geju Di Pingjia Yu Juece
(Evaluation and Policies Regarding the Pattern of Income Distribution Among the
Chinese People).* Beijing: Zhongguo Laodong Chuban She (Chinese Labour Press).

Westwood, R.I. and S.M. Leung, 1996. 'Working under the Reforms: The
Experience and Meaning of Work in a Time of Transition', in *China Review
1996.* Ed. by Maurice Brosseau, Suzanne Pepper and Tsang Shu-ki. pp. 367–424.
Hong Kong: The Chinese University Press.

Whyte, Martin K, 1991. 'State and Society in the Mao Era', in *Perspectives on
Modern China: Four Anniversaries.* Ed. by Kenneth Lieberthal et al., pp. 255–74.
Almonk, NY: M.E. Sharpe.

Whyte, Martin K. and William L. Parish, 1984. *Urban Life in Contemporary China.*
Chicago and London: The University of Chicago Press.

Wistow, Gerald. et al., 1994. *Social Care in a Mixed Economy.* Buckingham: Open
University Press.

Wolf, Margery, 1985. *Revolution Postponed: Women in Contemporary China.*
Stanford, CA: Stanford University Press.

Womack, Brantly, 1991. 'Transfigured Community: New-Traditionalism and
Work Unit Socialism in China', *China Quarterly*, Vol. 126, pp. 269–89.

Wong, Christine P. W., Christopher Heady and Wing T. Woo, 1995. *Fiscal
Management and Economic Reform in the People's Republic of China.* Hong Kong:
Oxford University Press.

Wong, Linda, 1992. *Social Welfare Under Chinese Socialism – A Case Study of the
Ministry of Civil Affairs.* PhD Thesis, London School of Economics, London.

Wong, Linda and Stewart MacPherson, eds., 1995. *Social Change and Social Policy
in Contemporary China.* Aldershot: Avebury.

Wright, Mary Clabaugh, 1957. *The Last Stand of Chinese Conservatism: The T'ung-
Chih Restoration, 1862–1874.* Stanford, CA: Stanford University Press.

Xue, Mu-qiao, Su King and Lin Tse-li, 1960. *The Socialist Transformation of the
National Economy.* Peking: Foreign Languages Press.

Yang, C. K., 1959. *The Chinese Family in the Communist Revolution.* Cambridge,
Mass.: Harvard University Press.

Yang, Mayfair Mei-hui, 1994. *Gifts, Favors & Banquets: The Art of Social
Relationships in China.* Ithaca, NY: Cornell University Press.

Yeh, Kung-Chia, 1993. 'Economic Reform: An Overview', in *China's Economic
Reform.* ed. by Walter Galenson. pp. 11–32. South San Francisco, CA:
The 1990 Institute.

Yu Xian-yang, 1991. 'Danwei yishi di shehuixue fenxi' ('A Sociological Analysis
of *Danwei* Culture'), *Shehuishe Yanjiao (Sociological Studies)*, No. 5. pp. 76–81.

Yuan, Lun-qu, 1991. *Zhongguo Laodong Jingjishi (History of Labour Economics in China)*. Beijing: Beijing Jingji Xueyuan Chuban She (Beijing Institute of Economic Studies Press).

Yue, S.D, 1991. 'The Reform of the Chinese Social Welfare System', in *Management World*, Vol. 4, pp. 171–6. Cited in Leung (1992: 6).

Zhan, Huo-sheng et al., 1993. *Zhongguo Dalu Shehui Anquan Zhidu (Social Security System in Mainland China)*. Taibei: Wunan Tushu Chuban She (Wunan Press).

Zhang, Chun-yuan, ed., 1990. *Zhongguo Laonian Renkou Ynjiu (Studies on the Elderly Population in China)*. Beijing: Bejing Daxue Chuban She (Beijing University Press).

Zhang, Wen-shou, 1996. 'Zai dierci quan guo houqin guanli xueshu yantao hui shang di zhongjie fayan' ('Concluding Speech at the Second National Conference on Domestic Management'), in *Zhongguo Houqin Gaige Zonglun (An Overview of Reforms in Domestic Services in China*. Ed. by Quanguo Houqin Guanli Yanjiu Hiu (National Association for Research on the Management of Domestic Services). pp. 1–10. Beijing: Zhongguo Qingongye Chuban She (Light Industry Press).

Zheng, Jing-ping and Zheng Chun-xian, 1993. 'Dui wo guo shouru fenpei xian zhuang di tantao' ('A Study on the Current Situation of Income Distribution in China'), in *Guomin Shouru Fenpei Geju Di Pingjia Yu Juece (Evaluation and Policies Regarding the Pattern of Income Distribution Among the Chinese People)*. Ed. by Weng Tian-zhen et al., pp. 34–47. Beijing: Zhongguo Laodong Chuban She (Chinese Labour Press).

Zheng, Xian-shu, 1995. 'Gongshang baoxianx zhidu gaige' ('Reforms of the Industrial Accident Insurance System'), in *Shehui Baozhang Tizhi Gaige (Reforms of the Social Security System)*. Ed. by Guojia Jingji Tizhi Gaige Weiyuanhui (State Economic Restructuring Commission), pp. 175–80. Beijing: Gaige Chuban She (Reform Press).

Zhou, En-lai, 1993. *Zhou En-lai Jingji Wenxuan (Selected Works of Zhou En-lai on the Economy)*. Ed. by Zhonggong Zhongyang Wenxian Yanjiao Shi (Research Office of the Chinese Communist Party Central on Documents and Records). Beijing: Zhongyang Wenxian Chuban She (Party Central Documents and Records Press).

Zhou, Zhen-hua, ed., 1995. *Qiye Gaige (Enterprise Reform)*. Shanghai: Shanghai Renmin Chuban She (Shanghai People's Press).

Zhu, Qing-fang, 1995. '1994–1995 nian renmin shengghuo zhuangkuang' ('Living Conditions in 1994–1995'), in *1994–1995 Nian Zhongguo Sshehui Xingshi Fenxi Yu Yuce (China in 1995–1996: Analysis and Forecast of Social Situations)*. Ed. by Jiang Liu et al., pp. 189–201. Beijing: Zhongguo Shsehui Ke Xue Chuban She (Chinese Social Science Press).

—— 1996. '1995–1996 nian renmin shenghuo zhuangkuang' ('Living Conditions in 1995–1996'), in *1995–1996 Nian Zhongguo Shehui Xingshi Fenxi Yu Yuce (China in 1995–1996: Analysis and Forecast of Social Situations)*. Ed. by Jiang Liu et al., pp. 143–56. Beijing: Zhongguo Shehui Kexue Chuban She (Chinese Social Science Press).

Zhu, Qing-fang et al., eds., 1993. *Shehui Baozhang Zhibiao Tixi (A System of Social Indicators on Social Security)*. Beijing: Zhongguo Shehui Kexue Chuban She (Chinese Social Science Press).

Zhu, Ying, 1995. 'Major Changes Underway in China's Industrial Relations', *International Labour Review*, Vol. 134, pp. 37–49.

Index

accident insurance, 154
allowances and subsidies, 8
alternatives and choices, 158, 165

Bankruptcy Law, 69
bao xia lai, 45–6
Berlin, Isaiah, 175
Bian, Yanjie, 1, 11, 46, 52, 83, 183
Bo, Yi-bo, 46
Boisot, M., 12
border region economy, 39–43; *see
    also* guerrilla war experience
Burawoy, Michael, 27

canteens, 132–5, 138–9
Castells, M., 22
chaogang, 83–8
Child, John, 12
Chinese Communist Party, 42–3,
    107–9
Chinese occupational welfare
    burden on state enterprises, 18–22
    calculative uses, 98–102
    concept, 7–8
    coverage, 8–11
    danwei responsibility, 120–1
    economic implications, 14–23
    government responsibility, 124–6
    instrumental use of, 122
    model of welfare pluralism, 173–5
    origins, 33–81, 159–61
    social implications, 11–14
Chow, Nelson, 50, 58, 178, 185–6
Ch'u, T'ung-Tsu, 36, 37
citizenship, 176
clientelistic ties, 13
Cohen, Myron S., 1, 12, 178
collective welfare, 8
Confucianism, 33
contract responsibility system, 65–9
convergence, 173–4

Dai, Yuan-chen, 72, 81

daigan, 85
Davis, Deborah, 5, 12, 63, 73
Davis-Friedmann, Deborah, 12, 90
Deacon, Bob, 33
death benefits, 10
dependence
    near-complete and limited
        dependence, 24, 157–8, 161–2,
        169–70
    paternalistic dependence, 14
dingti, 12
distributing risks and responsibilities,
    140–56, 158
Donfang Heavy Machinery Works,
    28–9, 75–9

efficiency and inefficiency, 158, 165
employment reform, 70–3
Enterprise Law, 69
enterprise reform, 65–9, 110
entitlements and obligations, 7, 158,
    162–3
equity and inequity, 158, 163–4
Esping-Andersen, Gosta, 178

Fairbank, John King, 37, 44, 45, 46
family, impact on, 175
family strategy, 91–4, 98
Feng, Tong-qin, 73, 74, 75, 183
Field, Frank, 174
fieldwork
    case study, 28–9
    entry, 27
    participant observation, 26–8
    subjective perspective, 31–2

Gans, Herbert, 26
Gaulton, Richard, 48, 49
Gemeinschaft, 11, 175–6
gender differences, 88, 91–4
generational differences, 95–8
Giddens, Anthony, xii
Gold, Thomas B., 12, 18